THESE THINGS HAVE BEEN WRITTEN
STUDIES ON THE FOURTH GOSPEL

LOUVAIN THEOLOGICAL & PASTORAL MONOGRAPHS

2

THESE THINGS HAVE BEEN WRITTEN

Studies on the Fourth Gospel

RAYMOND F. COLLINS

PEETERS PRESS
LOUVAIN

WILLIAM B. EERDMANS PUBLISHING COMPANY
GRAND RAPIDS, MICHIGAN

Copyright © 1990 by Peeters Uitgeverij, Leuven

First published in Belgium 1990 by Peeters Uitgeverij,
Bondgenotenlaan 153, B-3000 Leuven
and in the USA 1991 by Wm. B. Eerdmans Publishing Co.,
255 Jefferson Ave. SE, Grand Rapids, Mich. 49503

ISBN 0-8028-0561-2

TABLE OF CONTENTS

ACKNOWLEDGMENTS vii

PROLOGUE ix

ABBREVIATIONS xi

I. JOHN'S CHARACTERS : 1
   1. Representative Figures 1
   2. Discipleship in John's Gospel 46
   3. Jesus' Conversation with Nicodemus 56
   4. The Twelve: Another Perspective 68

II. A SINGLE GOSPEL 87
   5. A Passion Narrative? 87
   6. The Search for Jesus 94
   7. Proverbial Sayings in John's Gospel 128
   8. The Oldest Commentary on the Fourth Gospel . 151

III. SIGNS AND FAITH 158
   9. Cana (John 2:1-12) – the First of His Signs or the
      Key to His Signs? 158
   10. Miracles and Faith 183

IV. COMING AND GOING 198
   11. "He Came to Dwell Among Us" (John 1:14) . . 198
   12. "A New Commandment I Give to You, That You
      Love One Another ..." (John 13:34) 217

INDEX 257
INDEX OF SCRIPTURAL REFERENCES 261
INDEX OF SUBJECTS 275

ACKNOWLEDGMENTS

On the occasion of the republication of these twelve essays on the Fourth Gospel, I would like to express my personal gratitude to the editors of the publications in which they first appeared. My thanks go out to them not only for the care with which they published them in the first instance, but also for granting me permission to publish them in this new version.

"Representative Figures" first appeared in the *Downside Review* (1976), "Discipleship in John's Gospel" in *Emmanuel* (1985), "Jesus' Conversation with Nicodemus" and "A Passion Narrative" in *The Bible Today* (1977; 1986), "The Twelve: Another Perspective," "Proverbial Sayings" and "He Came to Dwell Among Us' (John 1:14)" in the *Melita Theologica* (1989; 1986; 1976), "The Search for Jesus" and "'A New Commandment I Give to You, that You Love One Another ...' (John 13:34)" in *Laval théologique et philosophique* (1978; 1979), "The Oldest Commentary on the Fourth Gospel" in *Actualidad Pastoral* (1977, in Spanish, and in English in *The Bible Today* in 1978), "Cana (John 2:1-12)—the first of his signs or the key to his signs?" in the *Irish Theological Quarterly* (1980), and "Miracles and Faith" in *New Testament Miracles in African Context* , edited by Nlenanya Onwu (1989).

Since consistency is a desirable quality of any publication, it was decided to retouch the essays so that they would have a consistency of orthography, punctuation, system of references, and form of abbreviations in the present volume. A desire for consistency has also led to the use of the RSV for the biblical citations of the eleventh essay, "'He Came to Dwell Among Us' (John 1:14)," even though this title and the biblical citations in the original publication were taken from the NEB. Otherwise the text of each essay, apart, perhaps, from one or another minor correction, is as it first appeared in print.

PROLOGUE

The title chosen for this book is a sign that the essays which are published herein have previously appeared in print. The fruits of my reflection on the Fourth Gospel, they have been gathered together from a variety of publications on four continents. They were originally published over a fourteen year span of time, but herewith they appear together in print for the first time.

One who reads through the Fourth Gospel will certainly note that many expressions used by its author carry a double meaning. That stylistic device contributes to the fascination of the work of faith which the evangelist has left behind for subsequent generations to relish. At John 20:30 he uses the phrase "these things have been written," apparently the conclusion to his work at some penultimate stage.

In keeping with the Johannine tradition, the title chosen for this book is a double entendre. Not only does it evoke the fashion in which the present work was put together; it also recalls the way in which the Fourth Gospel was composed and the purpose for which it was written. While the present work is also the result of a composition in stages, it is hardly the last word on the testimony of faith which the evangelist has entrusted to us.

The anonymous evangelist wrote in order that his community might believe that Jesus is the Christ, the Son of God, and that believing it might have life in his name (John 20:31). It is my hope that the republication of these essays will not only contribute to a deeper understanding of the evangelist's work, but that it will also contribute to a life-giving faith for the members of the extended community of the Beloved Disciple.

Raymond F. Collins

ABBREVIATIONS

In addition to the standard abbreviations of the English language and those in common use for the books of the Bible and other works of ancient literature, the following abbreviations appear in this volume:

AB	Anchor Bible
AnBib	Analecta Biblica
Ang	*Angelicum*
AsSeig	*Assemblées du Seigneur*
BETL	Bibliotheca ephemeridum theologicarum lovaniensium
Bib	*Biblica*
BibLeb	*Bibel und Leben*
BJRL	*Bulletin of the John Rylands University Library*
BLE	*Bulletin de littérature ecclésiastique*
BT	*The Bible Translator*
BTB	*Biblical Theology Bulletin*
BZ	*Biblische Zeitschrift*
BZNW	Beihefte zur *ZNW*
CBQ	*Catholic Biblical Quarterly*
CSEL	Corpus scriptorum ecclesiasticorum latinorum
DR	*Downside Review*
EBib	Etudes bibliques
EstBib	*Estudios biblicos*
ET	English translation
ETL	*Ephemerides theologicae lovanienses*
EvQ	*Evangelical Quarterly*
ExpTim	*Expository Times*
FRLANT	Forschungen zur Religion und Literatur des Alten und Neuen Testaments
HNTC	Harper's New Testament Commentaries

HTKNT	Herders theologische Kommentar zum Neuen Testament
HUT	Hermeneutische Untersuchungen zur Theologie
ICC	International Critical Commentary
Int	*Interpretation*
ITQ	*Irish Theological Quarterly*
JB	Jerusalem Bible
JBL	*Journal of Biblical Literature*
JES	*Journal of Ecumenical Studies*
KNT	Kommentar zum Neuen Testament
LD	Lectio divina
LS	*Louvain Studies*
MeyerK	Kritisch-exegetischer Kommentar über das Neue Testament
MNTC	Moffatt New Testament Commentary
MTZ	*Münchener theologische Zeitschrift*
NAB	New American Bible
NEB	New English Bible
NICNT	New International Commentary on the New Testament
NIV	New International Version
NJB	New Jerusalem Bible
NovT	*Novum Testamentum*
NovTSup	Novum Testamentum, Supplements
NRT	*Nouvelle revue théologique*
NTD	Das Neue Testament Deutsch
NTL	New Testament Library
NTS	*New Testament Studies*
PL	Patrologia Latina
RB	*Revue biblique*
RechBib	Recherches bibliques
RevScRel	*Revue des sciences religieuses*
RevThom	*Revue thomiste*
RivB	*Rivista biblica*
RNT	Regensburger Neues Testament

RScEccl	*Revue des sciences ecclésiastiques*
RSR	*Recherches de science religieuse*
RSV	Revised Standard Version
SBLMS	Society of Biblical Literature Monograph Series
SBS	Stuttgarter Bibelstudien
SBT	Studies in Biblical Theology
SNTSMS	Society for New Testament Studies Monograph Series
Str-B	H. Strack and P. Billerbeck, *Kommentar zum Neuen Testament aus Talmud und Midrash*
TBT	*The Bible Today*
TDNT	G. Kittel and G. Friedrich, eds., *Theological Dictionary of the New Testament*
TS	*Theological Studies*
TTZ	*Trierer theologische Zeitschrift*
TZ	*Theologische Zeitschrift*
VD	*Verbum domini*
ZNW	*Zeitschrift für die neutestamentliche Wissenschaft*
ZTK	*Zeitschrift für Theologie und Kirche*

I. John's Characters

1. REPRESENTATIVE FIGURES

Some years ago, the Cambridge scholar C.F.D. Moule wrote an article on the individualism of the Fourth Gospel[1] in which he tried to demonstrate the thesis that the Fourth Gospel is one of the most strongly individualistic of all the New Testament writings and that the realized eschatology of this gospel results more from this individualism than from any profoundly new or different thought in the Gospel itself. Arguing from the fact that John is full of descriptive encounters between Jesus and various individuals and small groups, Moule held that the particular depth of the gospel lies in its penetrating analysis of the meaning of the individual's relationship with God in Christ. In a word, Moule held that a proper evaluation of the individualism of the Fourth Gospel is the key to an understanding of that gospel and of its eschatology.

Those of us who would be inclined to agree with the Cambridge scholar's position to some extent immediately come into conflict with an ancient tradition of the Church which has been, almost unseemingly, resurrected in the writings of many of the most critical commentators on the Fourth Gospel. This tradition is that which considers that the individuals who appear in the Fourth Gospel are to be considered rather as types of individuals than as historical persons. Already the Alexandrine school, strongly influenced by a neo-Platonist tendency and represented by such a luminary as Origen (d.255), was inclined to interpret the Fourth Gospel in an allegorical fashion. In the Middle Ages,

---

1. C.F.D. Moule, "The Individualism of the Fourth Gospel," *NovT* 5 (1962) 171-190.

Ruppert of Dietz (d.1135) was wont to consider at least some of the individuals of the Fourth Gospel in much the same manner as did the Alexandrines. As Catholic exegesis entered into the twentieth century and adopted the historico-critical method, it largely abandoned the allegorical method of interpretation and looked to the figures who appear in the Fourth Gospel in their historical individuality. A singular exception to this movement within Roman Catholic tradition has been a constant tendency to see in the mother of Jesus (John 2:1-11; 19:25-27) a type of the Church. Within recent years the studies of André Feuillet[2] have exposed most systematically and most forcefully the argumentation which would lead the interpreter to an eschatological interpretation of "the woman" in the Fourth Gospel.

Undoubtedly the Catholic reluctance to accept a typological interpretation of the individual figures of the Fourth Gospel has resulted from an acceptance of the historico-critical method of exegesis. Nevertheless this reluctance has been strengthened by an apologetic concern to reject the excessively symbolic interpretation of the personages of the Fourth Gospel that has been associated with the names of Alfred Loisy[3] and Rudolf Bultmann[4]. Loisy's stress on the symbolism of the Fourth Gospel led even such a venturesome scholar as Lagrange[5] to be somewhat cautious in interpreting the figures of John. In more recent times, Catholic scholars have been not a little uneasy with the work of a so-called ecclesiastical redactor posited by Bultmann in his epoch-

2. Cf. André Feuillet, "Les adieux de Christ à sa mère (Jn. 19,25-27) et la maternité spirituelle de Marie," *NRT* 86 (1964) 469-483; "L'heure de la femme (Jn. 16-21) et l'heure de la Mère de Jésus (Jn. 19,25-27)," *Bib* (47) 1966, 169-184, 361-380, 557-573; "The Hour of Jesus and the Sign of Cana," in *Johannine Studies* (New York: Alba House, 1964) pp. 17-37; "La signification fondamentale du premier miracle de Cana (Jo. II, 1-11) et le symbolisme johannique," *RevThom* 65 (1965) 517-535; etc.

3. Cf. Alfred Loisy, *Le quatrième Evangile. Les epîtres dites de Jean.* (2nd. ed., rev.: Paris, Emile Nourry, 1921).

4. Cf. Rudolf Bultmann, *Das Evangelium des Johannes*, Meyer K., 2. (18th ed., Göttingen: Vandenhoeck & Ruprecht, 1964; ET by G.R. Beasley-Murray, *The Gospel of John. A Commentary.* (Oxford: Basil Blackwell, 1971).

5. Cf. M.-J. Lagrange, *L'Evangile selon S. Jean.* EBib. (Paris: Gabalda, 1925).

making work on John. Similarly, Bultmann's contention that the apparent rivalry between the Beloved Disciple and Peter in the Fourth Gospel[6] represents the struggle between the Hellenistic Christian church and the church of Palestine has provoked not a little skepticism on the part of those who are concerned with maintaining respect for Petrine authority within the tradition of the Church, even that of the early Church. In like manner, the position advanced by Kragerud relative to the interpretation of the Beloved Disciple[7] has not won much adherance within Catholic circles. This Scandinavian scholar proposed that the Beloved Disciple represents not a single person, but a group, i.e., the Johannine church, possessor of the prophetic spirit, which is therefore superior to the ecclesiastical organization represented by Peter.

Nevertheless, the issue of symbolic personages in the Fourth Gospel continues to be with us. Not a few exegetes look to Nathanael, the Samaritan women and Thomas as representative, if not merely symbolic, figures.[8] On one level, a commentary on the role played by these individuals within the Fourth Gospel ought to be made within the broader horizon of Johannine exegesis, namely the obvious symbolism that pervades the entire Fourth Gospel. It is replete with symbolic images such as life and death, light and darkness, night and day, wine and bread, wind and water. The miracles of Jesus must likewise be treated within the symbolic categories of the prophetic 'oth and the properly Johannine sign theology. The reader of the Fourth Gospel cannot help but notice the frequent allusions to Old Testament types, such as the bronzed serpent and the manna. Nor can he overlook John's use of symbolic numbers, principally 7, the number of fullness—the seven titles of Jesus in John 1:29-51, the seven "signs"

6. Rudolf Bultmann, *The Gospel of John*, pp. 484-485 and *passim*.
7. Cf. A. Kragerud, *Der Lieblingsjünger im Johannesevangelium. Ein exegetischer Versuch* (Oslo: Universitätsverlag, 1959).
8. For example, Edward Bode. Cf. E.L. Bode, *The First Easter Morning. The Gospel Accounts of the Women's Visit to the Tomb of Jesus.* AnBib, 45 (Rome: Biblical Institute Press, 1970) p. 75.

of the Gospel, the seven uses of the *egō eimi* (I am) formula with a predicate nominative. Still another aspect of Johannine symbolism that continues to receive attention today, and that particularly from Catholic authors, is the Johannine sacramentary. Authors such as Cullman[9] and Vawter[10] would see a sacrament at every turn whereas others such as Bultmann[11] and the post-Bultmannians would ascribe the sacramentalism of the Fourth Gospel to the work of the ecclesiastical redactor. Somewhere between these two extremes lies the more critical and accurate evaluation of Johannine sacramentalism proposed by such authors as Niewalda, Brown and Klos.[12] Still other examples of the use of symbolism in the Fourth Gospel could be cited, but these several examples are sufficient to recall that it is difficult, if not impossible, to interpret the Gospel without taking into account its symbolism. Thus the very literary style which characterizes the Fourth Gospel should lead the interpreter and reader to question the symbolic characters of the individuals who appear within its twenty-one chapters. I would therefore propose that the individualism of the Fourth Gospel is a key to its interpretation, not in the sense that it determines the realized eschatology which is characteristic of the Gospel, as Moule holds, but in the sense that it provides a basic insight into the meaning of the Gospel, the tradition that lay behind it, and the purpose for which it was compiled.

If I look to individualism as an interpretative key for an exegesis of the Fourth Gospel, it is only because of a position which I would adopt relative to the pre-history of the Fourth Gospel. Basically the attempts to explain the literary provenance of the Fourth Gospel fall into three general categories. There are

9. Oscar Cullmann, *Early Christian Worship*. SBT, 10 (London: SCM, 1953).

10. Bruce Vawter, "The Johannine Sacramentary," *TS* 17 (1956) 151-166.

11. Cf. Rudolf Bultmann, *John*, pp. 138, n. 3; 218-219; 234-237; etc.

12. A good overview of the entire question has been provided by Herbert Klos. *Die Sakramente im Johannesevangelium*. SBS, 46. (Stuttgart: Katholisches Bibelwerk, 1970).

those who have recourse to a theory of sources,[13] those who opt for various displacements,[14] and those who hold to successive redactions[15] as well as those who opt for a combination of these as providing the most plausible explanation for the various aporias which exist in the Fourth Gospel. Perhaps Bultmann's commentary was the last major work to attempt to explicate the origin of this Gospel solely on the grounds of editors working with various literary documents at their disposal. Nowadays various documentary theories must be supplemented by appeals to the oral tradition out of which the Johannine Gospel grew. It was to the great credit of Bent Noack[16] that he reminded scholars of the influence that oral tradition had on the development of the Johannine tradition. In the sixties, such diverse scholars as Laconi,[17] Brown[18] and Schnackenburg,[19] opted for a relatively complex theory of composition to explain the Fourth Gospel in which they posited the influence of preaching as a most significant formative factor in the development of a specifically Johannine form of the Gospel tradition. Still more recently Barnabas Lindars[20] has appealed to the Johannine homily as the life situation of much of the Johannine material. This life situation has given a specifically Johannine cast to the material presently found in the Fourth Gospel.

13. R. Bultmann, H. Becker, G.H.C. MacGregor, A.Q. Morton, D.M. Smith, R.T. Fortna, etc.

14. R. Bultmann, J.H. Bernard, A. Wikenhauser, R. Olivieri, etc.

15. J. Wellhausen, E. Schwartz, E. Hirsch, R.E. Brown, R. Schnackenburg, etc.

16. Cf. Bent Noack, *Zur johanneischen Tradition. Beiträge zur literarkritische Exegese des vierten Evangeliums* (Copenhagen: Rosenkilde, 1954).

17. M. Laconi, "La critica letteraria applicata al IV Vangelo," *Ang* 40 (1963) 277-312.

18. Raymond E. Brown, *The Gospel According to John. I-XII*. AB, 29. (Garden City: Doubleday, 1966) pp. xxxiv-xxxix.

19. Rudolf Schnackenburg, *The Gospel According to St. John*, 1. Herder's Theological Commentary on the New Testament (New York: Herder and Herder, 1968; ET of *Das Johannesevangelium*, I, Freiburg: Herder, 1965) pp. 59-74.

20. Barnabas Lindars, *Behind the Fourth Gospel*. Studies in Creative Criticism, 3 (London: SPCK, 1971) pp. 43-60. *The Gospel of John*. New Century Bible (London: Oliphants, 1972) pp. 51-54.

It is my conviction that a process of oral tradition similar to that which lay behind the Synoptic Gospels also lies behind the Fourth Gospel. Within this homiletic tradition we should place the development of units of material, pericopes, in which various individuals appear—precisely as types of the point that the hom- ilist was trying to make. The evangelist and a final redactor would have compiled these several units of traditional Johannine homiletic material into his gospel where they remain as types which can serve to support the basic theme of his gospel. Obviously such an assertion requires that an extended treatment be given to the provenance of the Fourth Gospel, and that a study be made of the relationship between theology and history in the Fourth Gospel. To make either of these studies in a satisfactory manner would carry me far beyond the scope of the present essay. Hence I would simply have to say that in a general way I epouse the homiletic provenance approach urged by Laconi, Brown, Schnackenburg, Lindars, *et al.*, and that my vision of a redactional critical approach to the Fourth Gospel is that the redactor is working with traditional material, a good part of which has an historical basis. What that historical basis is, in the concrete, would have to be determined for each pericope—a determination that can properly be made only in a series of monographs or a voluminous study.

Fortunately one of the earliest, if all too superficial, redaction critical approaches to the Fourth Gospel was made by Juan Leal, S.J.,[21] who proposed that the Fourth Gospel ought to be consid- ered within the climate of faith. He drew attention to the frequent use of *pistuein* (to believe) in the Fourth Gospel and to the stated purpose of the Gospel as this is found in its first conclusion: "Now Jesus did many others signs in the presence of his disciples, which are not written in this book; but these are written that you may believe that Jesus is the Christ, the Son of God, and that believing you may have life in his name" (John 20:30-31). These

---

21. Juan Leal, "El clima de la fe e la Redaktionsgeschichte del IV Evangelio," *EstBib* 22 (1963) 141-177.

verses lead us to conclude that either the gospel in its penultimate stage[22] or the principal source used by the Evangelist pointed to salvific faith as the major purpose of the work. The most recent commentaries on the Fourth Gospel and a number of articles[23] have studied the purpose of the Fourth Gospel from a number of different vantage points. There are, indeed, a variety of ways of approaching the issue of the purpose of the Fourth Gospel. However, I find it difficult to disagree with the starting point urged by van Unnik,[24] namely that this brace of verses ought to receive prime emphasis in any consideration of the purpose of the Fourth Gospel. Granted it is difficult, on the basis of these two verses alone, with all the difficulties attendant upon their interpretation, to determine whether these verses reflect the situation of the missionary who is bent on enkindling faith in those who do not yet believe or that of the homilist and/or polemicist who intends to strengthen and confirm the faith of his audience, nevertheless it is clear that they point to faith as the purpose of the Fourth Gospel. I am personally inclined to the view that the faith to which these verses refer is the faith of one who already believes and that this faith is pre-eminently a christological faith.

In short, I would uphold that within the life-situation of the Johannine church we ought to envision a series of homilies directed to enkindling faith in Jesus. In the development of these homilies, various persons were chosen from the common gospel tradition or selected from his own tradition by the homilist in order to illustrate some point about the nature of faith, or lack of it, in Jesus Christ. Thus the various individuals of the Fourth Gospel do not stand as mere figments of the evangelist's imagination nor have they been chosen to demonstrate the relationship between the individual and God in Jesus Christ. Rather they

22. I.e., before the addition of the prologue and epilogue (John 1:1-18; 21).

23. A particularly valuable survey accompanies the personal opinion offered by A. Wind in "Destination and Purpose of the Gospel of John," *NovT* 14 (1972) 26-69.

24. Cf. W.C. van Unnik, "The Purpose of St. John's Gospel," in Studia Evangelica, I, Texte und Untersuchungen, 73 (Berlin: Akademieverlag, 1959) pp. 382-411.

have been selected from the homiletic tradition of the Johannine tradition to teach the evangelist's readers something about that faith in Jesus Christ which is life-giving. In this way it is appropriate to look at the several individuals who appear in the Fourth Gospel as individuals who have been type-cast. In their individuality they represent a type of faith (or lack of faith) -response to Jesus who is the Christ and Son of God.

At this point it must be obvious to the reader that the main thesis of this essay could be carried one step further than I have chosen to carry it. It is quite possible to speak of the Jews, the Greeks, his own, the world, and possibly also of Satan as having a representative character. I have not chosen to do so because I would gladly limit the scope of this essay. Thus I shall examine, only and briefly, those individuals in the Fourth Gospel who appear to have been definitely type-cast by the evangelist so that he might teach his readers about salvific faith and thereby enkindle and confirm that faith within them. Such individuals are John the Baptist, Nathanael, Mary (the mother of Jesus), Nicodemus, the Samaritan woman, the royal official, the lame man, Philip, the man born blind, Lazarus, Judas, Mary Magdalene, Thomas, Peter and the Beloved Disciple. These fifteen individuals reduced to somewhat of a stereotype insofar as they are representative figures, have characteristic traits that are not necessarily mutually exclusive. The Johannine characterization of each of these individuals illustrates something about the nature of a faith-response to Jesus. They have each figured as a "hero" in the homiletic tradition that lies behind the Fourth Gospel. It is therefore from the perspective of his/her representative capacity that the appearance of each of these personages in the Fourth Gospel must be understood.

John the Baptist

A clear indication that the Fourth Gospel belongs to the gospel *genre*, despite the striking particularities of its format and its theology, is the fact that it begins, as do the Synoptics,[25] with a narrative about John the Baptist. This introductory narrative (John 1:19-34) is followed by another scene in which John the Baptist appears (John 3:25-30) and two rather problematic passages, namely John 1:6-8, 15 and John 4:1-3.[26] Both of these problematic passages are such because they touch upon the issue of Johannine redaction at a late stage of the development of the Fourth Gospel. Undoubtedly John 4:2 has been inserted into the narrative as a corrective to John 3:26 and 4:1 in order to harmonize the Johannine narrative with that of the Synoptics who never present Jesus himself as a baptizer. The verses which have been intercalated into the prologue (John 1:6-8, 15) are problematic insofar as they may be considered as the original introduction to the Fourth Gospel[27] which were introduced into the prologue when this was added to the Gospel or they may be considered as the work of the final redactor of John, the same editor who was responsible for appending John 21 to the Fourth Gospel.[28] Indeed even the composition of both of the major passages which deal with John the Baptist poses something of a problem for those who are concerned with the redaction of the Fourth Gospel. Bultmann's position is well-known[29]. He considers that vv. 22-24 are an addition to John 1:19-34 made by a later editor and that John 3:22-30 can easily be divided into two pericopes, the first of which (vv. 22-26) is a literary composition of the author himself or of his tradition, whereas the second part (vv. 27-30) is clearly the evangelist's own composition. Bult-

25. Mark 1:9-11 and par.
26. In two other passages of the Fourth Gospel, the Johannine Jesus speaks of the Baptist. These are John 5:33-36 and 10:40-42.
27. Such is the opinion of Viteau and Boismard, supported by R.E. Brown. Cf. J. Viteau, "Sur le Prologue de S. Jean (Jn. 1,1-18)," *RevScRel* 2 (1922) 459-467; M.E. Boismard, *St. John's Prologue* (London: Blackfriars, 1957) pp. 24-25; R.E. Brown, *John. I-XII*, p. 21.
28. Among the authors who hold to this view, Ernst Haenchen may be cited. Cf. E. Haenchen, "Probleme des johanneischen Prologs," *ZTK* 60 (1963) 305-334.
29. Cf. R. Bultmann, *John*, pp. 85, 167-169.

mann's position is, however, but one among the several opinions
advanced by those authors who have studied the redaction of the
Fourth Gospel.

Apart from these several rather complex questions, it is immediately apparent to the reader who compares the Johannine
narrative with that of the Synoptics that the John of the Fourth
Gospel is quite different from the John of the Synoptics. To some
extent this might represent an apologetic concern on the part of
the Johannine author or of his tradition.[30] Nonetheless it
remains clear that the John of the Fourth Gospel is a distinctively
Johannine John. This is already apparent in the manner in which
the figure of the Baptist is introduced into the Fourth Gospel.
Nowhere is he characterized as the Baptizer or the Baptist; rather
he is simply introduced as "a man sent from God, whose name
was John" (1:6). Likewise in v. 19 the name of John is cited
without any descriptive titles. The reader is presumably aware
that John did baptize—otherwise the "Who are you?" of v. 19
hardly makes sense—but the fact of John's baptismal activity is
not introduced until v. 25.[31]

The John of the Fourth Gospel is a John of Christian faith and
Johannine characterization. It is the fact that he is sent from God
which marks him as a man to be understood within the light of
Christian faith; it is the fact that he is described as one who has
come for testimony, to bear witness to the light (John 1:7) that
gives to him a Johannine coloring. The Johannine John is pre-
eminently and almost exclusively a witness.[32] He has been sent by
God to bear witness to Jesus. That the function of John has been
reduced to the single role of giving witness is apparent from the

30. It is commonly accepted that a polemic motif accompanies the presentation
of the Baptist in the Fourth Gospel. According to this view part of the evangelist's
purpose in writing the Fourth Gospel was to counter claims, made by the
followers of John the Baptist, that he (the Baptist) was the Messiah. This view is
rather successfully opposed by Lindars in the two volumes which have been
previously cited.

31. Cf. 3:23; 10:40.

32. Commenting on John 1:19-28, Thomas Barosse has commented that "The
passage strips him down, so to speak, to his essential role as pointer to Christ."

multiple uses of the verb "to give witness" (*marturein*) and its cognates in the "Baptist" passages of the Fourth Gospel.[33] This impression is reinforced when we realize that "This is the Testimony of John" (1:19) serves as an introductory title to the first Johannine narrative.[34] Then when John does give direct testimony to Jesus as he does in v. 29, no mention is made of the public to whom John's testimony is addressed. He has been stripped down to an essential role, in which time and audience are almost unessential, that of giving witness. As such, John is the type of the Christian confessor. John represents the believer who confesses that Jesus is the Lamb of God (v. 29), and the one upon whom the Spirit remains (v. 32). His representative role is clearly stated in the verse, so full of Johannine vocabulary and theology, which stands as the climax of the first great pericope on the Baptist: "I have seen and have borne witness that this is the Son of God" (John 1:34). No more need be said than this to affirm that the John who appears at the beginning of the Fourth Gospel is no longer the one whose proper function is to baptize; rather he is a paradigmatic figure who represents the confessing Christian who bears witness to Jesus.

Nathaniel

The "Who are you?" question ostensibly addressed to the Baptist in John 1:19 is, in fact, a question about the identity of

Cf. T. Barosse, "The Seven Days of the New Creation in St. John's Gospel," *CBQ* (21) 1959, 507-516, pp. 508-509. Cf. also B. Marconcini, "Dal Battista 'storico' al Battista 'giovanneo': interpretazione storica e interpretatione esistentiale," *RivistB* 20 (suppl.) 1972, 467-480.

33. John 1:7, 8, 15, 19, 32, 34; 3:26, 28 (32, 33); 5:33, 34, 36. Particularly significant in this regard are John 3:26 and 5:33-36. In 3:26 a statement placed on the lips of the Baptist's disciples characterizes him as one whose role was to bear witness to Jesus. In 5:33-36 mention of the testimony of John (cf. v. 33: he has born witness to the truth) is inserted in a lengthier passage (John 5:30-47) which speaks of several other witnesses to Jesus: Jesus himself, the Father, Jesus' works and the Scriptures. Ultimately these several witnesses are reducible to one, the Father himself.

34. I.e. in the body of the Gospel itself.

the Messiah. The answer to that question is given in John 1:35-51
where Jesus is successively confessed to be the Lamb of God (v.
35), Rabbi (vv. 38, 49), Messiah (v. 41), the one of whom Moses
in the law and the prophets also wrote (v. 45), Jesus of Nazareth,
the son of Joseph (v. 45), the Son of God (v. 49) and the king of
Israel (v. 49). The seven-fold repetition of christological titles
indicates the fullness of Jesus' Messiahship and sets the stage for
the body of the Gospel in which the meaning of that Messiahship
is gradually unfolded for the Johannine community by the Gospel's description of the signs performed and the discourses uttered
by Jesus himself.

It is in the final pericope of this section on discipleship and
confession that Nathanael appears (vv. 43-51). He is an individual known only to the tradition of the Fourth Gospel,
appearing in this pericope and then again in John 21:2 where he
occurs among the seven disciples whom Jesus encounters on the
shore of the Sea of Tiberias and where he is identified as a native
of Cana in Galilee. The entire sequence of vocation and confession scenes[35] culminates in the encounter between Jesus and
Nathanael, who appropriately bears an Old Testament name.
John describes him as a man seated "under the fig tree." To the
perceptive reader this would recall the late Jewish tradition about
the study of the Scriptures under a fig tree.[36] Jesus, the all-
knowing divine man, perceives the true quality of the man who
bears both an Israelite name and is engaged in an activity which
is most characteristic of the people of the book and, using a
technical formula of revelation,[37] identifies him as "an Israelite
indeed, in whom there is no guile."

35. The traditional "vocation stories" have been transformed into "witness
stories" by the Johannine tradition. Commenting on the development of the
dramatic sequence of scenes in John 1, Lindars has commented: "Finally there is
the incident of Nathanael, in which the conversation is carefully contrived to lead
to the great testimony, 'You are the Son of God! You are the King of Israel!'" Cf.
B. Lindars, Behind the Fourth Gospel, p. 53.

36. Cf. S. Schulz, Das Evangelium nach Johannes. NTD, 4 (12th. ed.: Göttingen,
Vandenhoeck & Ruprecht, 1972) p. 42.

37. Cf. M. de Goedt, "Un schème de révélation dans le 4e Ev.," NTS 8 (1961-

As the true Israelite, Nathanael identifies Jesus as the "King of Israel," a traditional messianic title (cf. Mark 15:26). Thus Nathanael can represent the authentic Israel insofar as he recognizes and confesses that Jesus is the Messiah, the promised and anointed one. The evangelist has added to the traditional Messianic confession a Christian confession: Nathanael identifies Jesus as the "Son of God." On the one hand, this represents the evangelist's interpretation of "King of Israel." Jesus is Messiah in so far as he is the Son of God, a title to be understood not in the Old Testament sense as one who is particularly chosen, but in the specifically Johannine sense which points to the uniqueness of the relationship between the Father and the Son. On the other hand, it is this Christian (Johannine) interpretation of Nathanael's faith which allows him to be seen as a "true" Israelite. In the tradition of the Fourth Gospel, that which is true is not merely authentic; it is also the fulfillment of that which had been foreshadowed and promised of old.

If Nathanael represents the true Israelite, he stands in sharp contrast to "the Jews." They search the Scriptures and yet refuse to come to Jesus (John 5:39-40). Their father is the devil in whom there is no truth (John 8:44). They ask the question "Who are you?" (John 8:25), but do not understand what Jesus says (8:43). In contrast, Nathanael who had searched the Scriptures under the fig tree came to Jesus. He is one in whom there is no guile. Like the other disciples, whom he represents in so far as he is the true Israelite, Natnanael has no need to ask "Who are you?" (cf. John 8:25). He will come to know who Jesus is. Because Jesus has called Nathanael the true Israelite, with a call which constitutes him in this very capacity, Nathanael receives the answer to the unasked "Who are you?" question. Jesus is the Son of Man (v. 51). This answer is contained in a verse which has been added to the Nathanael pericope at a late stage in the development of the

1962) 142-150. This Johannine revelation formula is found in John 1:29-34, 35-39, 47-51; 19:24-27. It consists of a verb of seeing, the designation of the one seen, a verb of saying, the use of "behold" and a specific characterization of the person who is the object of the revelation.

Gospel tradition.[38] Yet it is important, not only by reason of the role which the Son of Man title plays in the Fourth Gospel, but also because the addition of the verse to the earlier tradition makes of Nathanael, the true Israelite, the first hearer of a formula of self-revelation coming from the Jesus of the Fourth Gospel, who is the self-revealing Son of God and Son of Man. What the true and believing Israelite perceives is the abiding and permanent union of the earthy Son of Man with the heavenly world.

Nicodemus

Quite different from the figure of Nathanael is that of Nicodemus. Outside of the Johannine Gospel (John 3:1-15; 7:50; 19:39), he, too, is unknown to the Gospel tradition. Nevertheless the description provided by the author of the Fourth Gospel is clear enough to give a type to Nicodemus. He is a representative of official Judaism. He belongs to the party of the Pharisees (John 3:1; 7:50) and, as a zealous Pharisee, is attentive to the observance of the law (7:50-51) and ritual piety (John 9:39). He is a ruler of the Jews (John 3:1). Obviously this indicates that the evangelist wants us to understand that the otherwise unknown Nicodemus is a leading man among "the Jews." Yet the title probably implies more than that. It would seem to indicate that Nicodemus is a member of the Sanhedrin.[39] With this frame of reference the allusive reference to Jesus' death in 3:14-15 takes on additional meaning. Finally, Nicodemus is a scribe (John 3:10; 7:50-51) whom the Johannine Jesus almost ironically styles "a teacher of Israel." As Nathanael represented the nation of Israel, the community of the elect who confess Jesus as the Messiah, Nicodemus represents the Jews, who study the Scriptures and

38. A number of inconsistencies between v. 51 and the preceding narrative show that this verse did not originally belong to the Nathanael tradition. Most probably it was a Son of Man saying which was circulated independently.

39. Cf. R. Bultmann, *John*, p. 133, n. 4.

know the Mosaic tradition, yet do not come to believe in Jesus, the Messiah and Savior.

Undoubtedly the dialogue with Nicodemus which appears in John 3:1-15 has been influenced by the wisdom tradition[40] and the tradition of the rabbinic dialogue.[41] The present pericope shows ample evidence of having been shaped within the Johannine tradition, to the point that Bultmann would consider it to be a composition of the evangelist himself. It is even more probable that the evangelist is presenting in written form a unit of Johannine oral tradition, marked as it is by typical Johannine traits. Following the law of stage duality, only two figures appear: Jesus and his interlocutor, Nicodemus. The latter, clearly marked as a representative of official Judaism, has become for the evangelist a type of the unbeliever. Nicodemus comes to Jesus by night (John 3:2). This is much more than a merely temporal reference—it is characteristic of the very encounter between Jesus and Nicodemus.[42] The encounter is basically noctural; it took place in darkness rather than in the light of revelation. If the stage has already been set from v. 2, the dialogue reaches its climax in the question which Jesus addresses to Nicodemus in v. 10: "Are you a teacher of Israel, and yet you do not understand this?" Misunderstanding is not a matter of understanding incompletely or inaccurately. It is rather a basic lack of understanding of the gospel teaching—it is expressive of a lack of faith.[43] Nicodemus has not received the gift of belief. He does not represent those for whom the signs are but a step towards belief; rather he represents those for whom the signs are the end as well as the beginning. This is even more apparent when we consider that the dialogue centers on being born anew. Such rebirth, as de la Potterie has

40. Cf. J.E. Bruns, "Some Reflections on Coheleth and John," *CBQ* 25 (1963) 414-416.

41. Cf. R. Bultmann, *John*, p. 132.

42. Cf. John 19:39.

43. Cf. M. De Jonge, "Nicodemus and Jesus: Some Observations on Misunderstanding and Understanding in the 4th Gospel," *BJRL* 53 (1971) 337-351; also S. Schulz, *Johannes*, p. 53.

shown,[44] does not only refer to the eschatological outpouring of the Spirit, but also to that outpouring of the Spirit which arouses authentic faith. Nicodemus has not understood what is meant by rebirth, he has not believed. As such he remains a leading man among "the Jews"—a type of unbelief.

The Samaritan Woman

At first reading, the narrative of the encounter between Jesus and the Samaritan woman offers a number of traits similar to those found in the Nicodemus incident. In both instances we meet a person who is otherwise unknown in the gospel tradition. In both cases we are dealing with a narrative composed by the evangelist[45] on the basis of a tradition which shows points of contact with Old Testament themes and rabbinic tradition. In each of the narratives, Johannine misunderstanding plays a major role in the point which the evangelist makes as he includes this bit of oral tradition in his gospel. Yet the point made by each of the pericopes is quite different.

The history of the narrative of the Samaritan woman is quite complicated. For instance, Schulz[46] contends that v. 1 is a post-Johannine gloss, that vv. 2-4 reflect the Synoptic tradition, that vv. 10-15 are a composition by the evangelist himself, and that he has preserved a Johannine tradition by including vv. 16-19 in his narrative. Certainly the present text shows points of contact with Gen 24:29 and Exodus 2.[47] Underlying the original story there lies quite clearly the issue of the relationship between the Jews and the Samaritans, but in the situation of the Christian church in which this account took shape there was the more urgent issue of the relationship between Jewish Christians and Samaritan

44. Ignace de la Potterie, "Jesus et Nicodemus: de necessitate generationis ex Spiritu (Jo. 3:1-10)," *VD* 47 (1969) 193-214.

45. Cf. *Inter alia*, S. Sabugal, "El titulo Messias-Christos en el contexto del relato sobre la actividad de Jesus en Samaria: Jn. 4:25, 29, *Aug* 12 (1972) 79-105.

46. Cf. S. Schulz, *Johannes*, pp. 74-75.

47. Cf. N.R. Bonneau, "The Woman at the Well, John 4 and Genesis 24," *TBT* 67 (1973) 1252-1259.

Christians. Indeed it may well be that in vv. 37-48 the Johannine tradition is addressing itself to the same concern that is resolved by the Lucan author of Acts 8:4-28.[48] Similarly it would appear that in v. 9 John is not so much concerned with showing that Jesus was willing to break a ritual prohibition imposed by the Pharisees, but that he destroyed the basis for any hatred between Jew and Samaritan.

As with the narratives of the encounter between Jesus and the other representative figures of the Fourth Gospel whom we have examined, our author's intention focuses primarily upon the encounter between Jesus and the representative individual. As in the case of Nicodemus, the misunderstanding of the Samaritan woman bears upon the gift of water which "wells up to eternal life." However, far from proving non-receptive, the woman requests the gift of Jesus. As a true disciple, she is invited to believe (v. 21) and is given a mission (v. 16). Her misunderstanding, then, was not that lack of understanding which was characteristic of Nicodemus. Rather her misunderstanding is similar to the inadequate understanding which is characteristic of the disciples.[49] Indeed the knowledge of the woman shown by Jesus (v. 16) recalls the all-knowing Jesus who knew Nathanael (1:48). In both cases, the knowledge of Jesus leads to a confession of faith, namely that Jesus is the Messiah. This confession of faith provokes a further response from Jesus, "I who speak to you am he" (v. 26). This is the first use of the *egō eimi* formula of self-revelation in the Fourth Gospel. John's Jesus once again interprets a Messianic confession,[50] this time by revealing that he

48. This is one of the points made by B. Prete, in "La Samaritana (Giov. 4, 1-42)," *Sacra Doctrina* 9 (1964) 252-268.

49. Cf. vv. 31-38. The addition of these verses into the account of the encounter between Jesus and the Samaritan woman serves, among other purposes, to place the Samaritan's "misunderstanding" in proper focus. Cf. S. Schulz, *Johannes*, p. 77.

50. Cf. John 1:51. Whereas Nathanael's confession proclaimed that Jesus is the King of Israel, the Samaritan woman must have proclaimed Jesus to be the *Taheb*, the one awaited by the Samaritans. The Messiah title would then be a Johannine insertion into the narrative. Cf. S. Sabugal, "El titulo." On the *Taheb*, cf. Wayne A. Meeks, *The Prophet-King. Moses Traditions and the Johannine Christology*.

is the Revealer, the one who speaks. Thus, as usual, the evangelist
reveals his christological interest when he narrates the encounters
between Jesus and the representative figures of the Fourth Gospel.

We would not, however, have sufficiently exploited the representative function of the Samaritan woman if we look to her
simply as a believer to whom Jesus responds with the words
which demand ultimate faith, "I am he who speaks to you."
Rather we must look ahead to vv. 39-42 where we are told that
the Samaritan woman testified to others about Jesus. As such she
represents the Christian messenger who brings others to faith.
The faith which results from the testimony of the believing
Christian is a faith which can be encapsulated in a formulaic
confession, "This is indeed the Savior of the World" (v. 42)[51]
and which leads to Jesus' abiding[52] with those who come to
believe in him (v. 40). We should not, however, accept too readily
Bultmann's contention that the faith of the Samaritans is a
"second-hand" faith of less value than that of the Samaritan
woman herself until such time as the Samaritans have come to
encounter Jesus himself.[53] Rather the faith described in v. 39 is

NovTSup, 14 (Leiden: E.J. Brill, 1967) esp. pp. 250-254; John MacDonald, *The
Theology of the Samaritans*. NTL (London: SCM, 1964) pp. 362-371.

51. It should be noted that Johannine Christology is also fundamentally
soteriological. Cf. John 20:30-31. A good study of the relationship between
Johannine Christology and Johannine Soteriology has been made by R.T. Fortna
in "From Christology to Soteriology. A Redaction-Critical Study of Salvation in
the Fourth Gospel," *Int* 27 (1973) 31-47.

52. A full discussion of the notion of abiding in the Fourth Gospel is offered by
Jürgen Heise, in *Bleiben. Menein in den Johanneischen Schriften*. HUT, 8 (Tübingen: Mohr, 1967).

53. Cf. R. Bultmann, *John*, pp. 200-212. I must agree with Bultmann that the
women symbolizes "mediatory proclamation which brings its hearers to Jesus."
But his further contention that "if the woman's witness was for people the
necessary condition of their faith, in itself it is of no importance; rather its
importance lies in the fact that it brings people to Jesus, or that faith becomes
faith *dia ton logon autou*, while human witness appears by contrast as *lalia*, as mere
words which in themselves do not contain that to which witness is borne," is
prompted by Bultmann's existentialist interpretation of the Gospel and stands in
need of further refinement. Bultmann's interpretation does not sufficiently take
into account the force of the verb *pistuein* in v. 39. Although it is true that the

full faith in the Johannine sense of the term. The evangelist's point is simple, namely, that the believer is one who brings others to belief in Jesus' word—to faith in Jesus, the Revealer. As such the believing Samaritan is a type of the Christian herald, the Christian messenger.

The Royal Official

Immediately following upon the narrative of the Samaritan woman comes the pericope which describes the encounter between Jesus and the royal official (John 4:46-54). Traditionally, and with good reason, the substance of the narrative has been assigned to the Sign-Source used by the evangelist in the composition of the Fourth Gospel. However, there are further problems related to the history of the tradition of this pericope which must be considered. First of all, it is clear that the Johannine narrative agrees in many details with the cure of the royal official's son which is described in Matt 8:5-13 and Luke 7:1-10, apparently the single miracle story which these Synoptists have taken from the Q-source. We can therefore conclude that all three evangelists narrate the same event,[54] even though considerable differences exist among the three versions of the event. Then, we must consider that some or all of vv. 51-53 have been added to the narrative in order to highlight the miraculous element in the narrative, i.e., that we are dealing with a cure effected from a distance. Finally, there is the problem of vv. 48-49 which have been added to the original and very brief narrative. Schnackenburg[55] rightly claims that they reflect a Johannine tradition and the specifically Johannine notion of sign, whereas Boismard[56] has

ultimate importance of Christian witness is that it brings people to Jesus, the value of the witness itself is not thereby denigrated. It leads to belief.

54. Cf. E.F. Siegman, "St. John's Use of the Synoptic Material," *CBQ* (30) 1968, 182-198.

55. R. Schnackenburg, "Zur Traditionsgeschichte von Joh. 4,46-54," *BZ* 8 (1964) 58-88.

56. M.-E. Boismard, "Saint Luc et la rédaction du quatrième évangile (Jn. IV,46-54)," *RB* 69 (1962) 185-211.

unsuccessfully tried to establish that these verses (as well as vv. 51-53) were added by the Lucan redactor and reflect a Lucan interpretation of the signs of Jesus.

The interpreter who understands this narrative in a merely symbolic sense and takes the royal official, whose son is cured from a distance, as the representative of the Gentile world is doing a bit of *eisegegis*. He is reading into the text. The royal official of John, unlike the centurion of the Synoptics,[57] need be no more than a high official in the employ of the Herodian court. His representative function is indicated in v. 50: "The man believed the word that Jesus spoke to him and went his way." As the faith of the centurion of Matthew and Luke[58] was the occasion for the cure of his son,[59] so it is the faith of the centurion in the word of Jesus that is the focal point of the Johannine narrative (vv. 50, 53). Nevertheless the Johannine narrative on this point is not as explicit about the faith of the royal official providing the occasion for the cure as is the Matthean.[60] When we compare the Johannine account with that of Matthew-Luke still further, another difference between the narratives comes to our attention. According to John, the word which the Johannine Jesus speaks is a word which gives life:[61] "Go, your son will live" (v. 50, cf. vv. 51, 53). Jesus' word in the tradition that is specific to the Fourth Gospel is not simply a healing word as it is in the Synoptics; it is rather a life-giving word. Thus the royal official of the Fourth Gospel stands as a representative of those who believe in Jesus' word, the word which alone brings life.

57. Luke 7:4-5, 9.
58. Matt 8:5; Luke 7:6-7.
59. Matt 8:13.
60. Cf. M.E. Boismard, "Saint Luc," p. 186.
61. Cf. B. Prete, "Beati coloro che non vedono e credono (Giov. 20,29)," *BeO* 9 (1967) 97-114, p. 103.

The Lame Man and the Man Born Blind

Both Rudolph Bultmann and J. Louis Martyn have pointed out that the story of John 5:1-18 and that of John 9:1-34 are constructed in a remarkably similar fashion.[62] Each of the dramas has a comparable sequence of scenes. Each begins with a miracle story (5:1-9b; 9:1-7) which is like that found in the Synoptics, with respect both to kind and to form. The classic tripartite schema of serious sickness (5:5; 9:1)—stereotyped command (5:8; 9:7a)—effect (5:9; 9:7b) is found in each narrative. Each miracle story leads to a controversy between Jesus and the Jews. The controversy is linked but loosely to the miracle story itself. In each case the juncture is established merely because the miracle is said, *post factum*, to have occurred on the Sabbath (5:9b, 10, 16, 18; 9:14, 16). Both narratives reflect a similar historical background, namely that of the relationship between the Christian church and the hostile Jewish synagogue.

When we compare the narratives still further, it is not immediately evident that the lame man is a representative figure, but the similarities between the narratives of John 5 and John 9 incline us to believe that the lame man is a representative figure. His representative status however can be understood only when he is compared to the man born blind who clearly has a symbolic function in the Fourth Gospel. The Johannine note of John 9:7 leads us to the conclusion that the evangelist would have us understand symbolically his account of the cure of the man born blind. This healing is treated by John as a symbol of the spiritual illumination which a man receives when he believes and is baptized.[63] The frequent references to washing point to the baptismal significance of the pericope, but vv. 35-39 show that it is the cured man and his faith which is the central point in the

---

62. Cf. R. Bultmann, *John*, p. 329; J. Louis Martyn, *History and Theology in the Fourth Gospel* (New York: Harper and Row, 1968) pp. 49-50.

63. Cf. J. Bligh, "Form Studies in St. John. I: The Man Born Blind," *Heythrop Journal* 7 (1966) 129-144.

theological reflection of the evangelist. Unlike the cured lame
man who, when queried by the Jews, did not know the identity of
Jesus, the man who received sight professed that Jesus was a
prophet. His initial confession of faith recalls that of the Samaritan woman who likewise acknowledged that Jesus was a prophet
(John 4:19). As Jesus had encountered the formerly lame man a
second time (5:14), so too he sought out the man who could not
see a second time (9:35). Jesus questions about his belief the man
who had been born blind but who could now see (v. 35). The
dialogue focuses on the Son of Man, recalling the revelation
made to Nicodemus (1:51), and inviting a still more profound
confession of faith on the part of the man who had been given the
gift of sight. Again, as in the dialogue with the Samaritan woman
(John 4:26), Jesus discloses himself as the Revealer: "It is he who
speaks to you" (5:37). The response is clearly that of a man
whose faith is renewed and developed for he confesses Jesus to be
the Lord and worships him.

A comparison of the dialogues following upon these two
Synoptic-like miracle stories permits us to appreciate the specifically Johannine character of the two dialogues and to contrast
the Johannine figure of the lame man with that of the man born
blind. For the evangelist and his tradition, the blind man represents the Jew whose experience of Jesus' healing power is such
that he is led to faith.[64] His faith places him in a critical situation
in which his belief leads him to defend his healer, to be excom-
municated from the synagogue, and to deepen his faith still
further. In contrast, the lame man represents the Jew who, having
experienced Jesus' healing presence, is also placed in a critical
position. While presumably thankful for his cure and presumably
sinning[65] no more, he is ignorant about Jesus' identity, appar-

64. Cf. J. Louis Martyn, *History and Theology*, pp. 55-56.

65. Although Jesus' exhortation to "sin no more" (John 5:14) recalls the
Jewish notion that sin is the cause of illness, it is particularly important in the
narrative of the cure of the lame man. First of all it suggests that his lameness was
the result of sin and contrasts his illness with that of the man born blind. In the
account of the latter cure a causal relationship between illness and sin is
specifically denied (John 9:3). Secondly, we can note a touch of Johannine irony in

ently sides with the Jews (5:15), and thus finds himself allied with those who persecuted Jesus (5:16). Thus both the lame man and the blind man are representative figures in the tradition of the Fourth Gospel, but they are antithetically symbolical to the point that one cannot be understood without the other.

Philip

The figure of Philip in the Fourth Gospel is a bit more complex than any of the representative figures whom we have thus far encountered. Apart from John the Baptist he is the only one of these figures to be named by both the Fourth Gospel and the Synoptic Gospels.[66] As is the case with the Baptist, Philip appears in the Fourth Gospel with quite a different function from that which is his in the Synoptic tradition. The Synoptics list Philip among the Twelve,[67] which is not a particularly Johannine theme, but the Fourth Gospel does not list Philip among the seven disciples to whom Jesus revealed himself by the Sea of Tiberias. Whom then does the Johannine Philip represent?

We find Philip in four pericopes of the Fourth Gospel: John 1:43-51; 6:1-15; 12:20-36; and 14:1-14. The first of these pericopes (1:43-51) clearly establishes Philip as a disciple with the mission of a disciple. He responded to the call "Follow me" (v. 43) and confessed that Jesus is "the one of whom Moses in the law and also the prophets wrote." Yet as a typical disciple, he is overshadowed by the figure of Nathanael whose call serves as the climax of the vocations sequence in John 1:35-51. Nevertheless, if we are to grasp the further characterization of him which occurs elsewhere in the Fourth Gospel, it is important to remember that the Johannine tradition clearly identifies Philip as a believing and witnessing disciple.

---

the "sin no more" exhortation. For John, sin is a matter of unbelief. The healed lame man is a symbol of unbelief. He only speaks of Jesus and is never led to what can be properly termed a confession of faith.

66. Mark 3:18; 6:17; 8:27; Matt 10:3; 14:3; 16:13; Luke 3:1, 6:14.

67. Cf. Mark 3:18 and par.

Philip's appearance (John 6:5-7) in the narrative of the multiplication of loaves is proper to the Fourth Gospel. It is clearly a
Johannine note to highlight the omniscience of the Johannine
Jesus and may well reflect the influence of Gen 22:1-14 on the
development of the Johannine tradition.[68] Although he appears
to stand as a foil for the action of Jesus, Philip represents in fact
the misunderstanding of the disciples. He reflects man's inability
to understand in the face of divine action. Already in John 4:31-
38, the evangelist had suggested that even the disciples were prone
to misunderstanding; now Philip is singled out among the disciples as a figure to represent their misunderstanding. Nonetheless
their misunderstanding is but a partial misunderstanding and
remains fully under Jesus' control—because Jesus said that only
"to test him, for he himself knew what he would do" (John 6:6).

Likewise in John 14:8-9, Philip appears as the figure of the
disciple who misunderstands. The evangelist uses the theme of
misunderstanding in a variety of ways. He uses it not only to
show that the world (i.e., as symbolized by the Jews and Nicodemus) remains in a state of disbelief, but he also uses it to show
that the disciple, and therefore the Church, is always in a
situation where he is confronted by some lack of understanding
when faced by the divine. Even though he was a disciple, Philip
does not really know Jesus; he has not fully understood the
revelation of him whom the final redactor of the Gospel would
call the Word (John 1:1). Philip misunderstood the revelation of
Jesus because he still sought a theophany[69] even after he had
received the revelation which Jesus had come to bring. He
expected that he might be the beneficiary of an appearance of the
God of Israel as had been Moses, Aaron and the elders of Israel
(Exod 24:9-10). No theophany was to be given; all that even the
disciple can expect in the here and now is the revelation of Jesus.

The appearance of Philip in the introductory verses (vv. 21-22)
of John 12:20-36 casts the figure of Philip in still another role.

68. Cf. C.T. Ruddick, Jr., "Feeding and Sacrifice - The Old Testament
Background of the Fourth Gospel," *ExpTim* 79 (1968) 340-341.
69. Cf. S. Schulz, *Johannes*, pp. 174-175.

Now it is a matter of wanting to see Jesus and those who wish to see him are "the Greeks." The text does not specify whether they are proselytes or God-fearers but there is reason to believe that they are not Hellenistic Jews. The text does specify, however, that Philip hailed from Bethsaida "in Galilee." John's temporal and geographic references are generally not lacking in significance. As is well-known, Galilee is the land of the Gentiles.[70] According to John 12:22 Philip went and told Andrew that the Greeks wished to see Jesus. Both of these disciples bore Greek names. The symbolism is apparent. Just as the Samaritans were introduced to Jesus through the testimony of a Samaritan (John 4:28), so the Greeks are introduced to Jesus by one who represents the "Greek disciples." Thus the Philip of the Fourth Gospel appears in different pericopes with different representative roles. On the one hand, he represents the disciple who misunderstands. On the other, he represents the Greek believer who introduces others to Jesus.

Lazarus

In his commentary on the Fourth Gospel, Bultmann[71] has attempted to show that, because he has not utilized the raising of Lazarus as a point of departure for the discussion which follows and because he has embellished the traditional narrative with various additions, the evangelist has thrust the person of Lazarus into the background and made of Martha and Mary the chief persons in the Lazarus account (John 11:1-44 and 12:1-11). It does not appear, however, that the figure of Lazarus should be dismissed so lightly. It is well known that the name of Lazarus appears only in John and in Luke 16:19-31, where "Lazarus" is again associated with the resurrection from the dead. Moreover, his very name is symbolic. "Lazarus" is an abbreviated transcription of El-azar, which means "God helps." Moreover,

---

70. Cf. the citation of Isa 9:1-2 in Matt 4:15-16.
71. Cf. R. Bultmann, *John*, p. 395.

Lazarus is to be reckoned among the disciples of Jesus in the full
Johannine sense of the term—he is loved by Jesus (John 11:3, 5,
36) and Jesus can call him his "friend" (John 11:11). Finally,
although the evangelist does not explicitly state that Lazarus
believed nor that he testified to Jesus, he does clearly affirm that,
because of Lazarus, others were brought to believe in Jesus (John
12:11). These features of a narrative which John has clearly
positioned as a prelude to the passion-resurrection account prompt
us to look for the symbolism present in a story which is recounted
not for its historical but for its theological value. This search
inevitably leads to the determination that Lazarus should indeed
be ranked among the representative figures of the Fourth Gospel.

At an earlier stage of the tradition, the story of Lazarus was
told as a miracle story. An important feature of that story was
the delay of Jesus (John 11:6). The four day motif (John 11:17,
39) harks back to the Jewish tradition that the spirit leaves the
area of the tomb on the fourth day and therefore underscores the
reality of Lazarus' death. For the purpose which was inherent in
the telling of the Lazarus story,[72] it was important that the
reality of Lazarus' death should be properly emphasized. Most
probably the story circulated in Johannine circles as a response to
the problem of the delay of the Parousia. The death of the
believer before the Parousia was problematic for the early Christian community.[73] Johannine tradition responded to this problem
by narrating a story in which Jesus' appearance is delayed until
after death has occurred and been finalized through burial and
the passage of four days' time. Jesus, nonetheless, raises the dead
man to life.

In the miracle story as it is presently told in the Fourth Gospel,
and particularly by means of the bandage and cloth motif of
v. 44, a subtle contrasting link is made to the resurrection of

72. Cf. James P. Martin, "History and Eschatology in the Lazarus Narrative,
John 11, 1-44," *Scottish Journal of Theology* 17 (1964) 332-343; W. Slenger, "Die
Auferweckung des Lazarus (Joh. 11:1-45). Vorlage und johanneischer Re-
daktion," *TTZ* 83 (1973) 17-37.
73. Cf. 1 Thess 4:13-18; John 21:21-23; Rev 6:10; 14:13.

Jesus. Jesus rose by his own power and carefully left the bandages behind (John 20:4-7), but Lazarus emerged from the tomb bound with bandages and with his head wrapped by a cloth. This subtle link not only contrasts the resurrection of Jesus and that of Lazarus but also serves to emphasize the Johannine theme that Jesus is the source of (eternal) life. Within this perspective Lazarus represents the disciple of Jesus who has died but who will be raised because of the glorification [74] of Jesus.

Within the present redaction of the Fourth Gospel, another representative person has been added to the Lazarus story. The dialogue with Martha seems to predominate over the Mary elements in the story and thus it is to Martha that we ought to look as a representative person. In fact, Martha and Mary are described as saying the same thing to Jesus: "Lord, if you had been here, my brother would not have died" (vv. 21, 32), but it is with Martha that Jesus enters into dialogue and who is led to a christological confession of faith. The Johannine author would have us understand that Martha's declaration in v. 24 is to be understood in a Christian sense, because he has Jesus direct the statement to Himself. As was the case in the accounts of Nathanael, the Samaritan woman and the man born blind, Martha's confession of faith becomes the occasion for Jesus to reveal himself. This time the self-revelation is effected by another use of the *egō eimi* formula: "I am the resurrection and the life" (v. 25). Then, in typical Johannine fashion,[75] the self-revelation leads to a further confession of faith: Jesus is the Christ, the Son of God (v. 27). Martha's faith is both christological and resurrectional. Within the Fourth Gospel she stands as the type of the believer who, during the period of the Church (i.e., before the Parousia), confesses a belief in final resurrection after death because of her belief in Jesus as the source of resurrection and life.

74. = passion and resurrection; cf. John 11:40.
75. Cf. 9:38.

Judas

Judas[76] is the third of the representative figures of the Fourth
Gospel who are named in the Synoptic tradition. There is no
doubt that John is reflecting the common tradition when he
mentions Judas. Already in John 6:67-71, Judas appears as one
of the Twelve. Mention of "the Twelve" is infrequent in John and
thus leads the reader to conclude that the tradition presented in
John 6:67-71 reflects that tradition which is embodied in the call
of the Twelve according to Mark 3:14-19. From the standpoint
of Johannine perspective however, the insertion of "one of the
twelve" into the description of Judas, the betrayer, in John 6:71
underscored the heinousness of his sin.

Judas reapperas in the Fourth Gospel in the account of Jesus'
anointing (John 12:1-8)—a passage which is paralleled in all
three Synoptics.[77] But, it is only in the Johannine narrative that
Judas is explicitly mentioned. He is cited in John 12:4 as "one of
his disciples (he who was to betray him)" and further characterized as a thief in v. 6. The Synoptic parallels, by comparison,
simply write of "some who said to themselves" (Mark 14:4) or
"the disciples" (Matt 26:8). It is clear, then, that it is the
evangelist or his particular tradition that has introduced the
figure of Judas into the anointing scene.

The remaining passages of the Fourth Gospel in which Judas
appears are each likewise paralleled by the Synoptics. In the
Supper scene, John 13:2 finds its parallel in Luke 22:3 and John
13:26 (expanded by vv. 27-30) is parallel with Mark 14:20, Matt
26:23 and Luke 22:21. In the Johannine account of the Passion,
John 18:2-5 is part of a larger pericope (18:2-12) which is
paralleled by Mark 14:43-52, Matt 26:47-56 and Luke 22:47-53.
When the narrative of John 18:2-5 is compared with its Synoptic
parallels it appears at once that the Johannine tradition has
omitted the kiss of Judas and that vv. 2-5 bear the specific mark

76. Cf. Bertil Gartner, *Iscariot* (Philadelphia: Fortress, 1971) pp. 23-29.
77. Mark 14:3-9; Matt 26:6-13; Luke 7:36-50.

of Johannine tradition.[78] Jesus asks the ironic question, "Whom do you seek?"[79]—a question that recalls his earlier and programmatic question, "What do you seek?" (John 1:38). That question, which is the christological question *par excellence*, receives an answer in the gradually unfolding christology of the Fourth Gospel. In the pericope which opens the Johannine passion narrative, it is Jesus himself who provides the answer to *the* question. When the band, almost as if in unison, replies, "Jesus of Nazareth," Jesus responds by answering his own question" "I am he"—*Egō eimi* (vv. 5,6,7). Used absolutely, it is a formula of divine self-revelation.[80] Confronted by the deity, the band "drew back and fell to the ground" (v. 6). Awe was the only attitude appropriate to the revelation of the Son of God. The moment of Jesus' passion is the hour, the moment of Jesus' manifestation as King of Israel and Son of God. The Jesus who goes to the passion in the Fourth Gospel is a Jesus who willingly lays down his life. Hence the superfluity of the mention of a kiss by Judas, and its consequent omission by the Johannine tradition. That Jesus remained the master during the time of his own passion was indicated earlier in the gospel when—and in John alone—Jesus says to Judas, "What you are going to do, do quickly" (John 13:27).[81] Not even the betrayal was beyond the realm of Jesus' control.

That the moment of the passion is the moment of the revelation—glorification and exaltation—of the God-man provides a clue to the role which Judas plays in the Fourth Gospel. The evangelist has borrowed from the common tradition of the early Church that Judas was the betrayer (even though the christology of the Fourth Gospel renders a "betrayal" in the strict sense somewhat unnecessary). To this common trait the Johannine

78. The use of the *egō eimi* formula is typically Johannine. Cf. John 6:20,35,51; 8:12,24,28,58; 9:5; 10:7,9,11,14; 11:25; 13:9; 14:6; 15:1,5; 18:5.

79. Vv. 4,7. Cf. v. 8.

80. Cf. S. Bartina, "'Yo soy Yahweh' Nota exegética a Io. 18,4-8," *EstBib* 32 (1958) 403-426; R.E. Brown, *John I-XII*, p. 534; *The Gospel According to John. XIII-XXI.* AB, 29A (Garden City: Doubleday, 1970) pp. 810-811.

81. Cf. S. Schulz, *Johannes*, p. 176.

tradition adds a further characterization. Like Nicodemus, Judas is a figure of the night (John 13:30). He can be described as a thief who usurps that which is not properly his own (John 12:6; 13:27-30). More specifically, Judas is the one into whom the devil has entered (John 13:2; cf. 13:27). As a result, Judas allied himself with the chief priests and the Pharisees (18:3), the representatives of the Jews. At the moment of the Passion, there are two worlds which stand in conflict with one another—that of the Father, of whom the person of Jesus is the supreme revelation, and that of Satan, represented by the figure of Judas.

Mary

From the time of the Fathers, the figure of Mary in the Fourth Gospel has been interpreted symbolically. Ambrose,[82] for example, after having considered the pericope of Mary at the foot of the cross (John 19:25-27) as one which both illustrated Jesus' own filial piety and expressed the Johannine acknowledgement of the virginity of Mary, claimed that Mary was a figure of the Church. The majority of modern commentators continue to take the Johannine figure of Mary symbolically. Briefly stated, their interpretations of Mary fall into three camps. Loisy, Bultmann and Schulz look to Mary's appearance in the Cana narrative (John 2:1-11) and at the foot of the cross (John 19:25-27) as a representation of Jewish Christianity.[83] In the latter case they would look to Mary as the counterpart of the Beloved Disciple who represents Hellenistic Christianity. On the other hand, a rather strong Roman Catholic tradition, represented by the studies of Schürmann, Dauer and Balducci, present Mary as the representative of the community of believers, the Church.[84]

82. "Expos. in Luc X," PL 15, p. 1931; CSEL, 32, p. 506.

83. Cf. A. Loisy, R. Bultmann, S. Schulz, op. cit., ad. loc.

84. Cf. Heinz Schürmann, "Jesu letzte Weisung," in F. Hoffmann, L. Scheffczyk and K. Feiereos, eds., Sapienter ordinare. Kleineidam Festschrift. Erfurter theologische Studien, 24 (Leipzig: St. Benno-verlag, 1969) 105-123; Anton Dauer, Die Passionsgeschichte im Johannesevangelium. Eine traditionsgeschichtliche und theologische Untersuchung zu Joh. 18, 1-19,30. SANT, 30 (Munich: Kosel, 1972) pp. 318-

André Feuillet[85] has been most consistent in promoting the ecclesiological interpretation of Mary in the Fourth Gospel, but with his own particular nuance, namely that Mary represents the eschatological Zion. Most recently, Ignace de la Potterie has defended the ecclesiological interpretation but again with a particular twist, namely, that Mary represents the Church in so far as the Church is the mother of believers.[86] A somewhat mediating position has been held by such exegetes as Uzin and Crossan[87] who look to Mary as the model for all Christians by virtue of her faith-response.

Since I have already devoted a rather lengthy article to the figure of Mary in the Fourth Gospel,[88] it would be as repetitious as it is impossible to treat adequately the Marian symbolism of the Fourth Gospel within the scope of the present study; so I will content myself with some of the salient points. First of all, both the Cana account and the scene at the foot of the cross are proper to the Fourth Gospel and present several features characteristic of the Johannine tradition—to the point that more radical critics see each of these scenes as Johannine creations. The mention of "the hour" in the one and of the "beloved disciple" in the other are but just two indications of the Johannine character of the two narratives. Secondly, Mary's role in each of these passages is quite unlike that in which she is portrayed in other gospel passages. Nowhere else is Mary presented as requesting a miracle (= the Johannine sign) of her Son. Nowhere else is Jesus presented as a son concerned about his mother's welfare. Finally, in John 2:4 and 19:26-27 Jesus addresses his mother as *gunai*,

333; P. Ricca, L. Barsotelli, E. Balducci, *Evangelo di Giovanni* (Milan: Mondadori, 1973) p. 228.

85. Cf. *supra*, n. 2.

86. Cf. Ignace de la Potterie, "La parole de Jesus 'Voici ta Mère' et l'acceuil du Disciple (Jn. 19, 27b)," *Marianum* 36 (1974) 1-39.

87. D. Uzin, "The Believing Woman. The Virgin Mary in the Theology of St. John," *Dominicana* 52 (1967) 198-215; Dominic Crossan, "Mary and the Church in John 1:13," *TBT* 20 (1965) 1318-1324.

88. R.F. Collins, "Mary in the Fourth Gospel. A Decade of Johannine Studies," *LS* 3 (1970-1971) 99-142.

woman. This appellation is unique and patently symbolical. Moreover, in 19:26-27, Mary's qualification as "mother" is the characteristic epithet which serves as the culmination of a typically Johannine revelation formula.[89]

Little more need be said to indicate the importance of searching for the significance of the Johannine characterization of Mary. Feuillet has a point to make when he draws upon the Cana incident to contend that Mary represents Zion. The wine of the story obviously symbolizes messianic blessings and the abundance of wine symbolizes the superfluity of the messianic goods. Nonetheless it would seem preferable to look to Mary of the Cana incident simply as the faithful one who is in a situation of expectation *vis-à-vis* the Messiah and the awaited Messianic times. Jesus' enigmatic reply to Mary in 2:4 can hardly be taken as a reproach because Jesus does provide the wine, even though the Jesus of the Gospel tradition consistently refuses to perform signs for those who do not believe. By reason of its mention of the woman and the hour, which hour is the hour of Jesus' glorification, the Cana incident must be seen in relation to the scene at the foot of the cross. In his portrayal of Jesus' Passion, the evangelist is describing the birth of the Church. There the one who had waited in faithful expectation is united to the one who is the faithful disciple *par excellence*, the one whom Jesus loved. The *eis ta idia* (to his own home) of 19:27 does not so much represent a place, as it does a disposition[90]—in this case a unity of faith and a new reality brought into being because Jesus has called his mother "woman" at the very moment of his glorification and our salvation. Thus rather than to see in Mary principally a corporate personality, it is preferable to look to her as a representative figure.[91] She symbolizes the one who faith-

89. Cf. *supra*, n. 37.
90. Cf. I. de la Potterie, "La parole," p. 30.
91. More precisely it sholuld be stated that Mary is to be seen as a corporate personality only because she is a representative figure. Indeed the use of "mother" in John 19:27 as well as the points of contact between John 19:25-27 and other Johannine passages invite us to look beyond Mary simply as a type representing

fully awaits the messianic times. Consequently she is introduced into the community of salvation but becomes the beneficiary of the messianic blessings effected and communicated through the "glorification" of Jesus.

Mary Magdalene

One of the other Marys of the Fourth Gospel is Mary Magdalene. She appears in two passages of the Fourth Gospel, John 20:1-2 and 11-18. She ought not to be identified with Mary of Bethany, the sister of Martha and Lazarus, since it is highly unlikely that the author of the Fourth Gospel would have identified a single individual by the use of two different place locations. Like Mary, the mother of Jesus, Mary Magdalene is called by Jesus. Unlike the mother of Jesus who receives a symbolic name, Mary is called by her own name (John 20:16).[92]

Before one can consider the function of Magdalene in the Fourth Gospel, we must consider that John 20:1-2 represents a different stratum of Johannine tradition from that represented in 11-18. That the two pericopes come from two independent traditions is apparent when we consider that in 20:2 Mary has left the tomb, whereas the Mary of 20:11 is a Mary, still in the throes of grief, who is weeping at the tomb. John 20:1-2 is the Johannine version of the common evangelical tradition of the women at the tomb.[93] John 20:11-18 presents a dramatic scene developed by the Johannine tradition or composed by the evangelist himself in order to teach something about the nature of faith itself. The

the individual believer to an ecclesial interpretation of her role in the Fourth Gospel.

92. The vocative *gunai* in 20:15 should no more be taken in a symbolic sense than should the vocative *kurie* in the same verse be understood as having a pregnant theological meaning. John 20:14-15 is a scene of non-recognition, a Johannine creation which shows that the risen Jesus is materially not the same as the historical Jesus. The pair of verses thus thematically prepares the reader for v. 17. In the dramatization of vv. 14-15 the two vocatives should be understood merely as polite formulas of address.

93. Mark 16:1-8; Matt 28:1-8; Luke 24:1-12.

common evangelical tradition, represented by our present Synoptic Gospels, portrays several women approaching the tomb on
the first day of the week. The Fourth Gospel stands apart from
this tradition in so far as it describes a visit to the tomb by Mary
Magdalene alone. A comparison of the traditions would thus
incline us to the belief that the Johannine form of the visit-to-
the-tomb tradition has reduced the Galilean women to the single
figure of Mary Magdalene. This suggestion is confirmed by the
narrative itself. The plural use of the verb *oidamen* (we have seen)
in v. 2[94] indicates some tension between the traditional form of
the narrative and the account as it appears in the Fourth Gospel.
Thus on a first level of interpretation, we must look to Mary
Magdalene as being the representative of the Galilean woman
within the Fourth Gospel. This would be entirely within keeping
of the individualism of this gospel.

Yet the representative function of the Magdalene must be seen
at a still more profound level. It is to John 20:11-18 that we must
look if we are to specify her precise role in the Fourth Gospel.
Mary appears with an apologetic function; the objection that the
disciples had stolen the body of Jesus cannot be valid because the
possibility of grave-robbing is already raised by one of his
disciples. She also appears as the representative of a certain type
of belief. She is brought to faith in the resurrection, but only as a
result of a direct revelation of Jesus himself. She recognizes Jesus
when he calls her by name.[95] Even then her faith is inadequate
for she believes that Jesus' resurrection is a matter of his
resuscitation, of his being restored to his former state of life. That
such is the level of Mary's faith as portrayed by the evangelist is
indicated by the form of address which Mary directs to the risen
Lord. She calls him "Teacher" (v. 16) as did the first two disciples
(John 1:38) and Nicodemus (John 3:2). She wants to hold on to
him (v. 17). Jesus must interpret for her the meaning of his own
resurrection, and the Johannine Jesus does so in character-

94. Cf. Edward L. Bode, *Easter Morning*, pp. 74-75.
95. Cf. John 10:3,4,16.

istically Johannine fashion. Jesus' resurrection, unlike that of Lazarus, does not mean that he has returned to his former mode of life; rather it means that he is to ascend to his Father. After this revelation by Jesus himself[96] of the meaning of the resurrection, Mary can be counted among those who are truly believers and disciples for she can announce, "I have seen the Lord." In a word, the Mary Magdalene of the Fourth Gospel represents the believer whose response to Jesus' call is faith in Jesus as the ascending one, but whose belief is such only because of the Revelation of Jesus himself. Without the intervention of the ascending Revealer her resurrection belief is quite inadequate. Thus she typifies the believer whose act of faith is directed to the resurrection of Jesus as this is understood in Johannine terms.

Thomas

Another dramatic sequence composed by the evangelist to illustrate a theme related to faith that is already attested by the common evangelical tradition is found in John 20:24-29, the account of the appearance of the risen Jesus to the "doubting Thomas." The narrative is, in fact, peculiar to the Johannine tradition and would seem to be patterned after the narrative of the appearance of the risen Jesus to the disciples in John 20:19-23. Nevertheless a mention of the disciples' doubting the witness of those who had seen the risen Lord is common to the Gospel tradition. It is found in Mark 16:11, 14; Matt 28:17; and Luke 24:36-43. That the theme of the doubt of the disciples occurs only in the epilogue to the Markan Gospel but is a common feature of the gospel tradition, although developed in different fashion by Matthew, Luke and John, is an indication that the theme of the disciples' doubt is a late addition to the tradition of resurrection

---

96. This pattern of faith response, followed by a further revelation from Jesus himself, is common to the Johannine presentation of representative believers. The pattern is first clearly manifested in the Gospel version of Nathanael's vocation (John 1:43-50 + 51).

narratives. This addition to the tradition probably corresponds to an apologetic interest of the early Church.[97]

The gospel tradition borrowed the literary device of inclusion from the oral style. The Johannine Gospel makes frequent use of inclusion as a literary technique.[98] Thus John 1:19-2:12 can be compared with John 20 and the conclusion established that the two parallel narratives make of the body of the gospel a single whole.[99] Within this perspective the narrative of the appearance of Jesus to Thomas can parallel the account of Jesus and Nathanael, both pericopes describing encounters which are singularly important for the evangelist's notion of faith.

The final redactor of the Gospel has included Thomas, cited in traditional Johannine fashion as "Thomas called the Twin" (John 11:16, 20:24), among the group of seven disciples to whom the Risen Jesus revealed himself by the Sea of Tiberias (John 21:1-2). Thus the final form of the Johannine tradition preserved for us[100] points to the fact that Thomas was one of those disciples who had witnessed an appearance of the Risen Jesus. An earlier stage of the gospel tradition had made of Thomas a representative figure (John 20:24-29). The evangelist had prepared the way for the inclusion of that particularly dramatic sequence into his Gospel by two earlier mentions of Thomas, each of which is without parallel in the Synoptic traditions. John 11:16 presents Thomas as the courageous one and as a leader among the

97. A response of unbelief to the proclamation of Jesus' resurrection (cf. Acts 17:30) was undoubtedly problematic for early Christian preachers. The tradition that even the disciples doubted the first announcement of the Resurrection *kerygma* responded to that concern. As the disciples were convinced only by the vision of the Risen Lord, so some would hear the message of the Resurrection, even from the twelve themselves, but would remain unconvinced until the Lord appeared at the Parousia.

98. One striking example is the Johannine passion narrative which begins and ends with a scene in a garden (John 18:1; 19:41-42).

99. A brief study of the Johannine use of inclusion and of the consequent parallelism between the Nathanael and Thomas encounters is offered by Thomas Matus in "First and Last Encounter," *TBT* 42 (1969) 2893-2897.

100. I would concur with Bultmann, Brown, *et al.* in holding that John 21 is a redactor's addition to the Fourth Gospel.

disciples of Jesus.[101] Here Thomas appears in a passage which focuses upon resurrection. His appearance serves to heighten the drama of the entire sequence[102] by linking the resurrection of Lazarus to the death of Jesus.[103] Thomas reappears in John 14:5 where he is the figure of ignorance: "Lord, we do not know where you are going; how can we know the way?" Thus even before he meets the doubting Thomas scene, the reader of the Fourth Gospel knows that he has encountered in Thomas a leading disciple who epitomizes both the bravado and the ignorance of the disciples.

When we turn our attention to the appearance of Thomas and the other disciples in John 20:24-29, the principal point of the dramatic scene is undoubtedly the reality of the Resurrection of Jesus. The Jesus who was crucified is the risen Lord. Thomas who is invited to be believing, to be *pistos*, faithful, represents the disciples who have overcome their doubt to believe in the risen Jesus. He represents the believing disciple who believes because of the appearances of the risen Jesus—one of the most ancient and authentic of resurrection traditions.[104] In some ways Thomas' doubt is incidental to the main point of the narrative. It serves only to underscore his later belief, and sets the stage for the logion of v. 29. What is central to the narrative is that Jesus is truly risen and that Thomas truly believes: his faith is a resurrection faith.

To stop there is, however, to overlook the confessional formula of v. 28, Thomas' "My Lord and My God!" is the sole explicit confession of the divinity of Jesus on the lips of a disciple in the entire Fourth Gospel. Thus we ought to acknowledge that

101. The closest parallel to this passage is in Mark 14:29, par. with Matt 26:33, Luke 22:33, and John 13:37 where Peter is presented as the disciple who is ready to follow Jesus unto death.

102. I.e., the reflection on Jesus' glorification, especially his passion and resurrection, but including the farewell discourses of John 13-17. The Johannine theme of Jesus' glorification is introduced by the Lazarus story (cf. John 11:4).

103. John 11:16.

104. Cf. for example, Raymond E. Brown, *The Virginal Conception and Bodily Resurrection of Jesus* (London: Geoffrey Chapman, 1973) pp. 69-129.

Thomas represents for the Johannine community the fact that
resurrection faith is faith in the divinity of Jesus. Liturgical,
apologetic and paraenetic elements are certainly present in the
narrative. *Inter alia*, the account could well have served as a
useful device for showing that even Christ's chosen group lost
faith in him and that the risen Lord overcame those doubts
irrevocably. But these additional elements should not deter the
reader's attention from the central point of the narrative, the
reality of Jesus' Resurrection. Within this perspective Thomas
appears as a representative figure principally in so far as he is a
believer who recognizes in the Risen One the One who is Lord
and God.

Peter

Of the several individuals who appear in the Fourth Gospel,
none receives as much characterization in the Synoptic Gospels as
does the figure of Simon Peter. Yet the Johannine characterization of Peter is so vastly different from that of the Synoptics as
to raise a rather significant exegetical question about the importance which Peter played in the Johannine church. The appearance of Simon Peter in John 21 assimilates somewhat the Johannine Peter with the Peter of the Synoptics, the miraculous draught
of fishes recalling Luke 5 and the pericope dealing with Peter's
leadership role within the Church recalling the Matthean keys of
the kingdom passage (Matt 16:13-20). John 21, however, is a later
redactional addition to the Fourth Gospel, an addition which
some authors interpret as part of an ecclesiastical redactor's
attempt to harmonize the last of the Gospels with the earlier
Synoptic Gospels. What appears in the earlier strata of the
Fourth Gospel is a characterization of Simon Peter who appears
to be in competition with the Beloved Disciple—a rivalry that
leads such exegetes as Bultmann and Schulz to conclude that
Peter represents the Jewish Christian Church whereas the Beloved
Disciple represents the Hellenistic Christian Church, the true

Church.[105] Rudolf Schnackenburg would reject the contention that the author of the Fourth Gospel is portraying a rivalry between Peter and the Beloved Disciple,[106] whereas other commentators would reject the Bultmannian contention that the Beloved Disciple is merely an "ideal" figure. Nevertheless the fact that Peter and the Beloved Disciple stand in juxtaposition in John 13:21; 18:15-18; 20:3-10; and 21:20-23 makes of their "competition" a *crux interpretum* for the student of the Fourth Gospel. It is a point to which we must return, if only in passing, when we consider the figure of the Beloved Disciple. But what of Peter himself?

Peter appears rather frequently throughout the Gospel, where he is often cited as Simon Peter.[107] Many of the sequences in which he appears give some indication of contact or familiarity with the Synoptic tradition. Yet these same passages also give evidence of Johannization, frequently with the result that Peter appears to be in a position subordinate to that of the Beloved Disciple. Perhaps a brief overview of three passages in which Peter appears can help the reader of the Fourth Gospel to understand just who Peter is for the Johannine tradition. Peter first appears in John 1:40-42. This little pericope represents the Johannine version of two traditions independently narrated by the Synoptics, viz., the call of Simon[108] and the imposition of the symbolic name, Peter.[109] In the Johannine account, which combines these two traditions, Jesus acts as the God-man from the very beginning by conferring upon Simon the name of Cephas. Peter himself, however, is placed *among* the disciples. He is brought to Jesus through the testimony of his brother Andrew. To this extent he is a typical disciple.

105. Cf. R. Bultmann, *John*, p. 685.
106. Rudolf Schnackenburg, "On the Origin of the Fourth Gospel," *Perspective* 11 (1970) 223-246.
107. John 1:41; 6:8,68; 13:6,9,24,36; 18:10,15,25; 20:2,4,6; 21:2,3,7,11,15.
108. Cf. Mark 1:16-18; Matt 4:18-20; Luke 5:1-11.
109. Cf. Mark 3:16; Matt 16:17-18; Luke 6:14.

A second Johannine passage which reflects a contact with Synoptic (or Synoptic-like tradition) is the confession of Peter,[110] the only passage in the Fourth Gospel which makes mention of the Twelve. This fact alone reveals the traditional nature of the account. The Johannine confession of Peter has its parallels in Mark 8:27-30; Matt 16:13-20; Luke 9:18-21. Here and there, Peter is presented as the spokesman for the Twelve (= the disciples), but the Petrine confession of faith in the Fourth Gospel is radically different from that of the Peter of the Synoptics. John's Peter is a spokesman for the disciples who have come to explicit belief that Jesus is the Revealer, whose very words are the source of eternal life: "You have the words of eternal life; and we have believed, and have come to know, that you are the Holy One of God." No longer is Jesus' messiahship the focal point of Peter's confession of faith as it is in the Synoptics. Indeed, according to John, the acknowledgement of Jesus' messiahship seems to derive from an acceptance of Jesus as revealer.

The third passage in the body of the Fourth Gospel to which attention should be drawn is John 20:3-10. The Greek text of v. 3 and a glance at the critical apparatus for that verse indicates that the narrative itself is only loosely joined to what precedes. The Greek text further indicates that the Johannine tradition has reworked a Petrine story by introducing the figure of the Beloved Disciple and thus contrasting the faith of the Beloved Disciple with that of Peter.[111] The Petrine tradition which lies behind John 20:3-10 is reflected in Luke 24:12.[112] The simpler (Lucan)

110. John 6:66-71.
110[a]. Cf. John 20:24.
111. Cf. G. Hartmann, "Die Vorlage der Osterberichte in Joh. 20," *ZNW* 55 (1964) 197-220.
112. Text critical considerations have led Nestle-Aland to omit Luke 24:12 from their twenty-sixth edition. [It is present in the twenty-fifth edition.] The editors of the United Bible Societies' edition have included the verse but acknowledge that "there is a very high degree of doubt" concerning the reading. In any event the appearance of Luke 24:12 in the Bodmer papyrus (P^{75}) and many of the major uncials makes of this verse an early witness to the tradition attested by John 20:3-10.

form of the tradition and the Johannine version of the account both point to the fact that Peter did not come to resurrection faith as a result of seeing the empty tomb.[113] Undoubtedly this is to acknowledge that Peter's resurrection faith was based on an appearance to him of the risen Jesus, an appearance cited by Luke 24:34 and 1 Cor 15:5.

Thus in the body of the Johannine Gospel, Peter is a representative of the twelve disciples of the common evangelical tradition. He is one among the disciples, as John 1:40-42 indicates. Yet he is more than simply one among others. He is the one who represents the Twelve in so far as they acknowledge that Jesus is the Revealer whose words bring eternal life. He is the spokesman for those who believe that Jesus is Messiah in so far as he is Revealer. The epilogue to the Gospel (John 21) adds to this characterization of Simon Peter a further description. The addition of this material undoubtedly is owing to a redactor's desire to flesh out the image of Peter so that it is more consistent with the more common description of Peter in currency at the end of the first century. In this epilogue we find Peter listed first among the disciples (v. 2), described as a fisherman (vv. 3,11), and cast as one to whom the risen Lord revealed himself (vv. 1,14). John 21 still bespeaks something of the rivalry between Peter and the Beloved Disciple (v. 7; vv. 20-23), but nonetheless manages to focus upon the image of Peter.[114] In vv.15-17, the triple scrutiny of Peter shows that Peter is Jesus' friend by choice[115] with responsibility for those entrusted to him. So Peter's role as leader of the community, chosen for a form of discipleship that leads (has led) to martyrdom is established. Vv. 20-23 indicate that even the Beloved Disciple follows after Jesus and his friend, Peter, and that one ought not to draw the wrong conclusion from the fact that the Beloved Disciple has outlived Peter. Yet all this

113. Exegesis of the pericope leads me to concur with Bode over against Bultmann. Cf. E.L. Bode, *Easter Morning*, p. 78; R. Bultmann, *John*, p. 684.

114. Cf. O. Glombitza, "Petrus—der Freund Jesu. Überlegungen zu Joh. XXI 15 ff.," *NovT* 6 (1963) 277-285.

115. Cf. John 15:13-16.

is so much didactic commentary, drawn ultimately from the common evangelical tradition, in order to harmonize the particular vision inherent in the Johannine tradition with that of the Church at large.[116]

The Beloved Disciple

In two pericopes of this Johannine epilogue, the figure of the Beloved Disciple[117] stands alongside that of Simon Peter (John 21:2-7, 19-24). He appears as the Beloved Disciple in three other passages of the Fourth Gospel, namely at the Last Supper (John 13:21-26), under the cross (John 19:25-27) and in the dramatic scene of the race to the tomb (John 20:2+3-10). In the latter passage the beloved is identified as the "other disciple" (vv. 2,3,4,7). Thus both by reason of the mention of the "other disciple" in John 18:15 and the Johannine tendency to place the Beloved Disciple alongside the more traditional figure of Peter, we have every reason to think that the other disciple who brought Peter into the court of the high priest (John 18:15-16) is the Beloved Disciple.

Each of these several passages is a composition of the evangelist or of the final redactor of the gospel. Over the course of the centuries, and even until most recent times, attempts have been made to identify the Beloved Disciple with John the son of Zebedee,[118] author of the Gospel. A minority view would seek to

116. Cf. B. Schwank, "Christi Stellvertreter: Jo. 21, 15-25," *Sein und Sendung* 29 (1964) 531-542.

117. Among the extensive literature on the Beloved Disciple, I would particularly refer the reader to articles by Arenillas, Dauer, Roloff and Moreno Jimenez. Cf. P. Arenillas, "El discipulo amado, modelo perfecto del discipulo de Jesus, segun el IV Evangelio," *Ciencia Tomista* 89 (1962) 3-68; A. Dauer, "Das Wort des Gekreugizten an seine Mutter und den 'Jünger, den er liebte.' Eine traditionsgeschichtliche und theologische Untersuchung zu Joh. 19,25-27," *BZ* 11 (1967) 222-239; 12 (1968) 80-93; J. Roloff, "Der johanneische 'Lieblingsjünger' und der Lehrer der Gerechtigheit," *NTS* 15 (1968-1969) 129-151; F. Moreno Jimenez, "El discipulo de Jesucristo, segun el evangelio de S. Juan," *EstBib* 30 (1971) 269-311.

118. A recent but unsatisfactory attempt to establish this identification has been made by B. de Solages, in "Jean, fils de Zébédée et l'enigme du 'disciple que Jésus aimait,'" *BLE* 73 (1972) 41-50.

identify him with Lazarus, John Mark, or John the presbyter known to Papias and Polycrates. Perhaps it is best to leave to him the anonymity which was certainly intended by the author of the final gospel. In his anonymity, he is a figure who served for the Johannine church a role similar to that which the similarly anonymous Teacher of Righteousness served for the Essene community.

The Beloved Disciple is not merely one among the several representative figures of the Fourth Gospel; rather he is *the* representative figure of the Johannine tradition. His traits are best described when thought is given to him as believer, as disciple, as beloved and as witness.

As a believer, the beloved disciple appears in contrast with Peter as both men peer into the empty tomb (John 20:6-9). Neither Magdalene nor Peter were brought to belief in the Risen Jesus by their experience of the empty tomb. Yet for the Johannine tradition the empty tomb is important. It is sufficient to bring to faith he who represents the believer *par excellence*, the Beloved Disciple. His is a resurrection faith in its purest state. Unlike Thomas whose faith was dependent on a "physical" vision of the risen Jesus, the Beloved comes to faith without seeing the risen Christ. To him, above all, the words of 20:19 can be applied: "Blessed are those who have not seen and yet believe."[119] Furthermore his faith in the Risen Jesus is not based on the testimony of the Scriptures, "for as yet they did not know the scripture, that he must rise from the dead" (John 20:9). Yet his is a resurrection faith in the fullest sense of the word. This is indicated by the absolute use of the verb *pisteuein* (believe) in 20:8. The ecclesiastical redactor of John 21 capitalized on this tradition that the Beloved Disciple believed in the Risen Jesus by having him proclaim the recognition formula "It is the Lord" to Simon Peter in John 21:7.

The redactor who added chapter 21 to the Johannine Gospel reminds us that the Beloved Disciple was a disciple who followed

---

119. No real problem should derive from the appearance of *Eiden* in 20:8 since John 20:3-10 derives from a tradition different from that of the logion of 20:29.

after Jesus (and Peter). In this way he dramatized the notion that
the beloved disciple continued to be a disciple of Jesus even after
the Resurrection. By so doing, he continues and reinforces the
earlier Johannine tradition which was consistent in describing the
beloved as a *mathētēs* (disciple).[120] On the lips of Jesus, discipleship implies belief in his word and the term disciple seems to
extend beyond the narrower circle[121] which tradition has identified with the Twelve. Thus there is no cogent reason for
claiming that the Beloved Disciple must have belonged to that
circle of Jesus' disciples. But there is reason for claiming that the
Beloved Disciple was characterized by the hallmark of all true
disciples of Jesus, namely that he was noted for his love of the
brethren.

Of all the disciples of Jesus, the anonymous other is the one
described as beloved. He is the disciple whom Jesus loved (John
13:23; 19:26; 20:2; 21:7,10). In a pre-eminent manner he deserves to be called a friend of Jesus (John 15:15). Indeed the
Johannine tradition is fond of representing the intimacy that
existed between Jesus and the Beloved Disciple. He is the one
who was lying close to the breast of Jesus at the Last Supper
(John 13:25; 21:20). He is the one who shared a same community
of faith with she who not only represents those who await the
Messianic times in hope but is also, and really, the mother of
Jesus himself (John 19:26-27).

The intimacy with Jesus which is so characteristic of the
Beloved Disciple is that which enables him to give the testimony
of and about Jesus to others. Within the tradition of the Johannine circle it is he to whom Peter addresses himself when he
would have knowledge of the events leading to Jesus' glorification
and it is to him that Jesus grants that knowledge.[122] This bond of
intimacy between the Beloved Disciple and Jesus establishes the
disciple as one qualified to be a witness unto others that they too

120. On the Johannine notion of discipleship, cf. F. Moreno Jimenez, "El
discipulo."
121. Cf. John 8:31.
122. Cf. John 13:23-26.

might believe and have eternal life. To bear testimony to Jesus is essential to being a disciple of Jesus, according to the Johannine tradition.[123] It is the Beloved Disciple who has witnessed (John 19:35) and whose testimony, according to the somewhat maladroit conclusion of the final redactor,[124] lies before the contemporary reader in the form of the Johannine Gospel.

The Beloved Disciple is not a figment of the imagination of the evangelist who wrote the Fourth Gospel. He is a real individual, just as were the Baptist and Peter. Yet within the Johannine tradition he typifies the disciple of Jesus *par excellence*. Thus his testimony could stand behind the Fourth Gospel. In its entirety this Gospel stands as the faith expression of the Johannine believer. Hence, even though he was a real person, the Beloved Disciple is described by the Johannine tradition with traits that characterize him as the one whose testimony had a special significance for the Church which appealed to his authority, the Church whose homiletic tradition gave rise to the Fourth Gospel.

Within this Gospel the Beloved Disciple is the epitome of discipleship. He has been transformed from a merely historical personage to the model of the authentic disciple of Jesus. In a sense, the tradition of the Fourth Gospel capsulizes in the single person of the Beloved Disciple the testimony of John, the receptivity of Mary, the faith of Nathanael as well as that of the man born blind, Peter, Mary Magdalene, and Thomas. In a word, he is no longer a representative figure for the evangelist; he is *the* representative figure, the one who epitomizes all that faith in Jesus Christ implies.

123. Cf. esp. John 1:35-51.
124. John 21:24-25.

2. DISCIPLESHIP IN JOHN'S GOSPEL

Those who study discipleship in the Fourth Gospel normally take one of two approaches. Some look to the general outline of the gospel and note that the beloved disciple looms large in the Johannine perspective, so large that this figure is the believer *par excellence*. In this sense the Beloved Disciple represents the epitome of the Johannine notion of discipleship.

Others approach the theme by comparing this gospel and the Synoptics, among which Mark is the major literary source. Discipleship is one of the key themes of Mark's narrative, as most of the recent scholarship on the gospel emphatically emphasizes. For Mark a disciple is one who follows, one who answers Jesus' call "Follow me." Among those called in this fashion were Simon and Andrew, James and John (Mark 1:16-20), and Levi (Mark 2:13-14). From Mark's point of view, the twelve are paradigmatic of discipleship. They are those appointed "to be with him, to be sent out to preach, and to have authority to cast out demons" (Mark 3:14-15).

John and Mark

While it is undoubtedly true that the Beloved Disciple is the disciple *par excellence* for the author of the Fourth Gospel, it is also true that his fashion of describing the disciple is quite different from that of Mark. John presents the call of the first disciples in a dramatic tale of a series of encounters with Jesus, which culminate in Jesus' self-revelatory assertion: "Truly, truly, I say to you, you will see heaven opened, and the angels of God ascending and descending upon the Son of man" (John 1:51, RSV). Three scenes lead up to this climax: the encounter with the first disciples (John 1:35-39), the encounter with Andrew and Simon (John 1:40-42), and the encounter with Philip and Nathanael (John 1:43-50).

When the Johannine description of these encounters is compared with the Markan account of the call of the first desciples, one quickly notices that the call of the brothers, Andrew and Simon, has been placed between two longer accounts (John 1:35-39; 43-50) and that neither of the longer accounts has any parallel in Mark or the other two Synoptics. Indeed the fourth evangelist seems to focus on the call of Nathanael, who is not identified by name in any of the other gospels. In all John describes an initial encounter between Jesus and five disciples, but only three of these are known from the Synoptic tradition, namely, Simon, Andrew, and Philip. John does not tell us about the call of the sons of Zebedee (Mark 1:19-20), nor does he narrate the call of Levi, the tax-collector (Mark 2:13-14).

What John shares with the Synoptic account is the call of Andrew and Simon, but the offers no indication that these Galileans were fishermen, a down-to-earth detail in the narratives of Matthew and Mark (Mark 1:16-18; Matt 4:18-20), and the basis of the evocative metaphor in Luke (Luke 5:1-11). Unlike Matthew who capitalizes on Simon's change-of-name (Matt 16:17-19), John offers a rather matter-of-fact description as he recounts his tale of the encounter between Jesus and Simon son of John (John 1:42). Strikingly, the fourth evangelist does not even give primacy of place to Jesus' encounter with Peter. His narrative account cites the encounter with Peter after the encounter with the initial pair, indeed in such a fashion as to have Andrew, Simon Peter's brother, presented as a disciple before Simon is even introduced.

A Closer Look

In studying the Fourth Gospel, it is necessary to take all of these differences into account. The evangelist has told his tale very carefully and has deftly structured the accounts which constitute Act I, Part II in the drama of his gospel (John 1:35-51). In particular one must focus on the interplay between Peter and the Beloved Disciple, a tension which heightens the dramatic account of the Fourth Gospel.

Nonetheless the Beloved Disciple is not explicitly mentioned in the first chapter of John's Gospel. At the outset of his story the evangelist presents us with the tale of an encounter between Jesus and two disciples. One of these is later identified as Andrew (v. 40) while the other remains anonymous. That, I think, is the point. The evangelist gives his readers a perspective on disciple-ship before he tells them about any one of the disciples, including Peter whose role among the disciples had long been told within the gospel tradition. The story of the first encounter does not appear in the Synoptics because it represents the insights of the evangelist's own community into what it means to be a disciple.

In the Johannine perspective, what does it mean to be a disciple? John 1:35-39 gives us the answer.

John's Testimony

The evangelist sets his story of Jesus' encounter with his first disciples in the context of testimony given by John: "Behold the Lamb of God" (John 1:29, 35). Hitherto the evangelist had as an almost overriding concern the need to portray John as the Witness (John 1:6-8, 15, 19-34). In fact the testimony of John is the highlight of Act I, Part I of his Gospel (John 1:19-34). The evangelist provided a title for Act I of his narrative: "This is the testimony of John" (v. 19). Then he dramatically builds up to the testimony itself, "Behold, this is the Lamb of God" (v. 29), an enigmatic statement whose full significance could be known only by one to whom it had been revealed, namely, that "this is the Son of God" (v. 34). By his literal repetition of the testimony of v. 29 in v. 36, the evangelist made it clear that he has intended to give, first the significance of the Witness' testimony (vv. 29-34) and only then the effect of that testimony (vv. 35-51). While the evangelist's attempt to cast John in such an exclusive, distinctive role is due to the circumstances which shaped the Johannine community, John's introduction to the encounter between Jesus and the first disciples derives from his appreciation of discipleship. For the fourth evangelist, one becomes a follower of Jesus because someone has witnessed to Jesus. In his perspective discipleship is a consequence of witness having been borne to Jesus.

Two Levels

By phrasing John's testimony enigmatically—"Behold, the Lamb of God"—John introduces the reader gently but firmly to symbolism without which it is impossible to understand the Fourth Gospel.

Indeed we really ought to read John's gospel on two levels. At one level, it is a narrative tale. It tells in a simple way, at times in an almost matter-of-fact fashion, the remembered tale of Jesus of Nazareth. The events which it recounts are onetime events in the life of a historical figure, who had died more than a half century before the Gospel was written.

On another level, the gospel of John is a symbolic tale. It tells the story of the Johannine community, its faith and its struggles. As the evangelist weaves his account of Jesus of Nazareth, he makes abundant use of symbolic language so that his readers get a glimpse into his faith convictions and the real-life confrontations that those convictions entailed.

A Symbolic Narrative

Having read the stylized account of John's testimony and having been introduced to Johannine symbolism in the words placed on the lips of the Witness, the reader is prepared to appreciate the tale of the first encounter (John 1:35-39) for what it really is, a symbolic narrative. The symbolism focuses on the use of four verbs which can be understood on a narrative level, but the narrative account serves merely as a backdrop for the symbolic account which the evangelist unfolds for his readers. In his tale, the key words are "to follow," "to seek," "to stay" and "to see."

Narrative Level

On the narrative level, the story of the encounter between Jesus and the first disciples is the story of two men who had been in the company of John, the baptizer whom the evangelist wants to cast in the role of the witness *par excellence*. These men were intrigued by their hero's testimony about Jesus. So they went running after him. Jesus heard their footfalls. He turned to them and asked them what they were looking for. They addressed him as "rabbi" and asked him where he was staying. Rabbi is a somewhat strange form of address in the Johannine narrative since Jesus has thus far been identified only enigmatically and Jesus' expertise in unfolding the meaning of the Scriptures has not yet been cited by the evangelist. Jesus said "come and have a look." They did and decided to stay, because it was getting late in the day.

Symbolic Level

Rereading the account on the symbolic level, with full attention paid to the Johannine notions of following, seeking, seeing, and staying, we realize that what John has offered us is a paradigm of discipleship. To appreciate that nuance of the story, one must note how the evangelist has woven this story (see vv. 35-36) into Act I of his gospel drama (John 1:19-51) and chosen action-packed words with rich connotations as well as observe the many signs of the evangelist's narrative skill. He used many of his favorite compositional techniques in designing the whole scene. His language is crisp. He uses the dialogue technique, the question and answer format, which characterizes so much of the Fourth Gospel. He employs traditional language, and then tells his reader what the tradition means with the help of an interpretive note. His references to time allow him to string his scenes together and invite the readers to participate in the drama that is unfolding before them.

To Follow

The story of Jesus' encounter with an anonymous disciple is thus a very Johannine tale. The disciple came to Jesus because he had been attracted to him by the testimony given by one who bore witness. Immediately he is characterized as a "follower." In the Synoptic tradition, to follow Jesus is to be his disciple. John the evangelist shares with the Synoptic authors this metaphorical use of the verb "to follow" (*akoluthein*). It is prominently featured, not only in the Johannine account of the initial encounters between Jesus and his disciples (vv. 37, 38, 41, 44), but also in two strong sayings on discipleship (8:12; 12:26), the allegory of the shepherd and his sheep (10:4, 15, 27), and the story of Peter's restoration to authentic discipleship (21:19, 20, 22). By his choice of the verb "to follow" in v. 38, an expression which is then cited as the technical and traditional vocabulary of Jesus' call to discipleship (v. 43), the evangelist lets us know that he is not so much telling the story of a man running after Jesus as that of someone who is really a disciple.

To See

According to John's story, Jesus was aware that the two were following: "He saw them following." It is well known that the evangelist employs different verbs of "seeing." On the narrative level, the verb "to see" (v. 38) obviously refers to physical sight. Yet on the symbolic level, "to see" (*theasthai*) suggests full appreciation of true reality. Perceiving that they were disciples, Jesus invites the pair to deeper intimacy with himself. Although discipleship is the result of testimony, true discipleship requires an initiative on the part of Jesus, an invitation to greater intimacy with him.

To Seek

Jesus directs his concern to the pair with the question "What do you seek?" These are the first words uttered by Jesus according to the Fourth Gospel. The Jerusalem Bible has well captured the ordinary narrative meaning of the question by translating the Greek *ti zēteite* as "What do you want?" Nonetheless the verb "to seek" (*zētein*) is a significant word used in rather striking fashion throughout the Fourth Gospel, where it occurs some thirty-four times.

Jesus' opening question introduces us to the search for Jesus, a search which ultimately leads to the cross where he is found as the revelation of the Father. A few manuscripts of the Greek text have caught the real flavor of Jesus' question. Their Greek reads, in literal translation, "Whom are you seeking?" Disciples are those who search for Jesus.

John's language recalls an ancient Hebrew usage according to which the verb *darash*, equivalently *zētein* in Greek, "to seek" in English, meant "to interpret (the Scriptures)." In fact, *midrash*, derived from *darash*, means an interpretation of the Scriptures. In the perspective of the fourth evangelist, to seek out the meaning of the Scriptures is to be led by Jesus. He not only interprets the Scriptures in an almost academic sense (see John 6:31-33). He is the one to whom the Scriptures point and in whom they are fulfilled.

The idea that the Scriptures point to Jesus is one of the leitmotifs of the subsequent scene: "We have found the Messiah ... we have found him of whom Moses in the law and also the prophets wrote ... you will see the heaven opened and the angels of God ascending and descending (Gen 28:12)." The evangelist anticipates his insight by having the first disciples address Jesus, not by his personal name, but as "Rabbi."

To Stay

Questioning is an important feature of the Fourth Gospel (see John 2:3-4; 2:18-19; 3:4-5; etc.), so the evangelist portrays the first disciples as those who question Jesus. Standing on the threshold of full discipleship, yet not fully understanding what it means, they ask "Where are you staying?" In Greek (*pou meneis*) this is a rather simple two-word question similar to the two word question (in Greek) which Jesus had posed to them. The narrative sense of the disciples' question has been well captured in the expression, "Where do you live?" the translation offered in the Bible of Jerusalem.

Yet one who is familiar with the gospel of John as a whole quickly realizes that, from the perspective of the evangelist, "to stay" is no ordinary verb. It does not indicate so much a temporary halt, as a permanent abiding. This full Johannine sense is already familiar to the reader who has twice heard John the Witness testify that the Spirit remains on Jesus (*menein*, vv. 32, 33). On the symbolic level, the disciples' apparently banal question means "where do you abide?" John uses the verb *menein* forty-one times in the course of his gospel. As his drama reaches its denouement, the reader comes to know that "the Christ remains forever" (*menei*; 12:34). The Father dwells in him (*menōn*; 14:10). This means "that I am in the Father and the Father in me" (14:11).

To See

The appreciation of where Jesus really dwells is, of course, not something to be contemplated from afar. The true disciple is invited to a deeper intimacy with Jesus and the Father. This invitation is tendered by Jesus who says to the exemplary pair, "Come and see." The disciples accepted the invitation: "They came and saw where he was dwelling." Once again the evangelist has made use of a verb of "seeing"—in fact, two different verbs (*horan* and *idein*) which are used almost interchangeably in the gospel. They suggest sight accompanied by a real understanding. They represent insight almost equivalent to that real comprehension which the evangelist suggests by his use of the verb "to see" (*theasthai*) in v. 38.

The acceptance of Jesus' invitation attests that the paradigmatic pair are indeed true disciples, whose following of Jesus has come to fruition. For them to have truly understood where Jesus abides, that he abides in the Father and the Father in him, was to abide with Jesus. Indeed of the forty-one Johannine uses of the verb *menein*, stay-abide, eleven are found in chapter 15, where the allegory of the vine and the branches (John 15:1-11, comp. v. 16) symbolizes that Jesus' disciples are to abide in him if they are to be fruitful. The disciple is one who abides with Jesus.

From this perspective, the dialogue between Jesus and his would-be followers focuses on the invitation to come and see. Those who perceive come to abide with Jesus. This dialogue takes place at the decisive hour. On the merely narrative level, the tenth hour suggests a time in the late afternoon, i.e., about four o'clock. Bultmann, however, reminds us that the tenth hour is the hour of fulfillment. The call to discipleship takes place at the decisive moment.

This is how the author of the Fourth Gospel understands discipleship. This disciple is one to whom testimony about Jesus has been made, and so he enters into dialogue with Jesus. He addresses Jesus with a faith that is as yet superficial ("Rabbi") but which will grow to greater fullness by interacting with Jesus. He finally appreciates where Jesus abides and comes to abide with him.

Such is the evangelist's interlude on the nature of discipleship. His narrative goes on and so it must, for the true disciple must in turn give testimony to Jesus (see 1:40-42). That is how things are on the narrative level, the real day-to-day world in which the disciples of Jesus live. But on the symbolic level, where the ultimate meaning of events unfolds, the reader knows that the disciple abides with Jesus. At first the reader may be puzzled that the evangelist has left one of the initial pair in anonymity. With Oscar Cullmann, the reader may even presume that the anonymous one is really the Beloved Disciple. In a sense, the presumption is true. Yet in another sense, the presumption is false since the anonymous one is the reader himself, for the story of the first encounter is the story of anyone who is truly a disciple of Jesus.

3. JESUS' CONVERSATION WITH NICODEMUS

As a result of form criticism and the study of the history of traditions, commentators on the gospels have sometimes noted that each unit of gospel material essentially contains within it the proclamation of the entire gospel. It is not the intention of these authors to contend that each and every pericope of gospel material contains a brief resume of salvation history. Nor would they contend that each isolateable unit of the gospel material contains the full proclamation of the meaning of Jesus of Nazareth. Rather, it is their contention that each pericope of the gospel contains within itself some formulation of the central message of the gospel. Thus the announcement of the immanence of the Kingdom of God, kerygmatically proclaimed in Mark 1:15, would be present in each of the Markan miracle stories as these had been preached in the Church.

While the somewhat unsophisticated presumption that the written gospels contain nothing but the kerygma of the early Church has lead to an uncritical generalization of this thesis, there is no doubt that many of the pericopes in our written Gospels do, in fact, contain the essence of the gospel message. This would appear to be particularly true of the Johannine material, so much of which has been influenced by a Johannine homiletic tradition. In particular it seems legitimate to claim that John's narrative of Jesus' conversation with Nicodemus contains the kernel of the gospel message, as that has been understood and articulated by the Johannine tradition.

The Role of Nicodemus

The story concerns a certain Nicodemus who came to Jesus by night. Nicodemus is unknown to the Synoptic tradition, but he might well have been known among the rabbis with whom the Fourth Gospel seems to be in constant dialogue. The Babylonian

Talmud (*b. Sanh.* 43a) cites a man named Naqai among a group of five disciples of Jesus. Naqai is a shortened form of the Hebrew name, Naqdimon, which would be the equivalent of the Greek name which we customarily transliterate as Nicodemus.

After his appearance in John 3, Nicodemus appears on two later occasions in the drama of the Fourth Gospel. In John 7:50-52 Nicodemus is found in discussion with his fellow Pharisees who reply in an *ad hominem* fashion to his suggestion that Jesus be judged according to the statutes of the Law. In John 19:39, Nicodemus is added, almost as an afterthought, to the story of Joseph of Arimathea who came to take the body of Jesus away for burial. The evangelist undoubtedly wants his readers to connect all three mentions of Nicodemus, since he calls his reader's attention to the initial conversation between Jesus and Nicodemus when he introduces the latter at 7:50 and 19:39.

Notwithstanding John's careful presentation of Nicodemus and the attestation of Nicodemus in the rabbinic tradition (which may well depend on the Fourth Gospel itself), there can be little doubt that the evangelist is more interested in the role of Nicodemus as a representative figure than he is in him as an historical person who belonged to Jesus' entourage. His account of the conversation between Jesus and Nicodemus introduces the rabbi as "a man of the Pharisees" (v. 1), "a ruler of the Jews" (v. 1), and "a teacher of Israel" (v. 10). Again, in his account of the gathering of the Pharisees, the evangelist takes care to note that Nicodemus was "one of them" (7:50). Thus there can be no doubt that the evangelist wants his readers to understand that Nicodemus is a member of the Pharisees' party and a leader of the Jews.

More specifically he is a scribe, learned in the law of his people. It is as a scribe of the Pharisees that Nicodemus has a role to play in the Fourth Gospel. What is that role? Barnabas Lindars has suggested that Nicodemus represents official Judaism in a situation of openness before the claims of Christ. B. Hemelsoet and J. Louis Martyn have argued that Nicodemus represents those Judeo-Christians who believed in Jesus, but did not confess their belief in public. It appears more likely that the evangelist has selected Nicodemus as a representative figure to describe a type of belief that is insufficient for salvation. Such is the opinion which I would hold along with Marinus de Jonge and Francis Moloney.

The Johannine Hand

To suggest that Nicodemus is typecast as a representative of inadequate faith is to suggest that the fourth evangelist has reworked the Nicodemus tradition in the pursuit of his own theological purposes. Even a cursory reading of his account of the conversation with Nicodemus is enough to confirm this suggestion. The pericope is redolent with evidence of the Johannine hand at work. So frequent are the Johannisms that the careful reader cannot escape the conclusion that 3:1-15 is, at least in its present redaction, a Johannine construction. Evidence of Johannine technique and style abounds, as do typically Johannine expressions. Taken as a whole, John 3 provides a major example of Johannine technique insofar as a unit of narrative material (3:1-10) is followed by discourse material (3:11-21, 31-36).

This technique is employed elsewhere in the Fourth Gospel, especially when a discourse of Jesus is introduced by a miracle story which provides an occasion for the discourse without necessarily entering into the substance of the discourse itself. The narrative-discourse technique is used by the evangelist in his account of the cure of the paralytic of Bethzatha (John 5) as well as in the narrative of the multiplication of loaves (John 6). Some authors would even find it in John 13, when the account of Jesus washing his disciples feet is followed by the farewell discourse(s).

Within the account of Jesus' conversation with Nicodemus itself, we find other typical examples of Johannine technique. The very appearance of Nicodemus as a representative figure (v. 1) is certainly a case in point. The narrative continues with a Johannine dialogue (compare with the dialogue with the Samaritan woman, 4:7-26), this time presented with traits of the rabbinic discussion. In the dialogue, the question is an important element (compare with the questions found in Jesus' initial encounter with his disciples, 1:38). In keeping with his "circular style," John makes use of the technique of repetition (compare the saying found in 3:3, and repeated in v. 5, with the saying of 7:34 repeated in v. 36). John is noted for his use of terms with a double meaning. Two of them occur in the conversation with Nicodemus: "anew" in v. 3, "lift up" in v. 14.

Misunderstanding is another significant literary device employed in the Fourth Gospel (8:21-22, 20:11-18). Nicodemus blatantly misunderstands what Jesus has to say about the Kingdom of God (v. 4). John's Gospel occasionally makes use of little parables in the development of its theology (compare 3:8 with the parable of the apprenticed son found in 5:19-20). Finally, our pericope includes three examples of the singularly Johannine stylistic device of introducing traditional material with a twice-repeated "Amen" (vv. 3,5,11).

In similar fashion, the language of the conversation with Nicodemus is clearly that of the evangelist and his tradition. "Rabbi" (v. 2) is one of the titles used of Jesus in the Fourth Gospel, but it is not as significant a christological title as is "Son of Man" (v. 14). The latter title appears as a major formulation of Johannine christology thirteen times in the Gospel. Other Johannine expressions which are integral to the formulation of the Fourth Gospel's christology are the statement that Jesus has "come from God" (v. 2), the ascent-descent motif (v. 13), and the use of "to lift up" to describe the crucifixion-exaltation of Jesus (v. 14). The emphasis on the Spirit recalls both John's adaptation of the story of Jesus' baptism and the oft-mentioned gift of the Spirit in the farewell discourses.

"To speak" and "to bear witness" (v. 11) recall not only the role of Jesus as revealer and so one who gives witness, but also the importance which John attaches to the theme of "witness" and "testimony" (compare with 1:19) throughout his Gospel. The mention of the "signs" of Jesus (v. 2) is undoubtedly a Johannine reference to the miracles of healing which Jesus performed (compare with 4:54), even if John does seem to single out the seven miracles which he describes at length as the "signs" of Jesus.

Signs are related to faith. Indeed the Gospel is written as an account of Jesus' "signs" so that we may believe that Jesus is the Christ, the Son of God, and that believing we may have life in his name (20:30-31). Sometime after Nicodemus' mention of Jesus' signs, Jesus himself introduces the issue of belief (v. 11). Finally John 3:15 offers the first full mention of "eternal life," an expression which epitomizes the gift of salvation some seventeen times in the Fourth Gospel.

The "Kingdom of God"

As the use of so many Johannine stylistic devices in the composition of 3:1-15 indicates that we have a typically Johannine passage at hand, so the presence of so much typical Johannine vocabulary indicates that we are dealing with a passage which has every likelihood of providing a compendium of Johannine thought, of being, in effect, a brief synopsis of the Gospel itself. There is, however, one element in the narrative which stands out as very unusual. This is "the kingdom of God" mentioned in vv. 3 and 5.

It is well known that the kingdom of God was a current theme in the apocalyptic literature of late Judaism. Those who phrased the hope of Israel in apocalyptic terms looked to the coming of the kingdom as the ultimate manifestation of the Lord's royal power. The comming of the kingdom was *the* eschatological event. Jesus borrowed the language of apocalyptic to announce his message of salvation. Subsequently the "kingdom of God" was taken over by the Church whose teaching was preserved in the Synoptic Gospels.

However, the perspective of "kingdom" language was always that of consequent eschatology. That is, mention of the kingdom looked to the final manifestation of God as king in mankind's history. For his part, the author of the Fourth Gospel has all but abandoned—with, of course, some significant exceptions, as in 5:25-29—the framework of consequent eschatology in view of his notion of realized eschatology. Consequently the evangelist has assiduously avoided any explicit mention of the "kingdom of God" with the singular exception of 3:3,5.

The presence of "the kingdom of God" as an unlikely theme in the conversation with Nicodemus prompts us to look for the sources from which the evangelist might have borrowed the material which he has incorporated into the scenario which he has constructed. Specifically, we, along with an increasing number of exegetes, can reflect that the Johannine tradition had contact with the Synoptic tradition. Most probably at an oral stage of the gospel's development, there was an interpretation of the Johannine and Synoptic traditions. Undoubtedly, the "kingdom of God" in 3:3,5 remains as a permanent trace of the influence of the Synoptic tradition upon the Johannine.

Is it possible to be even more specific and point to a passage in the Synoptic Gospels whose pre-history at the oral stage of development might have yielded the raw material for the logion which enunciates the basic statement of Jesus' conversation with Nicodemus? While admitting some formal similarity between John's account of the conversation with Nicodemus and the Synoptic story about paying tribute to Caesar (Mark 12:13-17 and par.), scholars are more inclined to look to the story of the rich young man (Mark 10:17-22 and par.) as providing the Synoptic analogue for John's account of the conversation with Nicodemus.

Perhaps the point is not to be pressed. Nevertheless, the reader will note that in both stories Jesus is addressed as "teacher" (John 3:2; Mark 10:17). In both accounts, Jesus is further qualified—he is called "good" (Mark 10:17) by the Synoptics and "one come from God" by John (3:2). Both accounts are concerned with eternal life (John 3:15; Mark 10:17). Both accounts narrate the tale of one who comes to Jesus with apparent enthusiasm but whose faith is ultimately found wanting. The Lukan version of the story describes Jesus' interlocutor as a "ruler" (Luke 18:18), the very qualification ascribed to Nicodemus by John 3:1. The point need not be pushed to the extreme, yet it must be affirmed that there is some similarity of form and content between the Johannine and Synoptic narratives of a scribal dialogue.

"Amen, Amen"

The Synoptic story of Jesus' encounter with the rich young man is preceded by the description of the children (Mark 10:13-16 and par.). It is, however, precisely this passage of the Synoptic Gospels which provides the closest parallel with the strange "Truly, truly, I say to you, unless one is born anew, he cannot see the kingdom of God" logion of John 3:3, repeated in a slightly different version in John 3:5. It is well known and commonly asserted that John's use of the double "Amen" to introduce a saying of Jesus is proper to him. The synoptics, as in Mark 10:15, occasionally record a saying of Jesus introduced by a single "Amen." The Qumran literature offers some examples of a double "Amen" at the end of a sentence for emphasis' sake. The Fourth Gospel is, however, unique in its use of an introductory "Amen" to render the logia of Jesus in a more formal and solemn manner.

Recent studies have shown, however, that the evangelist does not indiscriminately introduce the formula into this narrative. Rather, the formula is used when John is offering his readers a saying of Jesus that has been handed down to him from his tradition, the very tradition with which the Synoptic tradition has interacted. Thus it is not unreasonable to suggest that the traditional material which John introduces by his typical "Amen, Amen, I say to you" formula may well include formulae which have also been preserved by the Synoptic tradition.

Within the framework of this realization and given the similarities between John 3:3, 5 and Mark 10:15—the similarities are even closer between the Johannine logion and another version of the synoptic saying which Matthew offers in a different context, namely, 18:3—it seems that John 3:3,5, Mark 10:15, Luke 18:17 and Matthew 18:3 are so many different versions of the same traditional logion of Jesus. With the exception of John 3:3 which offers a more typically Johannine variant of the formula, the versions speak of "entering the Kingdom of God"—Matthew, of course, has "kingdom of heaven"—and all the versions introduce Jesus' saying with the "Amen, I say to you" formula. In all cases we are dealing with the divine initiative. The divine initiative would seem to have been concretized in Christian baptism insofar as a baptismal context seems to have shaped the logion as it was handed down in the tradition of the Christian church.

Christian Baptism and Faith

John explicitates the baptismal implications of the saying when he offers his explanation of what it means to be "born anew" in v. 5. It is a matter of rebirth in water and the Spirit. Some scholars, the most notable of whom is undoubtedly Rudolf Bultmann, claim that originally the saying mentioned only a rebirth in the Spirit. Thus they would further advance an interpretation of the Fourth Gospel whereby the discourses of Jesus represent a Johannine reworking of traditional themes taken from the myth of a Gnostic revealer. Such sacramentalism as appears in the Gospel would have been added by the later hand of a redactor who desired to make the Fourth Gospel more conformable to the belief and practice of the broader Church. Unfortunately for these authors there is not the slightest shred of textual evidence to suggest that the saying of Jesus found in John 3:5 ever spoke of anything other than a rebirth in the sacrament of baptism.

He is not, however, so concerned with the rite of the sacrament as he is with the effects of the sacrament. He makes no further mention of a rebirth in water. rather, he concentrates all his attention on the Spirit (John 3:6-8). For John, there is no middle ground. A man belongs to the Spirit or he does not. It is an "either—or" situation; either man is of the Spirit or he is of the flesh. In this situation, Christian baptism means that man is of the Spirit. To be such is not a matter of man's personal choice. Rather, it is a matter of divine election and the gratuitous nature of this choice. So John introduces a little parable (v. 8) into his narrative to show the sovereign freedom of the Spirit of God who chooses those who are born again.

Christian baptism ought not to be separated from Christian faith. So John introduces another question of a still incredulous Nicodemus (v. 9). Jesus proclaims Nicodemus' unbelief—the teacher of Israel does not understand—and then begins a monologue which reaches something of a climax in the announcement that the Son of Man must be lifted up. What follows this climactic utterance is a further development on the theme of belief in Jesus, John 3:16-21, essentially commenting on the notion of salvific belief (first expressed in v. 15), while 3:31-36 offers additional reflection on the notion that Jesus testifies to heavenly realities (v. 12).

In fact, Nicodemus disappears from the scene immediately after being called "a teacher of Israel" by Jesus. With Jesus' "Amen, Amen, I say to you" in v. 11 we have a new beginning. Now the verbs and pronouns are in the second person plural. The evangelist now can leave Nicodemus out of the picture since Jesus is beginning a discourse destined for those who *do* understand. The discourse bears upon Jesus' qualifications as the Revealer and the nature of the believer's faith.

Jesus the Revealer

Why is it that Jesus can testify to heavenly things? The reason is that he belongs to the heavenly realm. Already Nicodemus had suggested, on the basis of his response to Jesus' signs, that Jesus was a teacher come from God and that God was with him (v. 2). Nicodemus' language suggests that the signs worked by Jesus put him in a category similar to the Gnostic teachers who came from God or to that of the prophets of whom it could be said that God was with them (cf. Jer 1:8).

These categories, as important as they may be, are inadequate to describe the Jesus to which the Fourth Gospel gives witness. The Johannine Jesus is uniquely qualified to speak of heavenly things because he is the Son of Man. John's thought is that the Son of Man essentially belongs to the heavenly realm (cf. 1:18); since he is the one alone who belongs to heaven, Jesus is alone qualified to be the revealer of heavenly realities.

It is precisely the uniqueness of Jesus which prompts the evangelist to introduce a rather enigmatic saying into his narrative at 3:13. Some apocalyptists had claimed that one or other legendary hero of the Old Testament had gone to heaven where he was the beneficiary of visions and other communications which, upon his return to earth, he might share with men. In some Jewish circles, there was an expression of Mosaic piety which portrayed Moses as a man who had gone to heaven to obtain the Law, now identified with Wisdom. In response to these claims, John offers the classic rebuttal, "No one has ever seen God" (1:18). The only one who has ever seen God and is therefore qualified to speak of divine realities is he who has come from God, the Son of Man (cf. John 6:46). The title bespeaks Jesus' unique relationship to the Father and indicates the authenticity of his claim to be the sole Revealer.

With John 3:14-15, the evangelist gets closer to the heart of the matter. There is one moment which stands out from all the rest in the revelation and self-revelation of the Son of Man. The crucifixion of Jesus is not only a matter of his being exalted in glory by his heavenly Father. John uses the Old Testament Scriptures to make his point. A midrashic interpretation of Numbers 21:9 allows him to elucidate the meaning of Jesus' death. He capitalizes on two meanings of the verb "to lift up" to remind his readers that the crucifixion is both a lifting up on the cross and the exaltation in glory. That drama is the supreme act of Jesus' self-revelation.

We may speak of the "word of the cross," because there is no event in the earthly life of the Son of Man more revelatory than his crucifixion-exaltation. That act of revelation is the salvific event *par excellence*. However, the reader must not get the wrong idea. He should not become like Nicodemus who believes that merely physical, albeit extraordinary, acts are salvific (v. 4). No, it is not the material fact of Jesus' being lifted upon the cross which is salvific. The revelation of the Son of Man must be received in faith. Salvation, which John characteristically calls "eternal life," is God's free gift to those who believe. Eternal life is imparted through baptism to the man of faith, who understands that the crucifixion is the exaltation of the Son of Man who gives his Spirit to those who believe (John 19:30).

Unbelief and Belief

John's reflection on the true nature of Christian faith allows us to see the figure of Nicodemus in the proper light. He is truly a man of the Pharisees, a Jew who does not have an authentic faith in Jesus. The use of a midrashic exegesis and the trace of a polemic against a Moses-centered piety allow the reader of John 3:1-15 to understand that Nicodemus' "belief" is founded on earthly realities. His faith remains that of the one whose ex-egetical arguments will never produce authentic and life-bearing faith (cf. John 18:39-47, 9:24-34, etc.). As a teacher of Israel, Nicodemus is versed in the Scriptures of his people; yet his faith is inadequate.

Throughout John's Gospel misunderstanding is used as a lit-erary device to describe that sort of faith which is so inadequate as to really be unbelief. Nicodemus is portrayed as a first example of those who have such an inadequate faith. He exemplifies the faith of those described by John in the few verses which have been put together as an introduction to his account of the conversation with Nicodemus. Those verses (John 2:23-25) speak of those who believed in Jesus' name because of his signs. To those whose faith is founded on the signs which he performs Jesus did not entrust himself (v. 24). Nicodemus is typical of those who "believe" but only on the basis of signs. To such as him Jesus has not entrusted himself.

Thus Nicodemus serves as a foil which John uses to present the meaning of authentic faith in Jesus. That faith is a faith which is grounded upon the testimony, the revelation, of Jesus himself. It is a testimony which Jesus is alone qualified to give. It is testimony to the very reality of Jesus himself. It is the self-revelation of the Son of Man exalted on the Cross. Belief in this self-revelation of the Son of Man is salvific. It bears with it eternal life, as God's gift of salvation to those who are born anew, in the Christian sacrament of baptism. All this is of the essence of the message of the Fourth Gospel. It is summed up in John's account of Jesus' conversation with Nicodemus, an account which truly serves as a compendium of the entire Gospel.

4. THE TWELVE: ANOTHER PERSPECTIVE

Almost from the beginning of Christian history it has been recognized that the Fourth Gospel is radically different from the other three gospels in the New Testament. During Patristic times, the difference was epitomized in the characterization of the Fourth Gospel as "the spiritual gospel" and the choice of the eagle as a symbol to represent its author who was, as it were, considered capable of soaring to the heights of heaven.

In the early years of the historical critical era, the difference between the Fourth Gospel and the others was summed up in the characterization of Matthew, Mark, and Luke as "the synoptic gospels," a category from which the Fourth Gospel was obviously—and for good reason—excluded. The difference between the Synoptics and the Fourth Gospel received symbolic expression in the printed synopses, beginning with Griesbach's work in 1774, which contained only the first three of the canonical gospels.

In the late nineteenth and early twentieth centuries, the difference between the Fourth Gospel and the Synoptics was summed up in the views of radical critics, such as Alfred Loisy, who considered that only the Synoptics provided material useful for historical investigation into the life of Jesus and relegated the Fourth Gospel to the status of an imaginative theological exposition on a Jesus who had become virtually a myth.

In popular piety, the difference between the Fourth Gospel and the synoptics is symbolized in the choice of "John the Divine" to identify its author, while the authorship of the Synoptic gospels is simply attributed to Matthew, Mark, and Luke or, at best, Saint Matthew, Saint Mark, and Saint Luke.

As historical-critical scholarship has continued to probe the Fourth Gospel during the past four decades, these views of earlier times have been virtually abandoned. It is now almost universally recognized that the Fourth Gospel also has its roots in the historical ministry of Jesus of Nazareth. Published synopses of the gospels now commonly print in parallel columns Matthew, Mark, Luke and John. These names are generally considered to be but symbols designating whoever the author of the respective texts might have been. With regard to the fourth gospel, there is a wide consensus of opinion that it was not written by John, at least, not by the John who was the son of Zebedee.

Despite the fact that contemporary biblical scholarship is now accustomed to treat the Fourth Gospel in the same way, and for the same purposes, that it examines the other three canonical gospels, contemporary biblical scholarship shares with the older ecclesiastical, critical, and pious views the conviction that the Fourth Gospel is quite different from the Synoptics. The difference, quite obvious when the plan of the Fourth Gospel is compared to that of the Synoptics, is a difference that goes down to small details and extends to a wide variety of viewpoints. As a case in point, this essay will briefly consider the appearance of "The Twelve" in the New Testament.

The Synoptics

Christians commonly speak and write about "the twelve apostles" and Jesus' "twelve disciples." Whenever they do so, they are, in fact, echoing the language of the Synoptic gospels. To speak about the twelve apostles or Jesus' twelve disciples is a manner of speaking that is foreign to the tradition of the Fourth Gospel.

Mark

The earliest of the gospels to mention "The Twelve" is Mark, the first of the gospels. He does so on only one occasion, that is, when he lists the names of twelve men, Simon, James, John, Andrew, Philip, Bartholomew, Matthew, Thomas, James the son of Alphaeus, Thaddaeus, Simon the Cananaean, and Judas Iscariot whom Jesus appointed to be with him, to go out to preach, and to have authority to cast out demons (Mark 3:14-19a).

A Textual Problem

Although the three-fold mission of the twelve is clearly described in Mark 3:14b-15, the status of Mark's presentation formula (Mark 3:14a) is not so clear. "And he appointed twelve" (*kai epoiēsen dōdeka*) is the simple formula used by the RSV to introduce the mission statement of vv. 14b-15. However, many editions of the RSV offer a footnote to the effect that in v. 14a "other ancient authorities add *whom also he named apostles*."[1] Similarly, many of these same editions provide for v. 16 a footnote which reads "*So he appointed the twelve*."

In fact, the twenty-sixth edition of Nestle-Aland includes *hous kai apostolous onomasen* ("whom also he named apostles") in 3:14a as a bracketed part of the Greek text. The editors have included the disputed words because of the weight of the manuscript tradition (including the Sinaiticus, Vaticanus, and Ephraemi Rescriptus codices). However, they have given the disputed words only a C rating[2] and opine that the the clause is most likely an interpolation into the Markan text brought about because of the influence of Luke 6:13.[3]

At the beginning of v. 16, a bracketed *kai epoiēsen tous dōkeka* ("So he appointed the twelve") appears in N-A[26]. With the inclusion of these words, a neat *inclusio* is formed around the triple mission statement of Mark 3:14b-15. However, the editors once again offer but a C rating for the bracketed clause, opining that the words have come into the text as a result of scribal dittography.[4]

1. For example, Nestle-Aland, *Greek-English New Testament* (3rd. ed. : Stuttgart, Deutsche Bibelgesellschaft, 1985) p. 96.

2. Meaning that there is "a considerable amount of doubt."

3. See Bruce M. Metzger, *A Textual Commentary on the Greek New Testament* (London/New York: United Bible Societies, 1971) p. 80.

4. See B.M. Metzger, *A Textual Commentary*, pp. 80-81.

The revised edition of the NAB, following N-A²⁶, includes both sets of disputed words in brackets. In contrast, most of the principal recent English-language editions of the NT do not admit the disputed words of v. 14.[5] Generally, however, they do incorporate the disputed words of v. 16 into the English-language text.[6]

A group of twelve

Mark does not particularly speculate on the significance[7] attached to the fact that this group of Jesus' special companions, appointed by him to share in his ministry of preaching and exorcism, were twelve[8] in number. However, given the eschatological nature of their mission it is likely that their being twelve in number had some eschatological significance.[9]

Indeed, other texts in the New Testament suggest that "twelve" is symbolic of the twelve tribes of Israel and therefore points to the eschatological nature of the mission to which these twelve were appointed. Matthew and Luke (Matt 19:28 = Luke 22:30) have taken a logion on the Son of Man and the twelve tribes of Israel from their Q source and incorporated it into a short discourse on discipleship. Horsley suggests that that this saying of

5. In addition to the RSV, JB, NEB, NAB, and NJB do not include the disputed words, while the NIV does include the words in the text of v. 14.

6. The JB, NEB, NIV, NJB, NAB include the words, while the RSV does not.

7. Similarly, the evangelist does not speculate on the significance of the enigmatic names "Peter" and "Boanerges," notwithstanding the fact that he does translate the latter expression into Greek.

8. Cf. Ernest Best, "Mark's Use of the Twelve," *ZNW* 69 (1978) 11-35, pp. 32, 34. Best holds that "the twelve" is an element of the tradition that has come down to Mark.

9. The point is emphasized by Jean Giblet, "Les douze, histoire et théologie," in J. Giblet, *et al., Aux origines de l'Église.* RechBib, 7. (Bruges: Desclée de Brouwer, 1965) 51-64, pp. 61-64. In this article Giblet strongly defends the view that the twelve were, in fact, a group which was gathered together during Jesus' historical ministry—a view rejected by many modern critics. Since the present essay is dealing with the way in which the different evangelists treat of the tradition about the twelve, we will not enter into a discussion of the relationship between the tradition and the Sitz-im-Leben Jesu in the present essay.

Jesus on the twelve thrones evokes a concrete social context.[10] If so, the Q-logion is concerned with a concrete manifestation of the "reign of God," a powerful eschatological symbol in the apocalyptic context within which Jesus spoke. In any event, the Son of Man is patently an eschatological quantity, as is the notion of the judgment to come. Applied to the disciples in Matthew and Luke, the Q-logion highlights their eschatological role.[11]

Similarly, within a single, relatively short passage (Rev 21:10-14), the book of Revelation speaks of the twelve tribes of Israel and mentions the names of the twelve apostles, without, however, citing each of the names in turn.

While Mark does not explicitly exploit the eschatological significance of the twelve, it is clear that "the twelve" has qualitative significance for his gospel.[12] In his narrative of Jesus' feeding the five thousand, Mark indicates that the pieces of the broken bread and the fish that had been gathered up after the meal filled twelve baskets (Mark 6:43), apparently in reference to the appointed group of twelve (see Mark 6:37,41). The Markan Jesus subsequently draws attention to those twelve baskets (Mark 8:19) as he confronts the disciples' lack of understanding.[13]

10. See Richard Horsley, *Jesus and the Spiral of Violence: Popular Jewish Resistance in Roman Palestine* (San Francisco: Harper & Row, 1987) pp. 201-202.

11. Trilling correctly notes that this does not necessarily imply that the logion was originally addressed to a group of twelve. Cf. W. Trilling, "Zur Entstehung des Zwölferkreises: Eine geschichtskritische Überlegung," in R. Schnackenburg, ed., *Die Kirche des Anfangs.* H. Schürmann Festschrift (Leipzig: St. Benno, 1977) 201-222, pp. 213-222.

12. Since Rigaux' 1960 study it has become common for commentators to note that Mark's mention of the twelve is frequently found in the redactional verses of the gospel. The redactional insertion of the twelve does not take away from the fact that "the twelve" is an element of the tradition received by Mark. See B. Rigaux, "Die 'Zwölf' in Geschichte und Kerygma," in H. Ristow and K. Matthiae, eds., *Der historische Jesus und der kerygmatische Christus: Beiträge zum Christusverständnis in Forschung und Verkündigung* (Berlin: Evangelische Verlagsanstalt, 1960) pp. 468-486.

13. The discussion is not found in Luke. It is present in Matthew, but Matthew's syncopated version of the confrontation (Matt 16:8-12) is focused more on the teaching of the Pharisees and Sadducees than on the disciples' misunderstanding *per se*. In abbreviating the dialogue, Matthew has omitted any explicit reference to *the twelve* baskets in v. 9.

Moreover, in the Passion Narrative, Mark identifies Judas three times as "one of the twelve" (Mark 14:10,20,43), thereby underscoring the heinousness of the betrayal of Jesus by Judas. Mark's group of twelve are portrayed as having been Jesus' special companions (Mark 3:14; 4:10). They were the group with whom Jesus celebrated his final Paschal meal (11:11). To the twelve Jesus gave particular instructions. In fact, Mark emphasizes that Jesus specifically chose the twelve for this instruction (Mark 9:35; 10:32).[14] Finally, the twelve were sent out, in pairs, as an extension of Jesus' ministry of exorcising (Mark 6:7).

For Mark, the twelve are a group of special companions of Jesus,[15] who were especially taught by him and who were sent out into mission by him. From this perspective, the Markan resume which serves as in introduction to the list of the names of the twelve in Mark 3:14-16 provides a sketch of the image of the twelve which is then fleshed out in the remainder of the gospel.

Matthew and Luke

Mark's portrayal of "the twelve" is substantially reflected in Matthew and Luke, the canonical gospels clearly dependent on Mark. Despite their general similarity with Mark, each of these later gospels portray the twelve with nuances that are specific to the respective evangelists. The purpose of the present essay does not allow for an in-depth study of "the twelve" in Matthew or Luke. However, it might be useful to identify a few traits which differentiate the understanding of the twelve in Matthew and Luke from that found in Mark.

Twelve

To begin, although Matthew (5 times) and Luke (7 times) explicitly mention "the twelve" (dōdeka) less frequently than does

14. See also Mark 4:10.
15. Best, however, states that "although the twelve are commissioned to be with Jesus this does not imply a special relation between them and Jesus." E. Best, "Mark's Use," p. 34.

Mark (10 times), each of these evangelists patently portrays "the twelve" as representing a full complement. Unlike Mark,[16] both Matthew and Luke identity the group as "the eleven" after Jesus' passion and death (Matt 28:16; Luke 24:9,33). Judas was one of the twelve (Matt 26:47; Luke 22:47). Because of his defection the group was not up to its full complement; they were only eleven in number.[17]

At the beginning of the second part of his two-part work, Luke tells the story of the choice of Matthias as the group is brought up to its full numerical strength. Then, after the mission-enabling gift of the Spirit. Peter, standing with the eleven (Acts 2:14) utters his speech at Pentecost, the paradigm of Acts' kerygmatic (missionary) speeches. According to Luke the twelve continue to enjoy a leadership function within the church of Jerusalem (Acts 6:21).[18]

Disciples and Apostles

Matthew and Luke identify the twelve as disciples and apostles (Matt 10:1-2; Luke 6:13). The similarity stops, however, with the nomenclature. Each of the evangelists has a particular view of the relationship between discipleship and apostleship.

Matthew's list of the twelve (Matt 10:2b-4) is formally introduced with the statement: "The names of the twelve apostles are these" (Matt 10:2a). This is the only place in the New Testament where the expression "twelve apostles" (dōdeka apostoloi) occurs;[19] and it is the only time that Matthew writes about the "apostles." Matthew, however,clearly identifies these twelve apostles with the disciples of Jesus. In his vision of Jesus' ministry,

16. See, however, Mark 16:14. This verse belongs to the canonical gospel but textual critics generally hold that the entire passage (Mark 16:9-20) was not part of the original gospel text.

17. Significantly, these passages (Matt 28:16; Luke 24:9,33) along with Acts 1:26 and 2:14 (+ Mark 16:14) are the only places in the NT where the numerical adjective "eleven" (endeka) is to be found.

18. Where "twelve" (dōdeka) is a hapax occurrence in Acts.

19. See, however, "the eleven apostles" (hoi endeka apostoloi) in Acts 1:26.

there are (only) twelve disciples (Matt 10:1)[20] and these twelve are identified as the twelve apostles in Matt 10:1-4.

While formally acknowledging that the twelve are disciples, Luke states that the twelve have been chosen from among the disciples. It is only the select group of twelve that are named apostles (Luke 10:13). Luke has highlighted the importance of Jesus' selection of the twelve by presenting Jesus at prayer during the night before he made his choice (v. 12).

In sum, Mark's significant group, identified as "the twelve," have become Matthew's "twelve disciples" and Luke's (twelve) "apostles." The difference of terminology is apparent in the three evangelists' description of Jesus' passover meal. While Mark tells that Jesus came with "the twelve" (Mark 14:17), Matthew states that Jesus sat at table with "the twelve disciples" (Matt 26:20) and Luke states that Jesus sat at table with "the apostles" (Luke 22:14).

Matthew, of course, has his own view of what it means to be a disciple of Jesus, emphasizing the point that the disciples are those who have been particularly formed by Jesus, much in the same way that a Jewish rabbi shaped his disciples by the teaching which he imparted. On the other hand, Luke has a particular understanding of apostleship, one that he "unpacks" throughout the Acts of the Apostles.[21]

The Names in Matthew

The names of the twelve appear somewhat differently in Matthew and Luke from the way that they are given in Mark.

---

20. Cf. Matt 11:1; 20:17; 26:20.
21. The word *apostolos* occurs twenty-eight times in Acts. This is the highest concentration of the term in the entire New Testament.
22. Thus, the fifth-century Codex Bezae Cantabrigiensis, as well as Origen.
23. Thus, the Codex Koridethi, the minuscules of the Lake family, and the majority of the medieval Greek manuscripts.
24. Thus, some Old Latin manuscripts.
25. The traditional patronym for this gospel.

According to N-A[26], Matthew's roster of "the names of the twelve apostles" (Matt 10:2-4) includes the twelve names found in Mark 3:16-19a. However, some ancient manuscripts read "Lebbaeus,"[22] "Lebbaeus called Thaddaeus,"[23] or "Judas the Zealot"[24] in Matt 10:3. By listing "Lebbaeus" as the tenth name on Matthew's rota, the King James Version and the NEB attest to the confusion present in the manuscript tradition.

A comparison of Matthew's list with that of Mark shows that the name of Andrew appears in second rather than in fourth place and that the sequence of the names of Matthew and Thomas (the seventh and eight names) has been inverted. Matthew has also omitted the enigmatic Boanerges as an epithet for the sons of Zebedee and has qualified Matthew[25] as "the tax collector."

The call to discipleship of a tax collector named Levi is narrated in Mark 2:13-17 and Luke 5:27-32. A similar story, obviously based on Mark, appears in Matt 9:9-13, but here the tax collector appears as a man named Matthew. Since it is quite unlikely that a Semite would have two Semitic names, it is probable that the evangelist changed the name of Levi to that of Matthew in Matt 9:9.[26] The change of name was influenced by the evangelist's theory of discipleship. He identifies the disciples of Jesus with the twelve. The tax collector was obviously called to discipleship.[27] His name ought, therefore, to appear on the list of the twelve. Yet it did not appear on Mark's list of the twelve. So the evangelist, known to tradition as Matthew, substituted the name of the relatively obscure Matthew[28] for the traditional name of Levi in the story of the call of the tax collector. He completed his editorial work by identifying Matthew as a tax collector on the roster of the twelve, the only one of the twelve to be identified by a reference to a profession.

---

26. See Rudolf Pesch, "Levi-Matthäus (Mc. 2.14/Mt. 9:9; 10:3): Ein Beitrag zur Lösung eines alten Problems," *ZNW* 59 (1968) 40-56.

27. Cf. "follow me" (*akolouthei moi*) in Matt 9:9; Mark 2:14; Luke 5:27.

28. No particular function is otherwise attributed to Matthew in the canonical NT.

The Names in Luke

As Matthew did, so Luke lists Andrew in second place among the twelve, but otherwise his sequence of the first nine names (Luke 6:14-15) is similar to that found in Mark. Luke has, however, deleted the name of Thaddaeus from the tenth position. Thaddaeus' place on the list is taken by Simon, whom Luke identifies as a Zealot rather than as a Cananaean (Luke 6:15). A Judas, the son of James, who appears neither on the Matthaean nor on the Markan list, occupies the eleventh position on Luke's list of "the twelve." All three Synoptic authors, of course, place the name of Judas at the end of their lists of the twelve.

In Acts 1:13, Luke offers another list of the names of the group, understandably without the name of Judas. Although the names are the same as those which appear in Luke 6:14-16, their order is quite different. Peter and John appear at the head of the list, a position which reflects their leadership role in the Jerusalem church. Subsequently, the names of James, Andrew, Philip, Thomas, Bartholomew, and Matthew occur in a sequence which is reproduced at no other place in the New Testament. The three final names on the list, James, Simon, and Judas appear in the same order as they do in Luke 6:15-16.

The Mission

By and large,[29] both Matthew and Luke have omitted Mark's mission statement from their respective introductions to the list of the twelve. However, Matthew, apparently making use of a Q tradition,[30] has placed a mission statement after the listing of the twelve. That mission discourse focuses on preaching (Matt 10:7), but contains, nonetheless, an incidental reference to exorcisms.

29. Matt 10:1 makes reference to the twelve's power to exorcise, but does not highlight the twelve's companionship with Jesus, nor their mission to preach. Luke 6:13 does not specifically cite any aspect of the triple mission which Mark assigns to the twelve.

30. Cf. John S. Kloppenborg, *Q Parallels: Synopsis, Critical Notes and Concordance.* Foundations & Facets (Sonoma, CA: Polebridge, 1987) p. 72.

Luke has a mission statement parallel to Matt 10:5-14 in 9:1-6, where it is clearly addressed to "the twelve" (Luke 9:1).

Each of these later evangelists, writing from perspectives that are different from that of Mark, has, moreover, yet another vision of the ultimate mission of the twelve. That perspective appear in the Matthean scene of the great commissioning (Matt 28:16-20) and the first two chapters of Luke's Acts of the Apostles. The great commission and the promise of the empowering Spirit (Acts 1:8) articulate the major mission of the twelve according to the views of the later Synoptists. Luke-Acts particularly insists upon the role of the twelve in the origins of the church.

The Fourth Gospel

In contrast with the many references to the twelve in the three gospels of the Synoptic tradition, there are only four explicit references to the twelve in the Fourth Gospel—and none in the rest of the Johannine corpus. Three of these references are in one small pericope, namely, John 6:66-71. The fourth mention of the twelve is in John 20:24.

Names

The fourth gospel provides no list of the names of the twelve. It's most complete listing of the names of the disciples of Jesus is found in the epilogue to the gospel, where seven individuals are cited, namely, Simon Peter, Thomas called the twin, Nathanael of Cana in Galilee, the sons of Zebedee, and two others, whose names are not identified (John 21:2). The gathering of Jesus' disciples into a group of seven reflects the evangelist's predilection for the number seven and may well be another instance of the way in which the author of the epilogue imitates the style of the gospel itself.[31]

31. See my "Proverbial Sayings in St. John's Gospel," *Melita Theologica* 37 (1986) 42-58, p. 45; in this volume, pp. 128-150, pp. 132-133

Nathanael's name does not appear in the Synoptic gospels. According to the tradition of the Fourth Gospel, however, Nathanael is clearly a disciple of Jesus. Indeed, in many respects Nathanael serves as a paradigm of discipleship (John 1:45-51).[32] Christian tradition has often identified Nathanael with Bartholomew,[33] most likely under the influence of the Matthaean theory on the twelve, but there is no historical evidence to suggest that the Fourth Gospel's Nathanael and the Bartholomew of the Synoptic tradition are one and the same individual. In any event, the fourth evangelist does not identifty Nathanael as one of the twelve.[34]

The Fourth Gospel does, however, specifically identify Judas as one of the twelve (John 6:71).[35] His name, obviously, is omitted from the group of seven to whom the risen Jesus revealed himself (John 21:2). In its explicit identification of Judas as "one of the twelve," the Fourth Gospel concurs with the Synoptic tradition. Unlike Matthew and Luke who focus upon the twelve as a paradigmatic complement and who specifically treat of the death of Judas (Matt 27:3-10; Acts 1:18-19), the Fourth Gospel does not mention the death of Judas.[36] His name occurs for the last time in the Fourth Gospel at John 18:5.

The Fourth Gospel also identifies Thomas as "one of the twelve" (*heis ek tōn dōdeka*, John 20:24), a designation attributed only to Judas in the Synoptic gospels. The fourth evangelist also makes mention of some, but not all, of the other individuals

32. See my "Representative Figures in the Fourth Gospel," *DR* 94 (1976) 26-46, 118-132, pp. 34-36, in this volume, pp. 11-14, and *John and His Witness*. Zacchaeus Studies: New Testament (Wilmington, DE: Glazier, forthcoming).

33. See my "Nathanael," in the *Anchor Bible Dictionary*, forthcoming.

34. Raymond Brown, nonetheless, opines that, since these was no standard list of "the twelve" in first century Christianity (see above), "Nathanael may have been counted in the never-given list of the Twelve accepted in Johannine tradition." See R.E. Brown, *The Community of the Beloved Disciple: The Life, Loves, and Hates of an Individual Church in New Testament Times* (New York: Paulist, 1979) p. 81, n. 149.

35. Cf. John 12:4.

36. Cf. John 17:12.

whose names[37] appear on the Synoptic lists of the twelve. These
are Simon Peter,[38] Andrew,[39] and Philip.[40] These three names,[41]
of course, appear on all three Synoptic lists of the twelve.[42] Since
these are the only names mentioned, recourse to the Fourth
Gospel does not provide any solution for the identification
problems that arise from the comparison of the Synoptics' lists of
the names of the twelve with one another.

John 6:67-71

The fourth evangelist's views on the twelve are summed up in a
small pericope, which has been structured into a single unit of
material by a kind of *inclusio*: John 6:67-71. *Dōdeka*, "twelve," is
the only term that appears in both verses 67 and 71, but a verb of
saying appears in each verse, and, in each case, the subject is
Jesus (expressed in v. 67, implied in v. 71). The entire unit, which
has no direct parallel in the Synoptic gospels, is stamped with
elements of Johannine style. Among its Johannine features are
the use of dialogue, Jesus' initiative in the dialogue, the use of
interrogation,[43] the name of Simon Peter, the name of Judas the

37. The aforementioned reference to the sons of Zebedee occurs in John 21:2,
but the names of the brothers are not given. This reference to the sons of Zebedee
is hapax in the Fourth Gospel. Elsewhere, the Fourth Gospel does not mention
the name of either James or John.

38. John 1:40, 42, 44; 6:8, 68; 13:6, 8, 9, 24, 36, 37; 18:10, 11, 15, 16 (2 ×), 17,
18, 25, 26, 27; 20:2, 3, 4, 6. Cf. John 21:2, 3, 7 (2 ×), 11, 15, 17, 20, 21.

39. John 1:40, 44; 6:8; 12:22. Andrew is not cited in the epilogue's group of
seven (John 21:2).

40. John 1:43, 44, 45, 46, 48; 6:5, 7; 12:21, 22; 14:8, 9. Since Philip is likewise
not mentioned in 21:2, it is reasonable to assume that the author of the epilogue
had Andrew and Philip in mind when he wrote about "two others of his
disciples."

41. Gunther has suggested that the Judas (not Iscariot) of John 14:22 is a
brother of the Lord and one of the twelve (cf. Luke 4:16). See John J. Gunther,
"The Relation of the Beloved Disciple to the Twelve," *TZ* 37 (1981) 129-148. In
my judgment the suggestion is without merit.

42. Four, if the list of Acts 1:13 is to be included.

43. This, and the following characteristics, are among the fifteen characteristics
of Johannine style which Boismard and Lamouille have identified in the five verses
of the pericope. See M.-E. Boismard - A. Lamouille, *Synopse des quatre évangiles
en français*, 3; *L'évangile de Jean* (Paris: Cerf, 1977) p. 520.

son of Simon Iscariot, and the expressions "eternal life," "believe," and "know."

The Johannine character of this unit, coupled with the absence of a parallel narrative in the Synoptic gospels, leads to the ready conclusion that John 6:67-71 is a Johannine construction. The theme of the pericope is the twelve (*dōdeka*), the framing term and a vocable which also appears in v. 70. That three of the four Johannine uses of this term appear in this single pericope makes it all the more clear that it is in John 6:67-71 that the evangelist has chosen to formally treat the tradition about the twelve.

The fourth evangelist is familiar with the existence of the twelve. He speaks of them collectively and mentions the fact that they have been chosen (v. 70).[44] He does not, however, explain the circumstances of their call[45] nor does he explain how they came to be assembled as a group of twelve. As a matter of fact, although the fourth evangelist narrates the call of some of those cited in the Synoptics as belonging to the group of twelve,[44] he does not tell about the call of either of the two individuals who are specifically identified as "one of the twelve."

The setting which the evangelist has provided for his reflection on the twelve in John 6:67-71 is the crisis which developed among Jesus' would-be disciples because of the teaching on the bread of life. As the evangelist portrays the scene, the defection of some disciples prompts Jesus to ask the twelve about their own intentions. Apparently the twelve represent a special group among Jewish Christians.[47]

Although Jesus' question is addressed to the twelve as a group,[48] it is Simon Peter who responds. In a manner similar to that in which Peter functions as a spokesperson for the twelve in

44. Cf. John 13:18; 15:16, 19.

45. Cf. R.E. Brown, *Community*, p. 187, n. 331.

46. That is, Andrew in John 1:35-41, Simon Peter in John 1:41-42, and Philip in John 1:43-46.

47. See R.E. Brown, *Community*, pp. 74, 82.

48. Note the use of the second person plural, and the use of an emphatic *humeis*, "you," in the Greek text.

the Synoptic tradition,[49] Simon Peter functions as a spokesperson for the twelve in the Fourth Gospel. In fact, Simon Peter represents[50] the twelve insofar as he serves as their spokesperson.[51]

As Peter made a confession of faith in response to a query addressed by Jesus in Mark 8:29 (= Matt 16:15-16, Luke 9:20), the Simon Peter of the Fourth Gospel responds with a confession of faith to a question coming from Jesus. Simon Peter's confession of faith (John 6:68-69) is, however, formulated in characteristically Johannine terms. Rather than confess Jesus to be the Messiah, as did the Peter of Mark 8:29, the Andrew of John 1:41, and the Martha of John 11:27, Simon Peter confesses Jesus to be the sole revealer. This point of view expresses the faith conviction of the evangelist and his faith community.[52] Both the function of Jesus as Revealer and his uniqueness in that regard are convictions that are repeatedly promoted throughout the gospel.[53] Thus Simon Peter, as the spokesperson for the twelve, is presented as one whose confession of faith is at one with that of the Johannine community itself.

Simon Peter's confession is then epitomized in the affirmation that Jesus is the Holy One of God (*ho hagios tou theou*). In some ways the Petrine confession anticipates Jesus' description of himself as "the one whom the Father consecrated" (*hon ho patēr hēgiasen*) and sent into the world" (John 10:36). To underscore the importance of this unique titular confession, the evangelist uses a formal lemma, "we have believed," with its emphatic "we" (*hēmeis*) and a verb in the perfect tense (*pepisteukamen*) which indicates that the confession formulated in the past continues to

---

49. Cf. Mark 8:29 and parallels.

50. See "Representative Figures," pp. 126-129; in this volume, pp. 38-42.

51. Cf. John 13:22-24; comp. John 21:10-11.

52. Note the presence of the Johannine "we" in vv. 68 and 69. The "we" of these verses are among the thirteen instances in the Fourth Gospel where a first person plural is used to express the point of view of the Johannine community with the affirmation being attributed to some character in the story. See Godfrey C. Nicholson, *Death as Departure: The Johannine Descent-Ascent Schema.* SBLDS, 63 (Chico, CA: Scholars, 1983) p. 31.

53. See John 3:13-14, etc.

have validity for the present. A verbal hendiadys, "we have believed and have come to know" (*pepisteukamen kai egnō-kamen*)[54] further highlights the Petrine confession of faith.

As the only titular confession of faith placed on the lips of Simon Peter in the Fourth Gospel, the affirmation that Jesus is the Holy One of God represents the Johannine version of Peter's traditional confession of faith.[55] Elsewhere in the canonical gospels, however, the confession that Jesus is the Holy One of God is found only as the baited utterance of the unclean spirit who had taken possession of the man in the synagogue of Capernaum (Mark 1:24; Luke 4:34[56]).

Simon Peter's confession does not earn the response of Jesus' self-revelation.[57] Rather Jesus responds by speaking about his betrayal.[58] The response indicates that the faith of those for whom Peter serves as spokesperson is not all that it ought to be. From the standpoint of the Fourth Gospel, the corporate faith of the twelve is somehow inadequate.[59]

54. See John 17:8; 1 John 4:16.
55. Maynard opines that the title is "obviously Messianic," while Schnackenburg notes its connection in the history of tradition with Peter's confession of Jesus' Messiahship. See Arthur H. Maynard, "The Role of Peter in the Fourth Gospel," *NTS* 30 (1984) 531-548, p. 534; Rudolf Schnackenburg, *The Gospel According to St John*, 2 (New York: Seabury, 1980) p. 76.
56. Cf. Luke 1:35.
57. Compare John 1:49-51.
58. A comparison with the Synoptic scene at Caresarea Philippi (Matt 16:13-23; Mark 8:27-33; Luke 9:18-22), to which John 6:67-71 is a parallel (see R.E. Brown, *The Gospel According to John, I-XII.* AB, 29. Garden City, NY: Doubleday, 1966, pp. 301-302; A.H. Maynard, "The Role of Peter," pp. 533-534), proves enlightening at this point. In the Johannine narrative, Simon Peter not specifically confess Jesus to be the Messiah. Moreover, Jesus' rejoinder does not introduce a new christological title into the dialogue. Jesus' response focuses on his "passion," not, however, in the passive voice as it is in the Synoptics. Rather, the "passion" is clearly identified as the result of a betrayal and one of the twelve is said to be responsible for the betrayal. In the Synoptics, Peter, as the spokesperson for the twelve, fails to understand that Jesus' Messiahship involves the passion; in the fourth gospel, one of the twelve is humanly responsible for the passion.
59. Nicholson characterizes Peter's confession as a "halting and inadequate statement of belief." See G.W. Nicholson, *Death*, p. 42. Brown, however, suggests that the disciples who drew back from Jesus (John 6:66) represent the Jewish Christian churches of inadequate faith, while in vv. 68-69 "we are hearing ... the

The words of Jesus in John 6:70-71 focus on the less than adequate faith of the twelve. It is true that it is only Judas who is identified as a betrayer. That is in keeping with the Synoptic tradition and corresponds to the historicity of the events of Jesus' life. Nonetheless, one of the literary characteristics of the Fourth Gospel is its introduction of individual characters in the gospel story. On the narrative level, these individuals serve the needs of Johannine dramatization. Beyond that, however, the various characters also serve a representative function.

In John 6:70-71, Judas somehow represents the twelve. He is clearly identified as "one of you" (*ex hūmōn heis*) and as "one of the twelve" (*heis ek tōn dōdeka*). Judas has even assumed Peter's satanic function: Jesus calls him a devil.[60] While the affirmation that Judas is "one of you" has been placed by the evangelist on the lips of Jesus, the affirmation that Judas is "one of the twelve" is a reflective comment on the part of the evangelist himself.[61] The presence of this patent Johannine note serves as a clear indication that the evangelist is pondering the significance of "the twelve" in vv. 67-71. Clearly, the betrayal of Judas indicates that the corporate faith of the twelve is to be found wanting.

John 20:24

The third representative of the twelve is Thomas, identified in John 20:24 as "one of the twelve." In accordance with the

voice of Christians of a more adequate faith for whom Peter and the Twelve are appropriate symbols." See R.E. Brown, *Community*, p. 82. I would contend that although the faith of the twelve, represented by Simon Peter, is clearly more adequate than that of the defectors, it is not presented as a fully adequate faith according to the standards of the evangelist and his community.

60. Cf. Matt 16:23; Mark 8:33. In the Synoptic tradition there is some interchangeability between "the devil" (*ho diabolos*) and "Satan" (*ho Satanas*). Cf. Mark 1:13 ("Satan") in comparison with its parallels, Matt 4:1 and Luke 4:1 ("the devil") and Matt 4:1, 5, 8 ("the devil") in comparison with Matt 4:10 ("Satan," cf. Matt 16:23).

61. See Gilbert Van Belle, *Les parenthèses dans l'évangile de Jean: Aperçu historique et classification. Texte grec de Jean.* Studiorum Novi Testamenti Auxilia, 11 (Louvain: University Press, 1985) p. 78. Van Belle draws attention to the number of modern commentators who identify v. 71 as a redactional notation by the evangelist.

dramatic techniques of Johannine composition, Thomas represents[62] the doubt entertained by the disciples with regard to Jesus' resurrection.[63] Alone he is made to bear the burden of their corporate disbelief. The demands of Johannine dramatization, however, set Thomas over and against the "other disciples."[64]

Confronted by the risen Lord, Thomas comes to full belief in the Risen One. "My Lord and my God" appears upon his lips as a full confession of faith. This may well be the confession of faith with the highest level of christology in the entire Fourth Gospel. In this respect, Thomas is fully a believer. Nonetheless, and despite the relative fullness of his faith, Thomas the believer pales in comparison with those who have not seen and yet believe (John 20:28). It is for them, rather than for Thomas, that the Lord reserves the pronouncement of beatitude.

Conclusion

Although a thorough study of "The Twelve" in the Fourth Gospel, let alone in the entire NT, would require far more textual analysis than the limited scope of the present essay allows, the portrayal of the understanding of the twelve which has been sketched with such broad strokes readily lends itself to the conclusion that the understanding of the twelve entertained in the Fourth Gospel is quite different from that developed in the Synoptic gospels.

The Fourth Gospel shares with the first, that is, Mark, a tradition that has been handed down. Both evangelists write about the twelve as an element of the Jesus tradition with which they have to deal. Both writers refuse to speculate on the significance of the number itself. Both evangelists share a common tradition as to the names of some individuals who belong to the twelve and that (Simon) Peter served as spokesperson for the group.

62. See my "Representative Figures," pp. 124-126; in this volume, pp. 35-38.
63. Cf. Matt 28:17; Luke 24:36-43; comp. Mark 16:11, 14.
64. See John 20:25, 26.

Subsequently their ways of handling this traditional topic differ. While Mark develops the role of the twelve with regard to their mission, a role greatly expanded by Matthew and Luke, especially by the latter who emphasizes the role of the twelve in the origins of the church, the Fourth Gospel fails to attribute such a paramount significance to the group. While recognizing that the twelve were disciples,[65] the author fails to make of this group the paradigm of discipleship and does not attribute the title of apostle[66] to the group or to any of its members.

From the standpoint of the Fourth Gospel, the twelve represent a faithful group of Jewish-Christian disciples. Although they recognized Jesus as the revealer, and shared this faith conviction with the evangelist and his community, their faith in Jesus is shown to be somehow deficient in comparison with that of the evangelist's own faith community. Judas and Thomas graphically represent the inadequacy of the twelve before the death and resurrection of Jesus. The spokesperson for the twelve is Simon Peter, a truly round and ambiguous figure in the Fourth Gospel. His faith is authentic—indeed, he represents the authenticity of their faith—yet even his faith is not on a par with that of the Beloved Disciple, the real hero in faith of the Fourth Gospel.

65. Cf. John 6:66-67, "After this many of his disciples drew back and no longer went about with him. Jesus said to the twelve, 'Do you also (*kai humeis*) wish to go away?;'" John 20:24-25, "Now Thomas, one of the twelve was not with them (i.e., the disciples, cf. v. 19) when Jesus came. So the other disciples (*hoi alloi mathētai*) told him, ..."

66. *Apostolos* is hapax in the Fourth Gospel, namely, at John 13:36. Nonetheless, the harmonized reading of the gospels which has characterized ecclesiastical tradition through the centuries tends to describe those who heard the (Johannine) farewell discourse as apostles. This harmonized reading entered into the church's liturgical tradition. See, for example, the order of Mass in the Roman Catholic Roman rite: "Lord Jesus Christ, you said to your *apostles*: I leave you peace, my peace I give you" (my emphasis; cf. John 14:27).

II. A Single Gospel

5. A PASSION NARRATIVE?

Toward the end of the nineteenth century Martin Kähler described a gospel as "a passion narrative with an extended introduction." He was principally writing about the Gospel of Mark which scholars, then as now, commonly believed to have been the first of the written Gospels. The Fourth Gospel is quite unlike the Gospel of Mark—so unlike Mark, in fact, that it is not classified as one of the Synoptic Gospels. Today, a number of scholars are convinced that the author of the Fourth Gospel did not make use of Mark's work as he composed his Gospel at the end of the first century. Many of these same scholars are of the opinion that this evangelist did not even know of the text of the Gospel of Mark, although he probably made use of some of the same oral traditions which eventually made their way into Mark's Gospel in a written form. Nonetheless the Gospel of John has been called a gospel from time immemorial, and its author has been identified as an evangelist. Are these designations appropriate if John's work is so different from that of Mark? In other words, is the Fourth Gospel really a "gospel," if we understand by that term a passion narrative with an extended introduction?

John and the Synoptics

The answer to the question is not as simple as it may appear at first sight. John's Passion Narrative is quite different from the Passion Narratives of the Synoptic Gospels. This is particularly true if we consider a passion narrative to be an account of suffering and of passivity, that is, suffering that occurs at the hands of others. The Jesus of John's Passion Narrative is not one who suffers at the hands of others, if the accent is on suffering and on what others do. A comparison of two scenes in John's Passion Narrative with the parallel accounts in Mark will make the point.

Mark's story of Jesus' agony and arrest in the garden of Gethsemane (Mark 14:32-50) is well known. It focuses on Jesus' prayer which proceeds from his greatly distressed and troubled heart, on his disciples who repeatedly fall asleep, on the betrayal of Jesus by means of Judas' treacherous kiss, and on the flight of the disciples upon Jesus' arrest. John begins his Passion Narrative with a garden scene (John 18:1-11), but his story lacks the pathos of the Markan tale. It does not contain any mention of a woeful prayer; nor does it cite the kiss of Judas. In the garden Jesus is in full control of the situation. He inquires of the band of soldiers and officers from the priests and Pharisees, asking whom they seek. When he reveals himself as Jesus of Nazareth, those who have come out to arrest him are so awestruck that they fall to the ground. In John the disciples are neither overcome by sleep nor do they flee in fear. Rather Jesus gives the arresting crowd the command to let the disciples go (John 18:8).

Mark's description of the crucifixion and death of Jesus (Mark 15:21-41) includes the help that Jesus received from Simon of Cyrene and the taunting of Jesus by the passers-by and the chief priests. The last words of Jesus on the cross are those of a man in his final agony, "My God, my God, why hast thou forsaken me?" (Mark 15:34), the first words of Psalm 22. Crying out in agony, Jesus breathed his last (Mark 15:37). In John's story of the crucifixion and death of Jesus (John 19:17-30), the evangelist makes the point that Jesus carried his own cross (19:17). Rather than mocking Jesus, the chief priests are portrayed as meeting with Pilate and begging him to remove the "King of the Jews" placard from the cross (19:19-22). According to John, Jesus' last words focus on providing for his mother (19:26). He cites Scripture as he says, "I thirst" (19:28), and solemnly proclaims, "It is finished" (19:30). Then, in a similarly solemn gesture, Jesus bows his head and hands over his spirit (19:30). With this description the evangelist wants the reader to focus on the gift of the Spirit.

The contrasts that exist between these scenes in Mark's narrative of the passion of Jesus and the corresponding scenes in John's Gospel make it clear that the perspective of John's Passion Narrative is quite different from that of Mark. John portrays the crucifixion of Jesus as the great moment of Jesus' self-revelation as the Son of Man. The death of Jesus is the moment of his glorification. His crucifixion is his exaltation. As John tells his story of the passion, he does not tell us about one who suffers at the hands of others; rather, he tells the story of one who takes the initiative and remains in full control until the consummation of his self-revelation.

Indeed were it only the Gospel of John that had been handed down to us, it it unlikely that we would speak of the "passion" of Jesus at all; that is language appropriate to the stories contained in the Gospels of Mark, Luke, and Matthew. Had we only the Gospel of John, we would rather have spoken of the story of Jesus' glorification because the glorification of Jesus is the perspective that is highlighted in the account contained in John 19-20.

The Farewell Discourse

Granted, then, that we must understand "passion" in a particularly Johannine fashion if we are to speak of the Passion Narrative of the Fourth Gospel. Should we still think of the Fourth Gospel as a "passion narrative with an extended introduction?" The evangelist himself provides a striking clue that an affirmative answer must be given to this question in the chapters that immediately precede his account of Jesus' revelation-glorification by crucifixion. In John 17, the writer has dramatically projected his perspective on Jesus' crucifixion as he presents Jesus in prayer to the Father. The prayer speaks of Jesus' "hour," of the glorification of the Son, and of the manifestation of the Father's name. These are the very categories within which the evangelist understands what happened at Golgotha.

The prayer of Jesus in chapter 17 is the culmination of a series of discourses of Jesus (John 13-17) which scholars describe as a "farewell discourse." This literary form was well known to ancient Jewish writers. As the evangelist adopted this mode of writing, he clearly emphasized the importance that he attached to Jesus' death as his departure. Almost twenty percent of his Gospel belongs to the farewell discourse(s).

The opening verse sets the tone for the whole: "Now before the feast of the Passover, when Jesus knew that his hour had come to depart out of this world to the Father, having loved his own who were in the world, he loved them to the end" (13:1). The words anticipate motifs that will recur later in John's story. The "hour" is John's way of indicating the momentous event which is Jesus' revelation by crucifixion and draws our attention to the beginning of Jesus' priestly prayer (17:1). In the Greek language, in which John's Gospel was written, the "end" of John 13:1 anticipates Jesus' final utterance, "It is finished" (19:30).

A Passover Story

John's mention of the Passover at the beginning of the farewell discourse reminds the reader that he understands his Passion Narrative to be a Passover story. As he tells the story of the interaction between Pilate and the officers of the high priest at the time of Jesus' trial, the evangelist reminds us that the officers were ironically concerned with maintaining the ritual purity appropriate to the celebration of the Passover feast (18:28). He tells of the ironic release (in fulfillment of a Passover custom) of Barabbas, a would-be usurper of political power, while Jesus, the king of the Jews, remains in custody (18:39-40). He also tells us about the fulfillment of the Scripture relative to the paschal lamb (Exod 12:46; Ps 34:21) in his account of the soldiers' coming to the scene of the crucifixion to ensure the death of the crucified prior to the celebration of the Passover feast (John 19:31-37).

The evangelist has prepared the reader for his Passover story by repeatedly citing Jesus' presence in Jerusalem for the feast of Passover. It is almost as a refrain that the verse "the Passover of the Jews was at hand" recurs in John's Gospel. By repeating this refrain on three occasions (John 2:13; 6:4; and 11:55), the writer increases the crescendo of his dramatic tale until it reaches its climax in the Passover story itself. Dramatist that he is, the evangelist cites the refrain only at strategic moments in his tale. The first mention of the coming of the Passover opens John's account of the purification of the Temple (2:13-22). As a narrative which sets a tone for the entire Gospel, John's version of the story of the cleansing of the Temple focuses upon Jesus' death and resurrection in fulfilment of the Scriptures. This early and manifest reference to the death and resurrection of Jesus makes it clear that this is what John's Gospel is all about. The evangelist also tells us not only that this event will take place in fulfilment of the Scriptures, but also that it will make the Temple redundant. Then he brings his story to a close by again reminding his readers of Passover time (John 2:33).

The second mention of the coming of Passover (6:4) is set within John's account of the feeding of the five thoasand, an account which comes to a close with a suggestion of the crowd's misunderstanding of Jesus' kingship (6:15). The kingship of Jesus is, in fact, the central theme of John's Passion Narrative, more tightly woven into a dramatic sequence than any other part of John's Gospel. John has drawn special attention to the importance of Jesus' kingship in many ways, not the least of which is the dialogue between Pilate and Jesus on the subject of what it means for Jesus to be "the King of the Jews" (18:33-38).

The last of the signs of Jesus narrated by the evangelist is the raising of Lazarus from the dead (11:1-44). In John's story this is the event which directly leads to the death and resurrection of Jesus since the report of this sign led the chief priests and the council to plan how to put him to death (11:52). The stage has been set for the drama to reach its denouement as the writer reminds the reader that "Now the Passover of the Jews was at hand" (11:55). From this moment on, events move foreward with increasing rapidity and intensity. Having been anointed and having solemnly entered the city, Jesus proclaims "I, when I am lifted up from the earth, will draw all to myself" (12:32, 34). Immediately thereafter the evangelist tells us about the unbelief of the Jews (12:36-43) and the resultant judgment (12:44-50). Then he can proceed to Jesus' farewell discourse.

The Son of Man

When John recalls Jesus' speaking of his being lifted up (12:32, 34) in the short discourse after the raising of Lazarus, he is using another expression that also occurs some three times in his Gospel, again almost in refrain-like fashion. All three sayings of Jesus which make use of the verb "to lift up" (*hopsoun* in Greek) speak of the Son of Man being lifted up. In the judgment of some scholars these three sayings are akin to the triple prediction of Jesus' passion that we find in the synoptic Gospels. All three of those passages (Mark 8:31; 9:31; 10:33) speak of the death and resurrection of the Son of Man.

It is as the "Son of Man" that the Johannine Jesus speaks of his being lifted up. The first time that he does so (John 3:14-15) is in the context of a discourse with Nicodemus, a ruler of the Jews: "And as Moses lifted up the serpent in the wilderness, so must the Son of man be lifted up, that whoever believes in him may have eternal life." Later, in a dialogue with Jews who did not understand whence he had come nor whither he was going, Jesus said, "When you have lifted up the Son of man, then you will know that I am he (*egō eimi*)" (8:28). These two sayings of Jesus prepare us for the dialogue which precedes Jesus' passion and death: "'I, when I am lifted up from the earth, will draw all to myself.' He said this to show by what death he was to die. The crowd answered him, '...How can you say that the Son of man must be lifted up? Who is this Son of man?'" (12:32-34).

These three Son of Man sayings must be taken together. John's language is deliberately evocative. By speaking of Jesus' being lifted up, John is not only reminding the readers of Jesus' being lifted up on the cross but also proclaiming that the crucifixion was the means by which Jesus was lifted up in glory. Each of the three Son of Man sayings fills out the significance of that unique lifting up. By referring to the bronze serpent being lifted up by Moses in the desert (Num 21:8-9), the evangelist proclaims that Jesus' crucifixion-glorification is a salvific event which fulfills the Scriptures (John 3:14-15). By placing a saying about Jesus' being lifted up in a controversy setting, the evangelist reminds us not only that "The Jews" ironically functioned as the instruments of Jesus' being lifted up, but that his death was also a revelatory event (John 8:28). In the third and final mention of Jesus' being lifted up, John speaks clearly of Jesus' death—whose moment was at hand—and tells us how decisive it in is the judgment of humanity.

Conclusion

John is too much of a dramatist to have omitted still other telling indications of the movement of his Gospel. This movement lies fully revealed in the crucifixion-glorification of Jesus. With each indication the writer has shown that he has truly written a Passion Narrative with an extended introduction. The introduction is a dramatic one, and the Passion Narrative is told in a very particular way, but the whole is indeed a gospel—not only in the sense of a passion tale with a lengthy introduction, but also in the more fundamental sense of the proclamation of good news.

6. THE SEARCH FOR JESUS

Within the vast body of literature published in an attempt to elucidate the meaning of the gospels for the benefit of men of faith, attention is sometimes drawn to the programmatic nature of the words first spoken by Jesus during his public ministry. After the descent of the Spirit at the time of his baptism, the Markan Jesus solemnly proclaims: "The time is fulfilled, and the kingdom of God is at hand; repent, and believe in the Gospel" (Mark 1:15). This Jesuanic announcement of the eschatological event prepares the reader of this oldest gospel for the subsequent proclamation, in word and in deed, of the coming of the Kingdom of God—surely one of the most important themes of Mark.

Mark's programmatic dictum is taken over and somewhat adapted[1] by Matthew who incorporates the saying of his Markan source in Matt 4:17. Matthew, however, first places the words "Repent, for the kingdom of heaven is at hand" on the lips of John the Baptist[2] (Matt 3:2). This prompts the attentive reader of Matthew to consider the Baptist's eschatological pronouncement as part of Jesus' public ministry.[3] Within this perspective,

---

1. Matthew has characteristically substituted his *hē basileia tōn ouranōn*, "the kingdom of heaven," for Mark's *hē basileia tou theou*, "the kingdom of God." Matthew has inverted the announcement of the coming of the kingdom and the call to repentance, adding an explanatory *gar* ("for") as he does so. Matthew has also omitted from Matt 4:17 both the call for belief in the gospel and the announcement of the fulfillment of time. The latter omission, coupled with the appearance of *plērōsai*, "fulfill" in Matt 3:15 serves to strengthen our contention that Matt 3:15 represents Matthew's version of Jesus' first public utterance.

2. The Baptist's words in Matt 3:2 are textually identical with the dominical logion of Matt 4:17. The identity of the proclamation of the Baptist and that of Jesus owes to Matthew's fulfillment notion (cf. Matt 5:17, etc.). We should also note that Matthew has effectively diminished the sharp contrast implied in the traditional John-Jesus sequence (Mark 1:14) by separating the mention of John's arrest (Matt 4:12) from Jesus' announcement of the coming of the kingdom (Matt 4:17) by means of an extended fulfillment citation (Matt 4:13-16).

3. Since the Baptist's ministry belongs to the public ministry of Jesus, the baptism of Jesus must be considered as a public event. That it is to be so

the first public utterance of the Matthean Jesus is found in the post-baptismal dialogue when Jesus responds to the Baptist: "Let it be so now; for thus it is fitting for us to fulfill all righteousness" (Matt 3:15). The logion, with its use of characteristic Matthean vocabulary (*plēroō*,[4] *dikaiosunē*),[5] is clearly the work of the evangelist's hand. It announces that Matthew will present Jesus as he in whom the divine plan of salvation, all righteousness,[6] will be fulfilled.

Unlike Matthew, Luke makes a sharp distinction between the ministry of the Baptist and that of Jesus. According to the third Synoptist, the public ministry of Jesus begins only after the ministry of the Baptist has been brought to its definitive close.[7] Accordingly, the first public utterance[8] of the Lucan Jesus is spoken in the synagogue of Nazareth when Jesus solemnly proclaims: "Today this scripture has been fulfilled in your hearing" (Luke 4:21). The characteristic use of "Today"[9] shows that we are once again dealing with a passage that comes from an evangelist's hand; the words are of Luke himself. It is true that Luke's Gospel does not particularly employ fulfillment formulae to show that Jesus has fulfilled the Scriptures. Nevertheless "Today" is an important idea in the Gospel of Luke. Today is

considered is confirmed by Matt 3:17. Matthew's third person announcement, "This is my beloved Son in whom I am well pleased" is a public announcement which replaces the private revelation of Mark 1:11, "Thou art my beloved Son; with thee I am well pleased."

4. Matt 1:22; 2:15,17,23; 3:15; 4:14; 5:17; 8:17; 12:17; 13:35,44; 21:4; 23:32; 26:54,56; 27:9.

5. Matt 3:15; 5:6,10,20; 6:1,33; 21:32.

6. Cf. Albert Descamps, *Les justes et la justice dans les évangiles et le christianisme primitif hormis la doctrine proprement paulinienne* (Louvain: Publications universitaires, 1950).

7. The imprisonment of John is cited in Luke 3:20, with the mention of Jesus' baptism being reserved until 3:21. Moreover, Luke interposes the genealogy of Jesus between the baptismal scenes and the temptation narrative. Cf. Hans Conzelmann, *The Theology of Saint Luke* (London: Faber and Faber, 1960) p. 21.

8. A logion of Jesus is cited in Luke 2:49. The evangelist does not, however, include the finding in the temple pericope within the account of Jesus' public ministry.

9. Luke 2:11; 3:22; 4:21; 5:26; 12:28; 13:32,33; 19:5,9; 22:34,61; 23:43.

the time of salvation; it is the day of Jesus. The latter is the
bearer of the Spirit. His ministry is to the *anawin*, the poor. His
miracles are written in such a ways as to recall the OT record of
the saving deed effected by God on behalf of his people.[10] The
"today" of Jesus is all-important because it is the time of the
fulfillment of the expectations of God's people.

To state that the author of the Fourth Gospel imitated the
Synoptists' use of the initial logion of Jesus to set a tone for his
narrative is to go beyond the evidence presently available.[11]
However, it is not unlikely that the first logion of Jesus found in
John introduces a major theme of the Gospel. Two of the major
twentieth century commentators on John, M.-J. Lagrange and
Rudolf Bultmann,[12] are as one in noting that the question,
"What do you seek?" (John 1:38) not only contains the first
words of Jesus found in the Fourth Gospel but also that it is a
question which is addressed to each reader of the Gospel. According to these exegetes, it is as imperative that the twentieth
century reader respond to that question as it was for the unnamed disciples of John 1:35-39 to do so. In a similiar fashion,
Adolf Schlatter attributes a certain timelessness to this inaugural
Johannine question by nothing that "There is no other require-
ment for his union with men than that they seek him and come to
him."[13] Given the significant placement of the "What do you
seek?" question in John 1:38 and the authority of commentators
such as Lagrange, Schlatter, and Bultmann, it appears legitimate

10. By way of example one might refer to Luke 4:25-27 which explicity recalls
the miracle stories of the Elijah-Elisha cycle, and to Luke 7:11-17 with its allusion
to 1 Kgs 17:17-24 and 2 Kgs 4:32-37.

11. The issue of John's awareness of and dependence upon the Synoptics
continues to be debated. During the 1975 Louvain Biblical Colloquium both
Frans Neirynck and Maurits Sabbe argued that specific Johannine passages
showed traces of literary dependence on the Synoptic account.

12. M.-J. Lagrange, *Évangile selon Saint Jean*. EBib (Paris: Gabalda, 1936)
p. 45. Rudolf Bultmann, *The Gospel of John* (Oxford: Basil Blackwell, 1971)
p. 100. Cf. Clayton R. Bowen, "The Fourth Gospel as Dramatic Material," *JBL*
49 (1930) 292-305, p. 300.

13. Adolf Schlatter, *Der Evangelist Johannes. Wie er spricht, denkt und glaubt.
Ein Kommentar zum vierten Evangelium* (Stuttgart: Colwer, 1930) p. 53.

to inquire as to the existence and meaning of the "search for Jesus" as a Johannine theme.

One might begin with Lindars' observation that the verb *zēteō*, "to seek," is a very common word in John.[14] Indeed the verb appears some 34 times in the Fourth Gospel.[15] The verb appears more frequently in John than it does in any of the Synoptics,[16] but the mere frequency of occurrence in John is not such as to establish the search for Jesus as a specifically Johannine theme. What is more significant in this regard is that the verb "to seek" occurs in passages which are manifestly Johannine constructions or at least bear clear traces of Johannine redaction. Moreover, one might note with Cullmann, Wead[17] and others, that John often uses terms with a double meaning. Boismard has pointed out that the Aramaic verb *be'a* means both "to seek" and "to want."[18] Consequently, one might find in the Johannine use of the verb *zēteō* a reflection of a Semitic tradition and a typical Johannine play on words. It is, however, not necessary to have recourse to the theories of Burney, Torrey, *et al.*, with respect to an Aramaic tradition lying behind our Gospel in order to propose the hypothesis that John's use of *zēteō* might represent another Johannine choice of a word with a double meaning. Both of Boismard's proposed meanings of the Aramaic verb are appropriate renderings of the Greel *zēteō*. In a word, *zēteō* belongs to the type of vocabulary easily appropriated by the author of the Fourth Gospel.

In asking whether John's use of *zēteō* represents a deliberate choice of a term with a double meaning and serves, therefore, as

14. Barnabas Lindars, *The Gospel of John*. New Century Bible (London: Oliphants, 1972) p. 295.

15. John 1:39... 20:15. Codex Bezae has an additional use of *zētein* in John 20:13.

16. Matt: 14 × ; Mark: 10 × ; Luke: 26 × .

17. Cf. Oscar Cullmann, *Early Christian Worship*. SBT, 10 (London: SCM, 1953) pp. 50-59; D.W. Wead, *The Literary Devices in John's Gospel*, Theologische Dissertationen, 4 (Basel: Reinhardt, 1970), Chap. 3: The Double Meaning, pp. 30-70.

18. M.-E. Boismard, *Du baptême à Cana: Jean 1,19-2,11*. LD, 18 (Paris: Cerf, 1956) p. 73.

an indication that the evangelist would have his gospel read in the
perspective of a "search for Jesus," we must also take into
consideration some elements of John's literary technique. It seems
appropriate to speak of two levels of the Johannine narrative.
The narrative pericopes are characterized by a dramatic flair. The
use of irony heightens the drama but also leads the reader to find
a deeper significance in the drama. In other words it is appropriate for the reader of the Fourth Gospel to distinguish
between the Johannine drama and its theological significance,
between the event and the meaning. Sometimes the author of the
Gospel explicitly draws his reader's attention to the theological
significance of his account; at other times he does not. The
Johannine note found in John 2:21 tells the readers that the
sequence on the destruction of the temple (John 2:13-22) is to be
understood of the death and Resurrection of Jesus. Without the
benefit of such an explicit attestation as is found in John 2:21 the
reader of the first few chapters of the Gospel must come to the
awareness that the story of the water become wine (John 2:1-12)
symbolizes the fulness of the messianic gifts given by Jesus.
Similarly the reader must exploit his own sensitivity to Johannine
style to come to the realization that the call of the first disciples in
John 1:35-39 is a paradigmatic narrative on Christian discipleship, viewed from a Johannine perspective. Within this perspective, the verb *akolouthein*, "to follow," in v. 37 is to be
interpreted both as an element of Johannine dramatization, i.e.,
insofar as the unnamed disciples are portrayed as physically
following at a distance behind Jesus as he went his way, and as an
element of the Johannine message, i.e., insofar as the disciples are
portrayed as being in the condition of disciples, i.e., "followers"
of Jesus.

It is likewise appropriate to speak of two levels of the Johannine narrative from still another but somewhat related point of
view. We must distinguish between the *Sitz-im-Leben Jesu* and
the *Sitz-im-Leben Evangeliums*. The author of the Fourth Gospel
is at once reflecting on the significance of the historical ministry
of Jesus of Nazareth (the life situation of Jesus) and the then

current situation of the Johannine church (the life situation of the author of the Gospel). In recent years, for example, two studies[19] have cited the importance of considering the Fourth Gospel within the perspective of the trial of Jesus. This is not simply a matter of reflection on the trial of Jesus before Pilate and the high priests; it is just as much an observation that Jesus is an object of contention between the Johannine church and the Jewish synagogue. In a word, the reader of the Fourth Gospel must be aware that John composed his narrative as a reflection upon his Church and its needs just as much as he attempted to offer his readers an interpretation of the historical ministry of Jesus of Nazareth. The realization that we must distinguish two levels of Johannine narrative with respect both to language (event—significance) and to perspective (Jesus—the Church), should make the discerning reader open to the possibility that within the Johannine texts which speak of the disciples' search for Jesus there lies a still deeper significance. It is true that the reader of the Fourth Gospel must be wary lest he read into the Johannine text more than the author intended. It is no less true that he must be sensitive to the technique of an evangelist who incorporates into his text a significance which can be discerned only by means of a reflection on the entire Gospel and the techniques which the evangelist has employed in his composition.

What Do You Seek?—The Disciples' Search for Jesus

One of the techniques used by the author of the Fourth Gospel is the question.[20] Some questions receive an unexpected answer;[21] still others are unanswered.[22] The question, "What do you seek?" which Jesus addresses to the unnamed disciples in

19. J.L. Martyn, *History and Theology in the Fourth Gospel* (New York: Harper and Row, 1968); A.E. Harvey, *Jesus on Trial: A Study in the Fourth Gospel* (London: SPCK, 1976).

20. Cf. A. Vanhoye, "Interrogation johannique et exégèse de Cana (Jn. 2,4)," *Bib* 55 (1974) 157-167.

21. 4:12; 8:53,57; 9:2.

22. 7:35; 8:22.

John 1:38 is, in effect, to be classed among the unanswered questions. The disciples respond to Jesus' question with another question, "Where are you staying?" To this Jesus responds, "Come and see."[23] In one sense Jesus' question is superfluous. There is no need for the Johannine Jesus who knows what is in the heart of man[24] to ask for information. In another sense, it is imperative that Jesus take the initiative in the drama of salvation. The first words which Jesus speaks in the Fourth Gospel are an initial invitation. It is Jesus who takes the initiative, Jesus who invites. From the very outset of the Johannine narrative it is clear that it is Jesus who chooses his disciples.[25] Nevertheless, the Johannine narrative does not immediately indicate the result of this initial encounter with Jesus. That is reserved for the following pericope (John 1:40-42) in which Andrew announces to his brother, "We have found the Messiah" (v. 41). The disciples of the Baptist responded to the witness of the Baptist and the invitation of Jesus. Thus they became the disciples of Jesus himself.

Both Zimmermann and Heise[26] have accurately noted that the pericope in which Jesus addresses his invitational question to the as yet unnamed disciples is full of plays-on-words and terms with a double meaning. Given the evangelist's choice of expressions, it would be absurd to think that any real interest is attached to the external details as such.[27] Rather, the five verses (John 1:35-39) contain a Johannine paradigm on discipleship. The style betrays the hand of the evangelist. He makes use of a characteristic revelation formula.[28] He reduces the Baptist to the role of

23. John 1:39. Cf. 1:46.
24. John 2:25; cf. 1:42,47; 4:17-18; 6:70; etc.
25. Cf. John 15:16.
26. H. Zimmermann, "Meister, Wo Wohnst Du? (Jo. 1,38)," *Lebendiges Zeugnis* 1 (1962) 49-57, Jürgen Heise, *Bleiben. Meinein in den Johanneischen Schriften.* HUT, 8 (Tübingen: Mohr. 1967) p. 49.
27. Cf. R. Bultmann, *John.*, p. 100.
28. M. de Goedt, "Un schème de révélation dans le Quatrième Évangile," *NTS* 8 (1961-1962) 142-150.

witness.[29] He interprets an Aramaic expression.[30] He makes use
of symbolism. Thus the whole scenario becomes a reflection on
discipleship in general. Discipleship comes as a response to
witness and as a response to the invitation of Jesus. It leads to the
knowledge of where Jesus lives. From the perspective of the
evangelist, the dwelling place of Jesus is not some inn or other in
which Jesus might pass the night. Rather the disciple learns that
Jesus abides with the Father. The farewell discourses will make it
clear that the place where Jesus abides is also the place where his
disciples abide.[31] Thus, the suggestion that the disciples will stay
with Jesus anticipates the description of their abiding in him even
as he abides in the Father.[32]

In his brief and paradigmatic reflection on discipleship, John's
key verbs are expressions with a double meaning. Following,
seeking, seeing, and dwelling are expressions which must be
understood on the level of Johannine drama. No less must they
be understood on the level of Johannine theology (reflection). At
the level of event, to follow after Jesus is to walk at some distance
behind him. At the level of Johannine meaning, to follow after
Jesus is to be his disciple. At the level of event, to see Jesus is to
observe him with one's eyes. At the level of meaning, to see Jesus
is to perceive who he is. At the level of event, the question about
his dwelling is an inquiry as to where Jesus would pass the
night.[33] At the level of meaning, it is a question as to where he
abides. At the level of event, Jesus' first words indicate no more
than "what do you want?" At the level of Johannine meaning, his
words initiate the history-long drama of man's search for Jesus.
By the use of these double-meaninged expressions the evangelist
has transformed a story about an initial encounter into a significant theological reflection on discipleship. That reflection can

29. Cf. R.F. Collins, "The Representative Figures of the Fourth Gospel," *DR*
93 (1976) 28-46, 119-132, pp. 33-34, in this volume, pp. 8-11.
30. Cf. John 1:40,42; 4:25 (19:13); 20:16.
31. Cf. John 14:2-3,25; 15:4,7,10; 17:24.
32. Cf. Edwyn C. Hoskyns, *The Fourth Gospel* (2nd. rev. ed.: London: Faber
and Faber, 1947) p. 181.
33. Cf. J. Heise, *Bleiben*, p. 49.

be briefly summarized by stating that the disciple is one who responds to Jesus' invitation to seek him out by perceiving who he is and coming to know where he truly abides. The disciple who responds faithfully to Jesus' invitation will also abide with Jesus and the Father.

That the Johannine narrative is to be understood in this sense is further underscored by the indication of time with which the pericope closes. The words "for it was about the tenth hour" (v. 39) were most likely inserted into the narrative by the Evangelist himself.[34] It is well known that John makes significant use of temporal expressions. The "hour"[35] of Jesus and the poignant comment that "it was night" (John 13:30) are but two cases in point. John's notation that "it was about the tenth hour"[36] can indeed be understood on the level of event. In which case, the encounter between Jesus and the disciples is described as having occurred at about four o'clock in the afternoon. On the level of Johannine significance, however, the tenth hour must be seen as the hour of fulfillment.[37]

Further confirmation of the notion that John 1:35-39 offers a schema for a theology of discipleship is to be found in the variant reading of Jesus' initial logion provided by the Codex Koridethi and a few other ancient manuscripts.[38] This ninth century text, a principal witness to the so-called Caesarean type of NT manuscript, offers "Whom do you seek?" (*tina zēteite*) as the Johan-

34. Cf. R. Bultmann, *John*, p. 100.

35. Cf. R.E. Brown, *The Gospel According to John. I-XII*. AB, 29 (Garden City, NY: Doubleday, 1968) pp. 517-518.

36. The RSV strengthens the importance attached to John 1:39's temporal indication by providing it with an introductory "for." No corresponding particle is found in the Greek text.

37. Cf. R. Bultmann, *John*, p. 100, esp. nn. 9,10; Siegfried Schultz, *Das Evangelium nach Johannes*, NTD, 4 (Göttingen: Vandenhoeck und Ruprecht, 1972) p. 41; F. Wulf, "'Meister, wo wohnst du?' (Joh. 1,38)", *Geist und Leben* 3 (1958) 241-244, p. 244.

38. Some editors (e.g. Kurt Aland) believe that the variant reading at John 1:38 is a corruption of the text under the influence of John 18:4. It may well be, however, that an "intelligent scribe" consciously altered the text in view of a theology of discipleship. Cf. R.E. Brown, *John. I-XII*, p. 74, n. 38.

nine Jesus' first public utterance. These words anticipate the question addressed by Jesus to the soldiers and officers from the chief priests and Pharisees (John 18:4,7). They foreshadow the question which the Magdalene directs to the risen Jesus in John 20:15.[39] Does not, then, the variant provide some indication of a theme whose presence provides a clue for a basic understanding of the Fourth Gospel?

Before pursuing our quest for such a theme by means of a brief examination of other Johannine passages in which *zēteō* appears, we ought to return to a further consideration of John 1:35-39 considered on the level of a Johannine dramatization of an event. That Jesus should be addressed as Rabbi by the unnamed disciples and that this title should be translated as "Teacher" are not unusual. As a title for Jesus, "Rabbi" occurs frequently[40] in the Fourth Gospel, and John manifests a definite tendency to translate Semitisms. The use of the title "Rabbi" implies that the disciples looked upon Jesus as a teacher and interpreter of the Law. It is not unlikely that the disciples sought out Jesus precisely because he was one who could interpret the Scriptures.[41] What they found was the Messiah himself, i.e., the one of whom Moses

39. Without adopting the variant reading, both Raymond Brown and André Feuillet see a parallel between John 1:38 and John 20:15. Feuillet further notes that the question, "What do you seek?," occurs four times in John: twice as a question addressed to those who are looking for their Savior (John 1:38; 20:15), once as a question from the Savior who is seeking after souls (John 4:27), and once (in fact a single question, uttered twice) as a question addressed by Jesus to those who has come out to arrest him (John 18:4,7). Cf. R.E. Brown, *John. I-XII*, p. 74, n. 38; André Feuillet, *Le mystère de l'amour divin dans la théologie johannique*, EBib, (Paris: Gabalda, 1972) p. 126.

40. John 1:39,50; 3:2,26; 4:31; 6:25; 9:2; 11:8 (cf. 20:16 *rabbouni*).

41. A number of commentators see in the evangelist's use of "Rabbi" in 1:39 more than a merely conventional designation of Jesus. Loisy, for example, notes that the question, "Where are you staying?," ought to be understood in the light of the rabbinic custom to teach sitting down rather than walking about. Schackenburg indicates that the disciples' question probably indicates a desire to hear Jesus expound the Scriptures. Cf. Alfred Loisy, *Le quatrième évangile* (Paris: Picard, 1903) p. 243. Rudolf Schnackenburg, *The Gospel According to St. John*, I. Herder's Theological Commentary on the New Testament (New York: Herder and Herder, 1968) p. 308. Cf. Siegfried Schultz, *Johannes*, p. 41.

in the law and also the prophets wrote (John 1:45). Andrew's
"We have found the Messiah" (John 1:41) must, in fact, be seen
in connection with v. 38. The verb "find" (*heurēkamen*) of v. 41
stands in contrast to the verb "seek" (*zēteite*) of v. 38. The verbs
"to seek" and "to find" are traditionally paired in biblical,
extrabiblical, and even in contemporary literature. Moreover, the
Johannine use of a Semitic title translated into Greek for the
benefit of his readers in v. 41 (Messiah, which means Christ)
corresponds to the use of Rabbi with its Greek translation in
v. 38.[42] In a word, v. 41 corresponds to v. 38; v. 38 calls for v. 41.
On the level of Johannine dramatization, the disciples' seeking for
one who can interpret the Law results in their finding the Messiah
of whom the Law speaks.

The use of the paired expressions, seek and find, provides a
further clue to the deeper theological significance of the passage.
In extra-biblical literature where *zēteō* is used with a religious
reference, the term generally indicates man's philosophical and
religious quest. Indeed *zēteō* is a technical term for philosophical
investigation.[43] In his unique fashion, Philo, the Alexandrian
Jew, uses *zēteō* to link the mind's philosophical inquiry with the
heart's seeking after God.[44] The link is another example of
Philo's tendency to wed philosophical concerns with his own
biblical tradition. In fact the Greek text of the Old Testament
(LXX) uses *zēteō* of man's search for God to such an extent that
to "seek God" (*zētein theon*) or to seek the Lord (*zētein kurion*)
becomes almost a technical term, to denote man's voluntary
turning to God.[45]

We find such a use of "to seek God" or "to seek the Lord,"
along with its correlative "to find the Lord" (*heuriskein kurion*),

42. In the NT, the Semitic "Messiah" is found only in John 1:38 and 4:25.
"Rabbi" occurs in the Synoptics, but it is found more frequently in John (9 ×)
than in either Matthew (4 ×) or Mark (4 ×). The Semitic title is not used by Luke.
43. Cf. Heinrich Greeven, "*zēteō, zētēsis, ekzēteō, epizēteō*," TDNT, 2, 892-
896, p. 893. Greeven notes that the NT contains at least one text (1 Cor 1:22) in
which the technical philosophical sense clearly appears.
44. *Abr.*, 87.
45. Georg Bertram, TDNT, 2, p. 893, n. 5.

or "to find God," (*heuriskein theon*) in the writings of the
prophets. The prophets call to man in order that he should seek
after his God, that he should turn to Him with all his being.
Typical are the words of Jeremiah, "For thus says the Lord...
You seek me and find me, when you seek me with all your heart,
I will be found by you, says the Lord." (Jer 29:10, 13-14a). The
Deutero-Isaiah's call to conversion is phrased in the same terms:
"Seek the Lord while he may be found, call upon him while he is
near; let the wicked forsake his way, and the unrighteous man his
thoughts; let him return to the Lord, that he may have mercy on
him, and to our God, for he will abundantly pardon" (Isa 65:6-
7). According to the understanding of the prophets, the search for
the Lord is of vital importance. It is matter of life or death. The
one who seeks the Lord and finds him receives the gift of life
itself. Thus Amos of Tekoa proclaimed the Lord's message: "For
thus says the Lord to the house of Israel: Seek me and live... seek
the Lord and live..." (Amos 5:4-6). To seek the Lord is all-
important. It is a matter of life and death.

Of course, not all Israelites heeded the prophets' call. The
situation of those who did not seek the Lord is poignantly
described by a post-exilic disciple of Isaiah: "I was ready to be
sought by those who did not ask for me; I was ready to be found
by those who did not seek me, I said, 'Here am I; here am I,' to a
nation that did not call on my name" (Isa 66:1). Yahweh desires
nothing more than to be sought and found by his people. Often
Yahweh's desire is not realized because of man's own lack of
conversion. Yahweh is not found because man is ill-disposed and
will not seek after his Lord. The prophets described this situation
by noting that Yahweh hid his face from his people. Those who
are not normally disposed to find the Lord cannot find him
because he is hidden from their eyes. Thus the Trito-Isaiah:
"There is no one that calls upon thy name, that bestirs himself to
take hold of thee; for thou has hid thy face (*apestrephas to
prosōpon sou*) from us, and has delivered us into the hand of our
iniquities" (Isa 64:7). By means of this anthropomorphic
language, the divine initiative in man's seeking and finding is

maintained—even in those cases in which man refuses to seek after his Lord!

The seeking and finding of the Lord which is an integral part of both the prophet's message and the prophetic writings[46] has been taken over by the biblical Psalms[47] and the Wisdom literature. Already the opening words of the book of Wisdom enunciate the theme: "Love righteousness, you rulers of the earth, think of the Lord with uprightness, and seek him with sincerity of heart (*en haplotēti kardias zētēsate auton*); because he is found by those who do not put him to the test (*hoti heurisketai tois mē peirazousin auton*)," (Wis 1:1-2a). In the Sapiential literature, however, it appears that divine Wisdom rather than the Lord himself is the object of man's search.[48] Thus the anonymous sage writes: "I loved her (= Wisdom) and sought (*exēzētesa*) her from my youth... I went about seeking (*zētōn*) how to get her for myself" (Wis 8:2,18).

As the prophets proclaimed the search for the Lord to be a matter of life-and-death, so the wise men announced that the search for personified Wisdom was a cause of vital import: "Happy is the man who finds wisdom,... Long life is in her right hand" (Prov 3:13,16)... "For he who finds me finds life and obtains favor from the Lord" (Prov 8:35). Similarly, the sages were aware that man may well refuse to heed the call of Wisdom. In the recalcitrance of his unconverted state, man will be unable to find divine Wisdom. The first chapter of Proverbs reflects on this unfortunate situation: "Because I have called and you refused to listen... I also will laugh at your calamity; I will mock when panic strikes you... Then they will call upon me, but I will not answer; they will seek me diligently but will not find me" (Prov 1:24-28).

46. Amos 5:1-6; 8:11-12; Hos 2:9; 5:6,15; 7:10; Isa 51:1; 64:1; Jer 10:21; 29:13-14; Lam 3:25; Zeph 1:6; 2:3; Mal 3:1; Dan 3:41; Zech 8:22.

47. e.g. Ps. 9:11; 24:6; 40:17; 69:33; 70:5; 83:17; 105:3-4; Cf. A. Feuillet, *Le mystère*, p. 120.

48. Cf. A. Feuillet, *Le mystère*, pp. 126-127.

The French exegetes Boismard, Feuillet and Weber[49] particularly point to Wis 6:12-16 as a Sapiential passage which succinctly articulates the theme of seeking and finding Wisdom personified. Boismard notes that this passage treats but one motif: Wisdom will be found by those who seek after her; to them she will manifest herself.[50] His comment appears to be quite accurate especially in view of the fact that it is not much more than a paraphrase of the first lines of the pericope: "Wisdom... is found by those who seek her. She hastens to make herself known to those who desire her..." (Wis 6:12-13). The Dominican exegete also suggests that John 1:35-42 is modelled after Wis 6:12-16. Capitalizing on a variant reading *prōi*, "in the morning"[51] in place of the generally accepted *prōton* reading in v. 41, Boismard is able to find a point of contact between the Johannine narrative and Wis 6:14, "He who rises early (*ho orthrisas*)...". Greater plausibility is afforded to his suggestion on the grounds that both passages use the verbs "seek" (*zētein*) and "find" (*heuriskein*). Both Wisdom and Jesus take the initiative in seeking those who would come to them (Wis 6:13,16; John 1:38,43). Boismard concludes his comparative analysis by noting that "It is difficult to attribute this series of similarities to chance. For the evangelist, Jesus is Wisdom who invites men to seek her out; she will let herself be found by those who seek her, she will manifest herself to them."[52]

Boismard's conclusion would indeed be stronger than the evidence adduced were it not for the fact that the language of John 1:34-39 (-42) resonates the language of the Wisdom literature and the additional, and salient fact, that the Fourth Gospel clearly contains the motif of Jesus as Divine Wisdom. Since studies on the use of Wisdom motifs in the Fourth Gospel

49. Cf. M.-E. Boismard, *Du baptême*, p. 78-80; A. Feuillet, *Le mystère*, pp. 126-127; E. Osty, J. Weber, "Le livre de la Sagesse," in L. Pirot - A. Clamer, *Le Sainte Bible*, 6 (Paris: Letouzey et Ané, 1943) pp. 365-528, p. 439.

50. M.-E. Boismard, *Du baptême*, p. 79.

51. The variant reading *prōi* is suggested by these use of *name* in two or three Old Latin manuscripts. It is also attested by the Sinaitic Syriac text.

52. M.-E. Boismard, *Du baptême*, p. 80.

abound,[53] we can easily omit an extensive examination of John's use of Wisdom from the present essay. Let it simply be said that two recent and widely respected commentaries on the Fourth Gospel coming from the hands of Catholic scholars[54] indicate that Jewish Wisdom literature provides meaningful links with the Fourth Gospel. F.-M. Braun has devoted a significant chapter of his work on the Fourth Gospel to its Wisdom Christology.[55] C.H. Dodd has artfully sketched the points of contact between John's prologue and the Wisdom literature.[56] A further variety of contemporary scholars have demonstrated that the Johannine notion of life,[57] the great discourses of the Fourth Gospel,[58] the multiplication of loaves pericope with its accompanying bread of life discourse,[59] and the pregnant "I am" logia[60] are to be interpreted—at least in part—against the background of Israel's Wisdom tradition. There can be no doubt that the Fourth Evangelist has made use of Wisdom motifs. More specifically, there can be no doubt that John presents Jesus as the Divine Wisdom Incarnate.

Given the author's predilection for a presentation of Jesus as Divine Wisdom and the fact that John 1:35-39 is a prototypical

53. Brief overviews are offered by Henry R. Moeller and Basil de Pinto, among others. Cf. Henry R. Moeller, "Wisdom Motifs and John's Gospel," *Bulletin of the Evangelical Theological Society* 6 (1963) 93-98; Basil de Pinto, "Word and Wisdom in St. John," *Scripture* 19 (1967) 19-27, 107-122.

54. Cf. R.E. Brown, *John. I-XII*, pp. cxxii-cxxv, etc.; R. Schnackenburg, *John*, 1, p. 523, etc.

55. F.-M. Braun, *Jean le théologien*, 2: *Les grandes traditions d'Israel et l'accord des écritures selon le quatrième évangile.* EBib (Paris: Gabalda, 1964) pp. 49-152.

56. C.H. Dodd, *The Interpretation of the Fourth Gospel* (Cambridge: University Press, 1963) pp. 274-275.

57. Cf. Ignace de la Potterie, "'Je suis la Voie, la Vérité et la Vie' (Jn. 14,6)," *NRT* 88 (1966) 917-926; John Painter, *John: Witness & Theologian* (London: SPCK, 1975) p. 49.

58. Cf. Robert Kysar. *The Fourth Evangelist and His Gospel: An Examination of Contemporary Scholarship* (Minneapolis: Augsburg, 1975) pp. 122-127.

59. André Feuillet, *Johannine Studies* (New York: Alba House, 1965) pp. 58-87.

60. Cf. R.E. Brown, *John. I-XII*, pp. 537-538. I. de la Potterie, "Je suis la Voie," pp. 917-926.

reflection on discipleship, it is not unlikely that it was the author's intention to present discipleship as the search for incarnate Divine Wisdom. In this regard it would prove worthwhile to recall that the unnamed, but typical disciples of John 1:38, addressed Jesus as Rabbi. Rather than merely assume that this form of address represents a Johannine attempt to show that the disciples did not fully understand the "Lamb of God" title proclaimed by John the Witness, Schnackenburg indicates that "Rabbi"[61] was the usual way for a disciple to address his master. He further notes that the disciples' question probably indicates a desire to hear Jesus expound the Scriptures.

In this light the "What do you seek?" question takes on a new shade of meaning. In the Septuagint *zētein* renders not only the Hebrew verb *'aheb*, but also the verb *darash*.[62] Since the 1948 discovery of the Dead Sea Scrolls, it has become commonplace for Johannine scholars to affirm the many affinities of thought and vocabulary that exist between the Scrolls and the Fourth Gospel.[63] In the Scrolls *darash ha Torah* has become almost a technical term for the study and explication of the Scriptures.[64] The Qumran sectarians are those who "search" (*darash*) the Scriptures. From this perspective, one might paraphrase the Johannine Jesus' first word as "What Scriptures are you searching out?" Then, as so often in the Fourth Gospel, the movement of thought would be from the Scriptures to the person of Jesus who is in union the Father.[65] At this juncture a commentator might be inclined to note that neither in our pericope nor in the remainder of the body of the Gospel is Jesus called "the Word." That designation appears only in the Prologue (John 1:1, 14).

61. R. Schnackenburg, *John*, 1, p. 308.

62. Cf. Lev 10:16; Deut 22:2; 1 Sam 28:7; 2 Sam 11:3; etc.

63. Among other studies, the reader might refer to James H. Charlesworth (ed.), *John and Qumran* (London: Chapman, 1972).

64. 1QS 6:6; 4QFl 1:11; CD 6:7; 7:118; CF. 1QS 5:11; 6:7; 8:24; 1QH 2:15,32; 4QpNah 2,7; CD 1:18.

65. In presenting his movement of thought, the evangelist frequently makes use of the "Son of Man" title. Cf. J. Louis Martyn, *History and Theology*, pp. 122-125.

There, the commentators generally agree, the *Logos* vocable is applied to Jesus in such a way as to encompass both Sapiential speculation on Divine Wisdom and rabbinic speculation on the Torah as the word of God. The tradition embodied in John 1:35-39 is not as explicit as that of the Prologue; it nevertheless points in the same direction.

The realization that the search for Jesus is the search for Divine Wisdom incarnate and the search for the full meaning of the Scriptures sheds a bit of light, which ought not to be over-emphasized, on the use of *zētein* in John 6:24,26. Commentators do not agree among themselves as to the division of the sixth chapter of John's Gospel into intelligible units. Some[66] opt for vv. 22-24 as the unit which links the Bread-of-Life discourse to the multiplication of loaves—walking on water narrative. Others[67] include vv. 22-25 in the transition pericope, while still others[68] believe that vv. 22-26 comprise the pericope. There is, however, agreement that the transition pericope is somewhat confusing, as indeed the number of textual variants indicate. This confusion may be due to the complicated history of the pericope[69] or to the author's confusing style.[70]

In any event the present redaction of the transition pericope is typically Johannine. The pericope is not found in the Synoptics. Verse 26 harks back to v. 24. The resumption of a previously cited theme is a typically Johannine technique.[71] The repeated theme of vv. 24, 26 is part of a pericope whose obvious purpose is to introduce the Bread of Life discourse. In the discourse Jesus reveals that he is the bread of life by means of the *Egō eimi* ("I am") formula of self-revelation (John 6:35). The bread of life is the revelation which he has come to give; that revelation is his

66. e.g. R.E. Brown, *John. I-XII*, pp. 257-259.

67. e.g. B. Lindars, *John*, pp. 248-249.

68. e.g. R. Bultmann, *John*, p. 216.

69. Cf. M.-E. Boismard, "Problèmes de critique textuelle concernant le quatrième évangile," *RB* 60 (1953) 347-371, pp. 359-371; R.E. Brown, *John. I-XII*, p. 258.

70. Cf. B. Lindars, *John*, p. 248.

71. Cf. John 1:29,36; 3:3,5; etc.

very self. The Bread-of-Life discourse is redolant with Wisdom motifs. Might it not well be that the search for Jesus with which John introduces the Bread-of-Life discourse is, in fact, the motif of the search for Divine Wisdom — Divine Wisdom incarnate who manifests Himself to those who would but seek?

Ultimately the search for Divine Wisdom is a search in which the initiative belongs to Wisdom itself. The notion of a divine initiative is present in the programmatic utterance spoken by Jesus himself according to John 1:38. It may also be present in a little noticed passage in the account of Jesus' encounter with the Samaritan woman. The Samaritan is an example of discipleship.[72] She represents the Christian messenger who brings others to the faith. She herself has come to faith in response to Jesus' invitation (John 4:7). In effect, Jesus seeks her out. That he should seek out a woman is cause for wonderment among the disciples. They recognize that Jesus has sought her out[73] and so do not dare to ask "What do you seek? (*ti zēteis*)"[74] (John 4:27). On the level of event, the level of Johannine drama, the question might indicate that Jesus was looking for food. The parallel question, "Why are you talking with her?" indicates that we must go beyond a merely banal interpretation of *ti zēteis* if we are to grasp its full import. The second question of the disciples, "Why are you talking with her?" makes use of the verb *lalein*, "to speak," the same verb used to introduce the *egō eimi* formula in v. 26. The second question of v. 27 thus indicates full well that

72. Cf. R.F. Collins, "Representative Figures," pp. 39-40; above, pp. 16-19.

73. John 4:34 implies that the "What do you seek?" of v. 27 is addressed to Jesus. J.H. Bernard interprets the question as one addressed to the woman. His view is consistent with that of some ancient witnesses. Brown, however, correctly notes that these few witnesses are dependant upon Tatian who, as an Encratite, eschewed the idea that Jesus took the initiative in talking to a woman. Cf. J.H. Bernard, *A Critical and Exegetical Commentary on the Gospel According to St. John*, ICC (Edinburgh: Clark, 1928) p. 152; R.E. Brown, *John. I-XII*, p. 173.

74. The RSV translates *ti zēteis* as "What do you wish?" Barnabas Lindars opts for a paraphrase of the Greek words. He writes: "Their unspoken questions should perhaps be translated: 'What are you asking? or what are you talking with her about?'" Cf. B. Lindars, *John*, p. 193. Both Lindars' paraphrase and the RSV translation weaken the meaning of the disciples' first question.

Jesus' search results in his speaking to her whom he has found. As Divine Wisdom, he reveals himself to those whom he seeks out.

The search undertaken by Divine Wisdom is ultimately the search of God himself. From the perspective of the Fourth Gospel, the search of Jesus is the embodiment of the Father's search for men. The evangelist reminds his readers of this by speaking of the Father's search even before he refers explicitly to Jesus' search: "such the Father seeks (*zētei*) to worship him" (John 4:23). The search of Divine Wisdom incarnate is the embodiment of the Father's search.[75] In the initiative of Jesus, the initiative of the Father is expressed. In effect, the faithful disciple is one who responds in faith to the embodied invitation of the Father.

To Seek and Not to Find—The Search Which is "Too Late"

Another Fourth Gospel passage in which Wisdom motifs occur and in which we also find the Johannine motif of the search for Jesus is John 7:32-36. Here we find the twice repeated "you will seek me and you will not find me (*zētēsete me kai ouch heurēsete*)" (John 7:34,36). Once again we might begin our consideration with a brief indication of the specifically Johannine character of the passage. From the standpoint of Johannine technique, we immediately note the reference to a preceding verse, the use of dialogue, and the use of interrogation with an ambivalent response. The pericope also makes use of characteristic words drawn from the Johannine vocabularly. Among the characteristic Johannine terms are "a little longer" (v. 33)[76] as an expression to indicate Jesus' expectation of the Passion, "he who sent me" (v. 33)[77] as a designation of the Father, and "the Jews" (v. 35) as

75. Cf. John 6:44,65.

76. Cf. John 8:21; 12:35; 13:3, 33, 36; 14:4-5, 12, 19, 28; 16:5, 16-19, 28.

77. Cf. John 3:17,34; 5:36,38; 6:29,57; 7:29; 8:42; 10:36; 11:42; 17:3, 8, 18, 21, 23, 25; 20:21 (with *apostellein*); John 4:34; 5:23, 24, 30, 37; 6:38, 39, 44; 7:16, 18, 28, 33; 8:16, 18, 26, 29; 9:4; 12:44, 45, 49; 13:16, 20; 14:24, 26; 16:5; 20:21 (with *pempein*).

a stylized expression to represent those who remain in their disbelief.[78] Perhaps we should add the verb "to seek" which is not only a Johannine expression but may well be used in John 7 as an example of Johannine irony.[79]

Unlike the pericope which we previously considered, John 7:32-36 admits of but minor textual variants. Two minor Greek manuscripts and the Vulgate read a present tense in place v. 34's generally accepted future *zētēsete*. Some important texts, including many of the major uncials do not include the complement *me* after *ouch heurēsete* (you will not find). Hence some editors omit the reading,[80] whereas others, on the basis of its insertion in the Codex Vaticanus and the third century *Bodmer papyrus* ($\mathfrak{P}^{75}$) include the pronoun. The United Bible Societies' edition is among the latter, but the editors note that the reading is of "dubious textual validity." These minor textual variants have but little bearing on the sense exegesis of the pericope. The manuscript evidence as well as the internal coherence of the text require a future reading of *zētēsete*, you will seek. If *heuresēte* is an eliptical expression, then *me* ("me") must be understood as its direct object. In brief, then, notwithstanding the issues raised by textual criticism, the RSV's "You will seek me, and you will not find me," correctly renders the sense of the Greek text.

More significant for an understanding of Jesus' dialogue with the Jews relative to his impending departure than a study of the transmission of the text is an examination of parallel material. The apodictic saying of John 7:34,36 "You will seek me and you will not find me" is also found in the third-century Gospel of Thomas and the Oxyrhynchus Papyrus,[81] manuscripts which respectively preserve the logion in Coptic and in Greek. We read

78. There is abundant literature on the meaning of *hoi Ioudaioi* in the Fourth Gospel. Among those who attribute this representative function to "the Jews" are R.E. Brown and Jeffrey G. Sobosan. Cf. R.E. Brown, *John. I-XII*, pp. lxx-lxxiii; Jeffrey G. Sobosan, "The Trial of Jesus," *JES* 10 (1973) 70-93, p. 86.

79. Cf. B. Lindars, *John*, p. 295.

80. e.g. Kurt Aland.

81. *Gos. Thom.* 38; Pap Oxy. 654. Cf. Kurt Aland, *Synopsis Quatuor Evangelium* (6th. ed.: Stuttgart: Deutsche Bibelgesellschaft, 1969) pp. 95, 522.

in the Gnostic Gospel of Thomas that "Jesus said: Many times
you have desired to hear these words which I speak to you, and
you have no other from whom to hear them. The days will come
(when) you will seek me (and) you will not find me."[82] This
Gnostic logion proclaims that Jesus is the unique revealer. According to Gnostic thought, it is necessary to hear his words in
order to attain to Gnosis, the source of life. A similar notion is
expressed in the first two logia of the Gospel of Thomas which
underscore the importance of the search for knowledge by means
of the correlative seek-find expression: "And he said: who finds
the explanation of these words will not taste death. Jesus said: He
who seeks must not stop seeking until he finds, and when he
finds, he will be bewildered, he will marvel, and will be king over
the All."[83]

In his presentation of the significant parallels for the Johannine
Jesus' "You will seek me and you will not find me," Barnabas
Lindars[84] suggests that John may be playing on the well known
promise of Jesus "Seek and you will find," found in the Synoptics' Q source and preserved both by Matt 7:7 and Luke 11:9.
The logion is, in fact, the central expression of a three-phase
saying on prayer, "Ask, and it will be given you; seek, and you
will find; knock, and it will be opened to you." The image of
knocking on a door and having it opened is associated by the
rabbis with the study of the Law and its interpretation, as well as
with prayer for God's mercy.[85] Similarly the expression "seek

82. A slightly different form of the first saying was attributed by Irenaeus to
the second-century Marcosians. The Gnostic saying may be based on Luke 17:22.
Cf. Robert M. Grant - David Noel Freedman, *The Secret Sayings of Jesus
According to the Gospel of Thomas* (London: Collins, 1960) p. 145. If *Gos. Thom.*
38 is dependent on Luke, then the Gnostic texts' substitution of "hearing the
words of Jesus" for the evangelical "seeing the Son of Man" accentuates the
Gnostic estimation of Jesus as the Revealer whose words are the bearer of
Wisdom.

83. *Gos. Thom.* 1-2.

84. B. Lindars, *John,* p. 296.

85. Cf. H.L. Strack - P. Billerbeck, *Kommentar zum Neuen Testament aus
Talmud und Midrash,* 1 (Munich: Beck, 1955) pp. 458-459; Eduard Schweizer,
The Good News According to Matthew (Atlanta: John Knox, 1975) p. 173.

and you will find" admits not only of a banal, every-day meaning, but also a religious meaning. As a religious expression it
referred to the study of the Torah, as well as to the search for
God in prayer.[86] In a word, the Q logion on prayer, of which
John 7:34,36 is a parallel, made use of traditional language which
was used of the study of the Torah, the searching of the Scriptures.

The rabbinic background of Q's "Seek and you will find" is
not without its significance for an understanding of John 7:34,36.
Adolph Schlatter has noted that the introductory lemma of our
saying in v. 36, viz., "What does he mean by saying," is a
typically Rabbinic expression.[87] The Jews of v. 35 look upon
Jesus as a rabbi since they suggest that he might go to teach
among the Greeks.[88] The rabbinic language of John 7:32-36
recalls the rabbinic language of the pericope with which we began
our analysis of the Johannine "search for Jesus theme," notably
John 1:35-39. Here, as there, we find the use of the question as a
Johannine literary technique. It would appear that the two questions of the Jews in v. 35 admit of a double answer.[89] On the
level of Johannine drama, the answer is an obvious "no." Jesus
does not intend to go into the Dispersion to teach there. Nor does
he go there in fact. On another level, however, the Jews' question
is answered with an ironic "yes." When we link John 7:32-36 to
the only other Johannine passage in which the Greeks appear,
viz., John 12:20, we find that the encounter with the Greeks takes
place at the hour of Jesus' departure. Jesus does not go to the
Greeks as such — even on the level of Johannine drama, it is they
who come to him — rather he goes to the Father.[90] When he has

86. Cf. *Str-B*, 1, p. 458.
87. Cf. Adolf Schlatter, *Johannes*, p. 199.
88. Somewhat implausibly, Theodor Zahn has even suggested that the Jews
thought that Jesus was alluding (v. 33) to a well-known teacher in the Diaspora,
and that Jesus was saying that it was this teacher who had sent him. Cf. Theodor
Zahn, *Das Evangelium des Johannes*. KNT, 4 (3rd. ed.: Leipzig, Deichert, 1912)
p. 391.
89. Cf. A. Vanhoye, "Intérrogation johannique," pp. 157-158.
90. John 13:1; 16:28.

returned to the Father, then he will attain the Greeks.[91] Thus, as in the case of John 1:35-39, it is to the significance of Jesus' being with the Father that John 7:32-36 points. The search for Jesus is for him who is in contact with the Father.

That Jesus will not be able to be found by those who search for him (vv. 34,36) recalls the traditional theme of unconverted man's fruitless search for God found in the prophetic writings as well as the Sapiential theme of Divine Wisdom which is not found by those who seek with an unrepentant heart. A significant detail of the Johannine logion, "You will seek me and you will not find me; where I am you cannot come" (vv. 34,36) prompts us to further interpret the saying in the light of its biblical background. One would expect Jesus to have said "Where I go, you cannot come;" instead the words of the Johannine Jesus are "Where I am, you cannot come." The evangelist's use of *eimi*, "I am," rather than *hupagō*, "I go" (cf. v. 33), is another example of his use of the divine *egō eimi*. Those who remain in their disbelief, "the Jews," cannot be with him who alone can speak the divine word "I am."

Thus, on the level of Johannine significance, something of symbolic quality[93] characterizes our narrative. Those who seek Jesus but remain in their disbelief are unable to find him. The manifestation of Jesus in his self-revelation can be a tragedy. There is the possibility that it is too late.[94] For the moment we can leave aside the search which will be rewarded with success. Our pericope speaks of the search which ends in frustration. For those who do not accept the salvation offered through the word of Jesus, there is a "too late." There is an *einmaligheit*, a "once only" quality, characteristic of the offer of salvation. That once only quality is rooted in the eschatological sending of the Son of

91. John 12:32.
92. Cf. John 8:21,22; 14:33.
93. Cf. R. Bultmann, *John*, p. 308.
94. Cf. R. Bultmann, *John*, p. 308; S. Schulz, *op.cit.*, p. 120. A. Wikenhauser, *Das Evangelium nach Johannes*, RNT, 4. (3rd. ed.: Regensburg, Pustet, 1961) p. 160.

God. If man does not seize salvation when it is offered to him, he finds that he comes "too late." Bultmann expresses the evangelist's thought so accurately when he writes that "In this 'too late' the judgment is present."[95]

The divine offer of salvation is contingent upon man's acceptance of the self-revelation of Jesus upon the cross. It is to the cross that the "a little longer" (*eti chronon mikron*) of v. 33 points.[96] The time of the cross is the hour of Jesus' glorification; it is the hour of the Father's glorification. It is then that Jesus is fully manifest as he who bears the divine name *egō eimi*. It is then that he is with the Father. For those who refuse to accept in faith this ultimate manifestation of the Word of God, there is a too late. Too late they will seek the salvation which he came to bring. Therein lies the tragedy of judgment; therein lies the judgmental character of the coming of the Son.

Jesus' crucial statement, "you will seek me and you will not find me; where I am you cannot come," is the subject of a Johannine reflection in John 8:21-29. In the clearest of terms, Jesus explains that once he goes away, there will be no other possibility of salvation. The entire passage is characterized by an urgency appropriate to the decisiveness of Jesus' presence. Jesus challenges his hearers to a decision before it is too late. The pericope begins with an editorial "again."[97] The passage is once again redolent with traces of Johannine technique and Johannine vocabulary. The reader will note the use of the question with an ambivalent answer (v. 22: "Will he kill himself?"), the use of terms with a double meaning, and the presence of misunderstanding as a literary device (v. 25, explicitated in the comment of v. 27). A detailed analysis of the pericope's vocabularly is not necessary. "The Jews" (v. 22), the "world" (vv. 23, 36), "believe" (vv. 24, 30), "I am" (vv. 24, 28), "lift up" (v. 28), "The Son of Man" (v. 28), "he who sent me" (v. 26, 29), strike the reader almost immediately as typical Johannisms. The dualistic world

95. R. Bultmann, *John*, p. 308.
96. Cf. John 12:35; 13:32; 14:19; 16:16-19.
97. John 8:21; Cf. John 8:12.

view and the sharp contrast between Jesus and the Jews give added Johannine flavor to the drama. We cannot escape the conclusion that again we are dealing with a passage which is clearly of Johannine construction.

In this Johannine reflection, Jesus again takes the initiative by uttering a definitive, "I go away and you will seek me and die in your sin; where I am going, you cannot come" (v. 21). The logion differs from that to which it harks back (i.e., John 7:34, 36)[98] in two significant respects. "Die in your sin" replaces "and you will not find me;" "where I am going" replaces "Where I am." The first change express the poignancy of the situation. The expression itself is a legal one (Deut 24:16) which generally occurs in a context of personal and national salvation.[99] John's use of familiar biblical terminology reminds his readers that the search for Jesus is a matter of life and death. Those who fail to find him will lose their only hope for salvation. As Jesus is the giver of life (John 8:12) those who fail to find him are deprived of the gift of life itself.

The replacement of "where I am" by "where I go" renders Jesus' enigmatic statement in a most natural manner within the context of the Johannine drama. It avoids the elipticism of John 7:34-36. It points immediately to the significance of Jesus' departure. It provides an occasion for the evangelist to dwell at length on the *egō eimi* ("I am he") expression, the formula of Jesus' self-revelation as a divine being. It is necessary to believe that Jesus truly bears the divine name, "I am," in order to avoid death. The Jews fail to comprehend that Jesus bears this name. Thinking that there must be a predicate, the Jews ask who he is. Jesus has no alternative but to reaffirm that he bears the divine name, that he is one with the Father. When, as the Son of Man, Jesus is lifted up in crucifixion-exaltation, it will be clear to those who believe that he is the bearer of the divine name.[100] Then it will be clear

98. Cf. B. Lindars, *John*, p. 319.

99. Cf. Ezek 3:19; 18:24,26.

100. Lindars correctly notes that "In this verse the various threads of the argument are drawn together... The Passion will confirm what Jesus has already said about his identity, that I am he." Cf. B. Lindars, *John*, p. 322.

that the Father has not left Jesus unto himself. Then it will be clear that Jesus has the power to draw all men to himself. Then, however, it will be too late for those who do not believe. In order that man live and not die in his sin, he must even now believe that Jesus is the one who is. The situation is urgent. Belief in Jesus as the bearer of the divine name is the great challenge; the alternative is a tragic "too late!"

To Seek and Not to Find—The Disciples' Search for One Who is Absent

A further Johannine comment on the strangely judgmental "You will seek me and you will not find me; where I am you cannot come" is to be found in John 13:33. In the first of his farewell discourses, the evangelist makes a deliberate cross-reference to the teaching of 7:33-36 and 8:21-29. Jesus says to his disciples "Little children, yet a little while I am with you. You will seek me; and as I said to the Jews so now I say to you, 'Where I am going you cannot come'" (John 13:33). An impression of contemporary pastoral concerns pervades the narrative.[101] Jesus must speak to the situation of the disciples who will be burdened by his absence. The hour of his passion is near, "yet a little while I am with you." Jesus has proclaimed that the Son of Man is glorified; but he must correct the impression that the moment of glorification has arrived for his disciples. The departure of Jesus marks a point of transition in their lives. They will no longer be with him. They cannot go where he has gone. They must live in a new relationship with him. In that interim inaugurated by his going to the Father, their mutual love is the modality of his presence with them.[102] In the interim, they will seek but they cannot go with him. It is not said that they will seek and will not find. That judgment is reserved for the Jews

---

101. Cf. B. Lindars, *John*, p. 463.
102. H. Zimmerman, "Struktur und Aussageabsicht der johanneischen Abschiedsreden (Jo. 13-17)," *BibLeb* 8 (1967) 271-290.

who disbelieve. For those who believe, Jesus' words "Where I am going you cannot come" bespeak an "until," not a "too late."

The new situation of the disciples in the time inaugurated by the hour of Jesus' crucifixion-glorification is again the subject of Johannine reflection in John 20:11-18.[103] The pericope, as I have noted in an earlier essay, articulates but poorly with John 20:1-2; yet these two passages offer the Johannine version of the Mary Magdalene tradition.[104] Undoubtedly the author is making use of material coming from different sources. Yet he has clearly imposed his hand upon the traditional material[105] which he is using as a vehicle for his own theological interpretation. The Johannine techniques of dialogue, misunderstanding (vv. 14, 15), and the interpretation of Hebrew words (v. 16) serve to mold the narrative into its Johannine form. Expressions such as the vocative use of "Woman" (v. 13, 14), the use of "to take away" (*airein*, vv. 13, 15) to describe the removal of Jesus' body, the pronominal use of *ekeinos* (they, she; vv. 13, 15, 16), and the "not yet" (*oupō*) of v. 17 are typical of the evangelist's language. Indeed were the variant readings of v. 13 offered by the Codex Bezae, the Sinaitic Syriac version and a few Greek miniscules to be accepted, we would have still another example of typical Johannine style and vocabulary present in the narrative. According to this variant, Jesus twice (v. 15 and v. 13) addressed the Magdalene with the words "Woman, why are you weeping? Whom do you seek?" The second question recalls the words which the Johannine Jesus first addressed to his disciples: "What do you seek?" (John 1:35), its repetition recalls the technique used in John 18:4,7.

Virtually all of the commentators on the Magdalene sequence note both the typically Johannine reworking and the unique

103. Cf. André Feuillet, "La Recherche du Christ dans la nouvelle alliance d'après la Christophanie de Jo. 20, 11-18. Comparaison avec Cant. 3, 1-4 et l'épisode des Pèlerins d'Emmaüs," in *L'Homme devant Dieu*. H. de Lubac *Festschrift*. Théologie, 56 (Paris: Aubier, 1963) 93-112.

104. Cf. R.F. Collins, "Representative Figures," pp. 122-123; above, pp. 33-35.

105. J.T. Forestell, *The Word of the Cross. Salvation as Revelation in the Fourth Gospel.* AnBib, 57 (Rome: Pontifical Biblical Institute, 1974) p. 97, n. 162.

description of a resurrection appearance which results from this redactional activity. Pierre Benoit classifies the appearance to Magdalene as a recognition appearance.[106] It belongs to that group of resurrection stories in which Jesus is not recognized by reason of his new condition. What distinguishes John 20:11-18 from other narratives of the same genre is the enigmatic logion of v. 17, "Do not hold me, for I have not yet ascended to the Father; but go to my brethren and say to them, I am ascending to my Father and your Father, to my God and your God." With these words Jesus interprets for Mary the meaning of his own resurrection. Jesus' resurrection, unlike that of Lazarus, does not mean that he has returned to his former mode of life; rather it means that he must ascend to his Father. It is not necessary to suppose that the appearance of the Risen Jesus to the Magdalene took place before the ascension and that the appearance of Jesus to the disciples (John 20-21) took place only after the ascension. To make such a distinction would be to impose the Lucan temporal sequence, Death-Resurrection-Ascension-Sending of the Spirit, upon the Johannine account. John articulates in successive narratives the meaning of the glorification of Jesus which his tradition considers to be but a single event. In addition to its apologetic function,[107] John's account of the appearance to Mary has an interpretative function. Apologetically, the Johannine narrative shows that the disciples could not have stolen the body of Jesus since it is a disciple who asks the question about the presence of the body; interpretatively, the narrative shows that Jesus' resurrection means that Jesus has returned to the Father. In this narrative, Mary Magdalene has a representative role to play. Thinking Jesus to be her teacher come back to life, she typifies the believer whose resurrection faith is inadequate. Jesus himself must take the initiative in bringing her to an understanding of what the resurrection means. The resurrection means

106. P. Benoit, "Marie-Madeleine et les disciples au tombeau selon Joh. 20, 1-8," in Walter Eltester, ed., *Judentum, Urchristentum, Kirche*. J. Jeremias *Festschrift*. BZNW, 26 (Berlin: Topelmann, 1960) 141-152, p. 150.

107. Cf. R.F. Collins, "Representative Figures,", p. 123; above, p. 34.

that Jesus goes to the Father; he must go there where the Father dwells.

Mary is the one who searches faithfully even after the resurrection. As such she represents every faithful believer. She searches; Jesus manifests himself to her. He does not utter the divine name; rather he says that he must be with the Father. His words are directed not to much to Mary Magdalene, a woman of history, as to the entire Church which must live in the great interim between the resurrection and the Parousia. It is the Church which seeks after Jesus; it is the Church which must deal with his absence. The church as faithful searcher must come to know that Jesus has gone to the Father. It is with the Father that he dwells. In his absence, the Church has faith, love, and the Spirit. It has the faith to understand who Jesus is and where he dwells. It has brotherly love which is Jesus' own love. It has the testimony of Jesus' Spirit who is with it forever (John 14:16). Moved by this faith, living this love, and strengthened by the Spirit, the Church must search—UNTIL. Such is the life of both the Church and the disciple in the great interim.

To Seek To Kill—The Ironic Search

The question which the Risen Jesus addresses to the Magdalene and through her to the Church recalls the question which Jesus puts to Judas and those who had come out from the chief priests and the Pharisees to arrest him. Of these Jesus dramatically inquired, "Whom do you seek?" (John 18:4,7). We will not dwell on the specifically Johannine character of Jesus' arrest in John 18:1-11 except to note the solemnity of the twice-repeated question, whose second use is introduced by an editorial "again" in v. 7. A reflection on the function served by the account of Jesus' arrest in the Fourth Gospel allows us to identify it as both a climax to a search for Jesus and as the introduction to the great self-manifestation of Jesus.

The reader of John's Gospel must bear in mind that most of the occurrences of the verb *zētein* are concentrated in the first part of the Gospel. Only seven times is the verb used in the so-called Book of Glory (John 13-21), and three of these seven uses of *zētein* occur in the narrative of Jesus' arrest.[108] Apart from the passage which we have already considered, it appears that John uses the verb "to seek" in a series of passages which culminate in the arrest which leads to his death. The Jews, those representatives of unbelief, sought to kill him (*zētein apokteinai*). The thought, as first expressed in John 5:18, is repeated in John 7:1,19,20,25; 8:37,40.[109] As variants on the theme, we read that the Jews sought to stone him (*zētein lithasai*)[110] and that they sought to arrest him (*zētein piasai*).[111] Ironically those who do not believe in Jesus — the Jews — seek to kill him, while those who believe in him — the disciples — seek to be where Jesus dwells. The search of the disbeliever reaches its climax in John 18:1-11 when the Jews, making use of the powers of this world, appear to have achieved a successful outcome in their search. They have sought, and apparently found, Jesus of Nazareth.

John's dramatic description of Jesus' arrest serves not only as the climax to the search for Jesus conducted by the Jews, it is also a dramatic introduction to the tightly structured Johannine Passion narrative.[112] The commentators note that it is the evangelist himself who has fashioned the scenario of Jesus' arrest.[113] John's narrative, like that of Mark 14:32-52, is located after the last meal and the final conversations of Jesus with his disciples. Like

108. John 18:4,7,8; Cf. 13:33; 16:19; 19:12; 20:15.

109. A few brief reflections on the theme and its relationship to Luke are offered by Rene Laurentin in *Jésus au Temple, Mystère de Pâque et Foi de Marie en Luc 2, 48-50*. EBib (Paris: Gabalda, 1960) p. 132.

110. John 11:8; Cf. 10:31.

111. John 10:39; Cf. John 7:30.

112. Cf. A. Janssens de Varebeke, "La structure des scènes du récit de la passion en John. xviii-xix," *ETL* 38 (1962) 504-522.

113. For example, Raymond Brown writes, "If John does draw on older independent tradition, the material from that tradition has been reworked in the interests of Johannine theology... In our judgment, in order to do justice to all the complexities of the Johannine account, one must allow for both a reliable independent tradition and a highly theological elaboration." R.E. Brown, *The Gospel According to John. XIII-XXI*. AB, 29A (Garden City, NY: Doubleday, 1970) p. 817.

Mark's account of Jesus' arrest, the Johannine narrative serves as a dramatic introduction to the entire Passion narrative. The Johannine account, unlike that of the Synoptics, however, omits the description of Jesus' poignant prayer (Mark 14:32-42). John's account, however, introduces new features into the scenario: Roman soldiers who also come out to arrest Jesus, and a description of Jesus' solemn conversation with Judas (John 18:4-8).

The presence of the Romans serves to heighten John's dramatization of a scenario in which two worlds stand in conflict—that of the Father, of whom the person of Jesus is the supreme revelation, and that of Satan, represented by the figure of Judas. In similar fashion, the omission of the prayerful struggle and the introduction of the conversation with Judas are apposite to John's understanding of the meaning of Jesus' passion and death. In the passion-death, Jesus is the glorified one (John 13:31). He can have no doubt and anxiety about his fate (John 18:4). He knows what will befall him. Even though Judas is the betrayer (John 18:5), it is Jesus who lays down his life. It is Jesus who is in command of the situation. It is Jesus who acts. Indeed, it is Jesus who takes the initiative by posing the question "Whom do you seek?" (v. 4). That the glorified Jesus is in control of the situation explains the superfluity of the mention of a kiss by Judas and its consequent omission from the Johannine narrative as well as the typically Johannine reworking of the tradition of the flight of Jesus' disciples. In the Synoptic account[114] the disciples forsake their Master and flee; in the Johannine narrative it is Jesus who gives the order that they should be let go. Jesus takes the initiative in being left alone. Yet he is not alone; the Father is with him (John 16:32).

It is useful to read the Johannine account of Jesus' arrest as a commentary on the entire Passion Narrative. From the very outset of his narrative, the evangelist has provided his readers with a scene which expresses the meaning of the passion. For John the passion is nothing other than the revelation, the glo-

114. Cf. Mark 14:50 and par.

rification and exaltation of him who bears the divine name. As always, it is Jesus who takes the initiative in his self-revelation. It is he who poses and repeats the question, "Whom do you seek?" (vv. 4,7). While, from John's dualistic perspective, a hostile band replies "Jesus of Nazareth," the glorified Jesus provides the answer to his own question. "I am he"—*Egō eimi*. Used absolutely, as here, this is *the* expression of the divine self-revelation.[115] Confronted by the one who bears the divine name and is alone qualified to utter an "I am he" in the language of man, the band "drew back and fell to the ground." Awe is man's only response to the revelation of the Son of God. They sought a man; they found the Son of Man revealed as the glorified one. Their awe yielded to their obedience and subjection. They had but to yield to his command to let the disciples go. Ironically the powers of darkness found him for whom they were searching.

Conclusion

With these brief comments upon the theophany of John 18:1-11, our reflections on the search for Jesus may be brought to a close. Given the subtleness of the evangelist's thought and the intricacy of his technique, it is difficult to isolate one Johannine theme from another. A study which purports to treat of but one theme in the Fourth Gospel necessarily touches upon other significant elements in the evangelist's thought. Likewise it must necessarily take a position relative to the way in which the evangelist composed his Gospel. We began our study with the conviction that the "search for Jesus" is a touchstone of the evangelist's thought. We were convinced that the first words of the Johannine Jesus provide a key to an understanding of the entire Gospel. Subsequent analysis revealed that the verb "to seek," *zētein*, is not used haphazardly in the Fourth Gospel. Rather it occurs in passages which are distinctively Johannine, in

115. Cf. S. Bartina, "'Yo soy Yahweh.' Nota exegética a Io. 18, 4-8," *EstBib* 32 (1958) 403-426.

passages where typical vocabulary and technique function as so many indications of the evangelist's hand. In reading these passages we must be attentive to that meaning which is indigenous to John's description of a once-only event in the life of the historical Jesus of Nazareth as well as to that "symbolic" meaning which John attaches to passages which he has so constructed or reworked as to elucidate the theological significance of Jesus of Nazareth.

The Johannine Jesus is, above all, the one who reveals himself to his disciples. To those who believe, he reveals himself as the one who bears the divine name. He alone can utter the awe-inspiring *Egō eimi*, "I am he." Jesus takes the initiative in his self-revelation. It is he who asks the question, "Whom do you seek?" Ultimately it is he who provides the answer in his own self-revelation.

The disciple is one who seeks. His search leads him to understand that Jesus says "I am he" because he dwells with the Father. The disciples, those who search faithfully, are likewise called to abide with the Father. There is, nevertheless, the great interim which comes between Jesus' death-exaltation and his return. His disciples know that the passion of Jesus' is the moment of his return to the Father. In the interim which it inaugurates, they must continue to search.

As John develops "The search for Jesus," he makes use of language which recalls that of the prophets who speak of the search for the Lord, of the sages who speak of the search for Wisdom, and of the rabbis, and the *Essenes* who speak of searching the Scriptures. For John, this multifaceted search coalesces in the search for Jesus who is the revelation of the Father, Wisdom incarnate, and the fulfillment of the Scriptures. The search leads to the foot of the Cross, for Jesus' death is the supreme act of his self-revelation. This act of self-revelation is the *krisis*. It is the judgment. Those who have searched with open hearts come to know that Jesus has returned to the Father there to prepare a dwelling place for his disciples. In contrast to the believing disciples stand the "Jews." They will be confounded by the drama in which the death of Jesus of Nazareth unfolds as the revelation of him who bears the divine name. They have sought in frustration. They have sought and have not found. Confounded by their disbelief, they are confronted by the inevitable. But it is "too late."

The authentic search for Jesus is the search for the divine revealer initiated by Jesus himself. To seek in faith is to find him who is absent so that man might live. This is the search unto which John's Jesus ironically challenges man when he confronts him with the question which is a matter of life-and-death, "What do you seek?" Only the believer knows that the "search for Jesus" is life's most authentic quest.

7. PROVERBIAL SAYINGS IN JOHN'S GOSPEL

For some time now, scholars have been in virtually unanimous agreement that the Gospel of John once ended at 20:31 and that the entire twenty-first chapter of John represents an epilogue to the original work. Indeed John 20:30-31 has such a concluding character that one would not expect the Johannine narrative to continue beyond the twentieth chapter except for the fact that there is a twenty-first chapter not only in our modern translations of the New Testament but also in the ancient Greek manuscripts and the ancient versions. In fact, there is no external textual evidence whatsoever that the Gospel of John ever circulated without the presence of John 21.[1]

Nonetheless the text of the Fourth Gospel that circulated within the church, at least from the beginning of the second century, and the text that was received as the canonical text by various orthodox Christian churches at the end of the fourth century[2] is a text which has had a rather complicated history. Conclusions that do not really conclude[3] are but one of the puzzling features of the Gospel of John as it is presently constituted. There are others and they are many. A quick comparison of John 16:5 with John 13:36 reveals but one of the many inconsistencies[4] encountered by the discerning reader of the Fourth Gospel.

During the course of this century scholars have advanced a variety of theories[5] in an attempt to place these inconsistencies

---

1. That is to say that, so far as the manuscript evidence is concerned, the Gospel of John began to circulate only after chapter twenty-one had been appended do it.

2. See further "The Formation of the New Testament" in my *Introduction to the New Testament* (Garden City, NY: Doubleday-London: SCM, 1983) pp. 1-40, esp. pp. 31-32.

3. See not only John 20:30-31 but also 14:31.

4. See also John 7:8, 10.

5. For an overview of the matter, see Raymond E. Brown, *The Gospel*

within a meaningful frame of reference. Some scholars have suggested that the author of the Fourth Gospel made use of various documentary sources which have been only imperfectly incorporated into the present text.[6] Others have considered that the present text of the Fourth Gospel results from a reordering of the original Johannine schema.[7] Still others have held that the extant twenty-one chapter work is the product of a long history, in which we must consider various stages in the oral tradition and successive redactions of the written text.[8] All three of these approaches towards an explanation of the inconsistencies in the Fourth Gospel are to be found in recent monographs and the best of the recent commentaries on the Gospel.

Increasingly, however, scholars are of the mind that the Fourth Gospel was produced within a "school"[9] and that the text of the Gospel was reedited at different moments in response to various situations within the Johannine community.[10] The break of the

According to John I-XII. AB, 29 (Garden City, NY: Doubleday, 1966) pp. xxv-xxiv.

6. The classic proponent of this approach is Rudolf Bultmann who identified a signs source, a revelation discourse source, and an underlying passion narrative. See R. Bultmann, *The Gospel of John. A Commentary* (Oxford: Basil Blackwell, 1971), the original German text of which appeared in 1940. The history of the possible use of a signs source by the evangelist has been chronicled by Howard M. Teeple in *The Literary Origin of the Gospel of John* (Evanston: Religion and Ethics Institute, 1964) and Gilbert Van Belle in *De Semeia-Bron in het Vierde Evangelie. Ontstaan en groei van een Hypothese* (Louvain: University Press, 1975).

7. See Bultmann's *The Gospel of John*, the order of which is laid out according to Bultmann's theorizing in this regard.

8. Among the recent major commentaries on John this approach has been adopted by Raymond E. Brown in *The Gospel According to John. I-XII; XIII-XXI.* AB 29, 29A (Garden City, NY: Doubleday, 1966, 1970) and Rudolf Schnackenburg, *The Gospel According to St. John*, Vol. 1, *Introduction and Commentary on Chapters 1-4* (New York: Seabury, 1980); Vol. 2, *Commentary on Chapters 5-12* (New York: Seabury, 1980); Vol. 3, *Commentary on Chapters 13-21* (New York: Crossroad, 1982). In the German original the volumes were respectively published in 1965, 1971, and 1975.

9. See R. Alan Culpepper, *The Johannine School. An Evaluation of the Johannine-School Hypothesis Based on an Investigation of the Nature of Ancient Schools.* SBLMS, 26 (Missoula: Scholars, 1975).

10. See especially Raymond E. Brown, *The Community of the Beloved Disciple* (New York-Ramsey: Paulist, 1979) and J. Louis Martyn, *The Gospel of John in Christian History. Essays for Interpreters* (New York-Ramsey: Paulist, 1978).

Johannine Jewish Christians from the synagogue would have been a major event in the life of the community[11] while the christological debate within the community itself would represent another significant situation in its history. Detailed analysis of this history would take us far beyond the thrust of the present essay, but it is necessary for us to recall that the Johannine community was a community very much alive at the time that the collection of Johannine writings was composed, that this dynamic community lived through certain pressures from without and certain tensions from within, that the community's theology developed[12] because of these pressures and tensions, and that the pressures and tensions, along with the responsorial theology which they evoked, are reflected in the community's literature. The present, somewhat confused state of the Gospel of John, reflects the development, under pressure, of the Johannine community. The Fourth Gospel was amended as the community which produced it evolved.

An examination of John 21 reveals that the entire chapter focuses on Simon Peter but that the figure of him which emerges from John 21 is somewhat different from the Simon Peter discovered by the reader of John 1-20. This difference of characterization is but one of the many inconsistencies that exist between John 21 and the rest of the Gospel of John.[13] One could also note that the phrase with which the chapter begins, "After this" (*meta tauta*), is a classic example of a loose connective;[14] but it hardly fits after the definite conclusion found in John 20:30-31. Moreover, verses 1 and 14 frame John 21:1-14 in such a manner that one must consider the miraculous catch of fish and the breakfast by the sea to constitute but a single story in the present

11. In addition to the works cited in note 10, see also J.L. Martyn, *History and Theology in the Fourth Gospel* (2nd. rev. ed.: Nashville: Abingdon, 1979).

12. Perhaps it may be more correct to say that it occasionally jumped forward in quantumlike leaps.

13. For an overview of some of these differences, see Ernst Haenchen, *John, 2.* Hermeneia (Philadelphia: Fortress, 1984) p. 229.

14. In John it is found at 3:22; 5:1, 14; 6:1; 7:1; 19:38; and 21:1; see also the use of *meta touto* in John 2:12; 16:7,11; 19:28.

Johannine account.[15] Verse 14 indicates that the narrative describes the third manifestation of the Risen Lord to his disciples, in apparent oblivion of Jesus' appearance to Mary Magdalene.[16] In addition to these various inconsistencies, there is the salient fact that the Gospel has been brought to a clear and classic conclusion in 20:30-31 and that the story has been reopened as chapter twenty-one begins.

In sum, the internal evidence offered by an examination of John 21 coalesces with contemporary theories about the history of the Johannine community to lead virtually all scholars to the conclusion that John 21 represents a rather late addition to the written Gospel of John. Thematically it focuses not only on Peter but also on a number of ecclesiastical issues, especially Jesus' presence at a meal.[17] These foci suggest that John 21 was added to an earlier edition of the Gospel in order to address issues bearing upon the relationship between the Johannine community and other Christian churches. In this way John 21 functions as a reflective postscript to the body of the Gospel.[18]

John's Gospel stands out among the canonical Gospels because it has an epilogue and a prologue which were appended to the written Gospel at a relatively late stage in its literary history. It may well be and indeed it is likely that John 21 was added to the Gospel at the same time as the prologue (John 1:1-18). Nonetheless there is a marked difference between the function and style of the prologue and the function and style of the epilogue.

Functionally, the prologue puts the Johannine Gospel and its Christ, the central focus of the Gospel narrative, in the broadest possible perspective. It serves as a broad commentary on the

15. The narrative framework is a classic example of *inclusio* (ring construction).
16. John 20:1,11-18.
17. See R. Schnackenburg, *The Gospel According to St. John.* 3, p. 409 and Pheme Perkins, *Resurrection: New Testament Witness and Contemporary Reflection* (Garden City, NY: Doubleday, 1984) p. 180.
18. A clear indication that John 21 serves as a reflection on the body of the Gospel is the fact that the triple scrutiny and triple commission of Peter (John 21:15-17) is linked to the triple denial of Peter (John 18:17,25,27).

Gospel, enabling the reader to focus attention sharply upon the central concerns of the written work.[19]

Stylistically, the prologue consists of an interweaving of poetic and narrative elements. Its language is clearly different from the language of the Gospel itself.[20] The stylistic and linguistic differences between the prologue and the body of the Gospel have led many commentators — perhaps the majority[21] — to opine that the prologue is a reworking of an earlier *Vorlage* which was probably composed outside the Johannine community.

Functionally, the epilogue is a reflection on the traditions of the other Christian churches[22] from the perspective of the Johannine community. Stylistically, the dialogue technique and the characterization of the disciples reflects that of the body of the Gospel. Linguistically, even though there are several Johannine *hapax legomena* in the chapter,[23] John 21 echoes the vocabulary of the main part of the Gospel itself. Indeed the style and language of the epilogue is such that one must unquestionably affirm that it has been composed within the Johannine community. Moreover, the citation of seven disciples in John 21:2 serves as an indication that the traditions which have been set down in writing in the epilogue circulated within the Johannine community.

Given this situation it might be well to characterize the style and vocabulary of the epilogue as an imitative style and vocabulary. The author of this chapter has consciously aped the style and vocabulary of a previously extant twenty-chapter work

19. See my article, "The Oldest Commentary on the Fourth Gospel," *TBT* 98 (1978) 1769-1775; in this volume, pp. 151-158.

20. Not the least of these differences is the use of *Logos*, "the Word" in vv. 1 and 14. The term does not appear as a proper noun in the body of the Gospel.

21. The tendency to interpret the prologue as a later edition of an earlier *Vorlage* is particularly pronounced in German-language scholarship. By way of example, we can cite the commentary on the prologue in the works of Haenchen (*John 1*, Philadelphia, Fortress, 1984) and Schnackenburg (see above, note 8) as well as articles on the topic written by these authors in various scholarly journals.

22. Especially the "apostolic church" associated with the Twelve.

23. In v. 2, for example, we find a partitive *apo* ("from") instead of *ek* and the "sons of Zebedee' (*hoi huioi Zebedaiou*).

with which he was quite familiar. The imitation of style and vocabulary is all more striking in that the themes of John 21 are not themes which have appeared in the main part of the Gospel— a seaside appearance to Simon Peter and the other disciples, fishing, a meal of bread and fish, the Petrine commission, and death. In the epilogue these non-Johannine themes are treated in a very Johannine manner.

Chapter twenty-one's technique of the dramatic sequence of successive little scenes is very Johannine.[24] It recalls not only the drama that followed upon the cure of the blind man (John 9), but also the call of the first disciples (John 1:35-51) and the story of water-become-wine at Cana in Galilee (John 2:1-12).[25] Stylistically, as has been noted, the dialogue technique is a typical ploy of the evangelist which has been imitated by the story-teller who has appended John 21 to the earlier narrative.[26] The interrogations in John 21, the questions and repeated questions found within the dialogue, recall the evangelist's predilection for interrogation as a literary device.[27]

As far as the characters who appear in the epilogue are concerned, the reader must surely note that Peter is called Simon Peter as he is throughout the Gospel. In direct address, Jesus calls him "Peter, son of John" (vv. 15,16,17). The formula calls to mind the words of Jesus in John 1:42.[28] Thomas is identified as the Twin (John 21:2), just as he is in John 20:24. In the epilogue the Beloved Disciple is identified as the one who had lain on Jesus' breast at the supper (v. 20). In this presentation the author of the epilogue has portrayed the Beloved Disciple by means of a

24. See especially J.L. Martyn, *History and Theology*.

25. See my "Cana (Jn. 2:1-12) — The First of His Signs or the Key to His Signs?" *ITQ* 47 (1980) 79-95, esp. p. 82; in this volume, pp. 158-182, esp. p. 165.

26. See, for example, the dialogue with Nicodemus in John 3:1-11.

27. See Albert Vanhoye, "Interrogation johannique et exégèse de Cana (Jn. 2,4)," *Bib* 55 (1974) 152-167, esp. pp. 157-158.

28. There is however a difference between the two formulae. In John 1:42 we find *Simon ho huios Ioannou* (literally, Simon, the son of John), the equivalent of Matthew's Aramaic Simon Bar-Jona (Matt 16:17); whereas in John 21:15,16,17 we have an elliptical *Simon Ioannou* (literally, Simon of John).

salient feature,[29] just as the evangelist himself had typified
Andrew as the brother of Simon Peter,[30] Nicodemus as the one
who had come by night,[31] Judas as the betrayer,[32] Lazarus as the
one who had been raised,[33] and Mary of Bethany as the one who
had annointed and wiped Jesus' feet.[34]

John 21:18

The fact that the author of the epilogue so consciously imitates
the style of the author of the Fourth Gospel brings into sharp
focus the technique employed in his story-telling at John 21:18-
19a. The passage lies within a pericope which sets in comparative
contrast the figures of Simon Peter and the Beloved Disciple. This
follows the example of the evangelist himself who similarly
contrasted Peter and the Beloved in John 13:22-26; 18:15-18;
and 20:2-10. The pericope begins with the formulaic expression
"Truly, truly I say to you" (*amēn amēn legō soi*, v. 18), a formula
found only in John's Gospel and used by the evangelist to
indicate that he is making reference to a traditional logion of
Jesus, albeit in his own fashion.[35] Moreover, the reflective
thought contained in v. 19a not only has the character of the
Johannine note[36] but also recalls John 12:33 where Jesus is
presented as indicating the death by which He himself was to die.
Just as Peter succeeded Jesus in the shepherding of the flock, so
he would succeed him in dying the death on the cross.[37]

---

29. See John 13:23,35.
30. See John 1:40 in comparison with John 6:8.
31. See John 7:50 and 19:39 in comparison with John 3:1.
32. See John 6:64,71 and 12:4 in comparison with John 13:21-30; 18:2.
33. See John 12:1,9 in comparison with John 11:43-44.
34. See John 11:2 in comparison with John 12:3.
35. See Barnabas Lindars, *The Gospel of John*. New Century Bible (London: Oliphants, 1972) p. 48; and "John and the Synoptic Gospels: A Test Case" *NTS* 27 (1981) 287-294.
36. See John J. O'Rourke, "Asides in the Gospel of John," *NovT* 21 (1979) 210-219.
37. The tradition that Peter was crucified head downwards, found in the apocryphal Acts of Peter and referred to by Eusebius, represents a much later embellishment.

The "follow me" of v. 19b has, in fact, a rather profound significance. On one level, it has a narrative function insofar as the story-teller is relating a tale of Jesus' being followed by Simon Peter with the Beloved Disciple, as it were, chasing after them.[38] Nonetheless Jesus' invitation to Simon Peter has yet a deeper meaning. Peter was to follow Jesus not only as the once-only conclusion to the narrated occurence, but also in sherpherding the flock and dying the martyr's death. Thus the story-teller's use of "follow me" in v. 19b recalls the evangelist's double-level technique. His words often have significance on the symbolic level in addition to their significance on the narrative level.[39]

These several points make it quite clear that the story-teller is imitating the style of the evangelist as he narrates his tale in 21:18-23. The tale begins with the classic Johannine *lemma*, "Amen, amen I say to you," and then Jesus addresses an enigmatic statement to Peter: "When you were young, you girded yourself and walked where you would; but when you are old, you will stretch out your hand and another will gird you and carry you where you do not wish to go." The utterance consists of three pairs of contrasting statements: 1) when you were young—when you are old; 2) you girded yourself—you will stretch out your hands and another will gird you; 3) you walked where you would—another will carry you where you do not wish to go. A number of authors have suggested that the story-teller has made use of an ancient proverb[40] which contrasts the vibrancy and autonomy of youth with the inertness and passivity of those who

38. See v. 20.

39. J. Louis Martyn has called attention to this technique in his *History and Theology*. Important hermeneutical reflections on its significance are to be found in Xavier Léon-Dufour, "Towards a Symbolic Reading of the Fourth Gospel," *NTS* 27 (1981) 439-456, and Sandra M. Schnieders, "History and Symbolism in the Fourth Gospel," in M. de Jonge, ed., *L'Évangile de Jean: Sources, Rédaction, Théologie*. BETL, 44 (Louvain: University Press, 1977) pp. 371-376.

40. Bultmann has observed that "v. 18 is a prophecy by parable, at the base of which clearly lies a proverb" (*John*, p. 714). His suggestion has received the warm endorsements of C.K. Barrett, Ernst Haenchen. Barnabas Lindars, and Rudolf Schnackenburg in their respective commentaries. Bultmann reconstitutes the proverbs as something like "In youth a man is free to go where he will; in old age a man must let himself be taken where he does not will."

have died in old age.[41] That the youth goes where he wants while the body of a dead man is carried to the grave is the reflection of the anonymous sage. Such a statement of gnomic wisdom is a truism which the story-teller has employed as he attempts to reflect respectively on the deaths of Simon Peter and the Beloved Disciple.

The traditional utterance did not specify any particular type of death;[42] it merely contrasted life and death. The story-teller, however, was interested in reflecting on Peter's death by crucifixion—a historical fact which had occurred well in the past when John 21 was set to writing. Accordingly he interpolated into the traditional proverb the middle contrast, girded—being girded. Peter's girding himself recalls his impetuous action in girding himself before jumping into the water (v. 7). His being girded may well recall the death shrouds which encompass the body of one who has died and is being carried out for burial. In any case, however, the mention of Simon Peter's "stretching out his hands" (*ekteneis tas cheiras sou*) interrupts the balance of the expanded proverb. It recalls the language used by classical and Christian authors in antiquity to describe the hands that are stretched out and tied to the beam of the cross prior to one's being led out to crucifixion.[43] In short, the story-teller has adapted an ancient proverb to his own ends by inserting a third contrast in the midst of the traditional contrasts. By doing so, he has applied the proverb to the situation of Simon Peter who died by crucifixion.

41. According to Bultmann, the proverb points to the helplessness of the old man who stretches out his hands while groping for a support or for someone to lead him. See R. Bultmann, *John*, p. 713, n. 7; p. 714, n. 1. More persuasive, in my view, is the argumentation of Haenchen who notes that "'Taking someone where he or she does not want to go' refers to the grave. The combination of old age and death is not uncommon." See E. Haenchen, *John, 2*, p. 226.

42. Bultmann not only argues that the reworked proverb does not specify death by crucifixion but also that the proverb refers simply to old age. Thus "the proverb needs the explanation" of v. 19a. See R. Bultmann, *John*, p. 714, n. 1.

43. Among others, Epictetus, Artemidorus, and Plautus; Josephus; *Ep. Barnabas* and Tertullian. See Barnabas Lindars, *John*, pp. 636-637, and E. Haenchen, *John, 2*, pp. 226-227.

Thereby he prepared the way for his own explanatory note, "This he said to show by what death he was to glorify God" (v. 19a).

The story-teller's use of an old proverb in this fashion is not only interesting in itself; it is also interesting because it is an indication that the use of proverbs[44] was one of the features of the Gospel which so caught the fancy of the story-teller that he was prompted to imitate it when he composed his epilogue. This is indeed striking because the evangelist's use of proverbs seems not to have particularly captivated the attention of today's scholars. There is, nonetheless, a significant number of proverbs scattered throughout the Fourth Gospel. These proverbs have been variously adapted by the evangelist to suit his own purposes. His way of dealing with ancient proverbs has been imitated by the story-teller responsible for John 21; perhaps it could also serve as a lesson for Christian story-tellers in our times.

John 2:10

The first proverb incorporated into John's Gospel is found in John 2:10, "Every man serves the good wine first; and when men have drunk freely, then the poor wine." Although there are no clear parallels to this proverb in extra-biblical literature, the saying seems to enjoy a proverbial character.[45] It speaks of a

44. With Bultmann, I would describe a proverb as a "saying of popular wisdom." See R. Bultmann, *The History of the Synoptic Tradition* (New York: Harper & Row, 1963), n. 38, n. 2. The proverb is characterized by its appeal to common human experience, its brevity, its use of generic utterance, and the present tense or gnomic aorist. The proverb (*stichwort*) is to be distinguished from the similitude (*bildwort*), even though a proverb may be used for comparison's sake. The latter is frequently the case in John's use of proverbs. His proverbs are often used allegorically. Thus it is often difficult to distinguish between proverbs and small parables in the Fourth Gospel. The proverbs frequently function as small parables.

45. Both Strack-Billerbeck and, following Hans Windisch, Bultmann indicate that the common practice of first century Palestine was otherwise. See H.L. Strack - P. Billerbeck, *Kommentar zum Neuen testament aus Talmud und Midrash*, 2 (Munich: Beck, 1924) p. 409; and R. Bultmann, *John*, p. 118, n. 4. *Econtrario*, F.F. Bruce comments that "the common practice was so well known as to be

common situation, generically citing "everyone" (literary, every man, *pas anthrōpos*) as the subject of the utterance. Strictly speaking it does not even fit easily into the Johannine narrative. In the social context to which John 2:1-11 refers, the statement is not particularly appropriate since wedding festivities were spread over several days. They were characterized by that coming-and-going which is still to be found in oriental gatherings. In such a situation late-comers would have been unable to compare the wine served to them with the wine served to the first set of guests. Moreover in its specifically Johannine context the logion is not particularly appropriate since the pericope contrasts the absence of wine with the abundant quantity provided by Jesus. The miracle story from which the Johannine narrative was fashioned focused on the quantity of wine; the proverb focuses on the quality of the wine.

This doubly inappropriate character of the logion serves to indicate that the evangelist has borrowed a saying from elsewhere. Nonetheless he has deliberately introduced the proverb into his narrative because it serves his purpose. One of the major concerns of the evangelist is to contrast the old dispensation (Judaism) with the new dispensation inaugurated by Jesus. The theme is interwoven throughout the Fourth Gospel. In his reworking of the miracle story of the water-become-wine the evangelist not only indicated that Jesus is the provider of the expected messianic blessings in abundance, but also that what Jesus has come to bring contrasts sharply with that which had been suitable up to the time of Jesus' coming—the various institutions of

proverbial." See F.F. Bruce, *The Gospel of John* (Grand Rapids: Eerdmans, 1983) p. 71.

Recognizing that v. 10 represents a "detached saying" (*The Gospel of John*, p. 131), Barnabas Lindars speaks of it as "a relic of an authentic parable of Jesus" (p. 319) and a parable derived from traditions of the words of Jesus (p. 32) in "Two Parables in John," *NTS* 16 (1969-1970) 318-329. These different observations recall that not only are there frequently no extant extra-biblical parallels to the Johannine proverbs but also that as they are presently found in John the proverbs are worded according to a Johannine formulation. Accordingly the characterization of a Johannine logion as a proverb (or reworked proverb) must be based on an analysis of the literary form of the saying in quastion.

Judaism which are ineffective in comparison with the gifts of Jesus.

John 3:8

Another proverb used by the evangelist is to be found in John 3:8 where the words "The wind (*pneuma*) blows where it wills, and you hear the sound of it, but you do not know whence it comes or whither it goes" are attributed to Jesus. In its Johannine context the proverb functions metaphorically[46] insofar as *pneuma* can denote either the wind or the spirit.[47] The point of comparison would seem to be either the freedom of movement of the wind/ spirit or its incomprehensibility.[48] Once again, however, the proverb does not appear to be entirely apropos in its Johannine context. On the one hand, the evangelist has retained the proverb's statement on the sound of the wind, but he has not exploited it in his use of the proverb. Moreover the application to one born anew is not entirely appropriate. Indeed the Johannine phrasing of the proverb is a bit strange in itself. After all it is possible to hear the rushing of the wind and even reeds shaking in the wind[49] indicate its direction. Nonetheless the internal consistency of the proverb seems not to have troubled the Johannine author. The point that he wanted to make in his presentation

46. This point is made by virtually all the commentators.

47. C.K. Barrett identifies the logion as an allegory while Lindars, with reference to Chrysostom, identifies it as a parable. He explains that "we can only deduce that this is a parable from the fact that it blows and its sound can be heard." For A.M. Hunter, v. 8 represents an authentic parable of Jesus. See C.K. Barrett, *The Gospel According to John* (London: S.P.C.K., 1960) p. 176; B. Lindars, *John*, p. 154; and A.M. Hunter, *The Gospel According to John*. Cambridge Bible Commentary (London: Cambridge University Press, 1965) p. 79.

48. Bultmann notes that the incomprehensibility of the wind is used more than once in the OT and in Jewish literature to provide a comparison for the incomprehensibility of God's ways. See R. Bultmann, *John*, p. 142, n. 3, with references to Qoh 11:5; Prov 30:4; and Sir 16:21. It is to be noted that each of these references, the only biblical references cited by Bultmann, come from the wisdom tradition. Strack and Billerbeck also cite Qoh 11:5 and make reference to the Targum. See Str-B., 2, p. 424.

49. See Luke 7:24; Matt 11:7.

of Jesus' dialogue with Nicodemus, a leading figure among the
Jews, was that the Spirit was as free in its operation as the wind
was apparently fickle in its movement.

John 4:35,37

Two more proverbs (John 4:35,37) appear in the Johannine
narrative of Jesus' encounter with the Samaritan woman. Each of
these proverbs is placed on the lips of Jesus as a saying addressed
to his disciples. The first, "There are yet four months, then comes
the harvest," has a rhythmic character in Greek which allows it to
be typified as a popular saying.[50] The proverb states that the
harvest will come in due time. As such, the adage can serve as an
exhortation to patience or as an expression of idolence.[51] In
Johannine context, the popular saying ("you say") is contrasted
with Jesus' own utterance ("I tell you"). Delays cannot be
tolerated because the moment of Jesus' mission has arrived: The
harvest is ready.

The proverb found in John 4:37, "One sows and another
reaps," is formally identified as "a saying" (*ho logos*), that is, a
proverb.[52] The use of a parable of this type is clearly paralleled in
biblical and extra-biblical literature. In his final defence Job said:
"Let me sow, and another eat."[53] "You reap an alien harvest" is
a saying transmitted by Aristophanes.[54] The widely quoted
proverb called attention to the wry injustice of fate, and this may

50. Thus, explicitly, F.F. Bruce, *John*, p. 114. C.H. Dodd observes that, in
Greek, the proverb is in iambic pentameter but Raymond E. Brown suggests that
this might be a felicitous accident of translation. He finds an indication that the
saying is a proverb in its brevity and construction. See C.H. Dodd, *Historical
Tradition in the Fourth Gospel* (Cambridge: University Press, 1965) p. 394; and
R.E. Brown, *John. I-XII*, p. 174. See also R. Bultmann, *John*, pp. 196, 198.
Skeptically, however, C.K. Barrett remarks that "there is no evidence that such a
proverb existed." See C.K. Barrett, *John*, p. 202.

51. Thus Bultmann, *John*, p. 196.

52. Barrett notes that this meaning is often the case in Greek. See C.K. Barrett,
John, p. 203.

53. Job 31:8.

54. *Equites* 392.

have been the commonly accepted point of the proverb in first century Palestine.[55]

In any event, the proverb, as used in the Fourth Gospel, is applied to the Johannine community's Samaritan mission. Its verisimilitude is endorsed by Jesus himself. This must be put into perspective. Among the canonical Gospels, the Fourth Gospel is distinctive by reason of its explicit concern for two generations of Jesus' disciples[56] and by its affirmation of the mission to the Samaritans.

Both of these concerns are expressed in John 4:31-38. Jesus' sending his disciples (v. 38) clearly represents a post-resurrectional perspective. Accordingly one must affirm that the proverb of v. 37 is related to the Christian mission in Samaria. What the application of the proverb implies is that the effectiveness of the mission to the Samaritans is dependent upon the work of the first generation of Jesus' disciples. Indeed the attribution of the proverb to Jesus himself would seem to suggest that the evangelist would have it that the Samaritan mission has been endorsed by Jesus himself.

John 4:44

Another proverb comes to Johannine expression in the introduction to the following pericope when Jesus reflects that "a

55. Bultmann states the saying is not attested anywhere else in this precise form, but the idea itself is common enough in the Old Testament and in Greek literature. See R. Bultmann, *John*, p. 198, n. 2. In the biblical literature the proverb is not about fate but highlights the idea as a form of punishment or misfortune. Because of this biblical usage Barrett holds that the Johannine proverb is Greek rather than Jewish. Sanders, however, has taken issue with Barrett, citing the references to the harvest in Luke 19:21 and Matt 25:24 and nothing that "the proverb reflects the bitter truth that men are often deprived of their labors." See C.K. Barrett, *John*, p. 203, and J.N. Sanders, *A Commentary on the Gospel According to St. John*, edited by B. Mastin, HNTC (New York: Harper, 1969) pp. 151-152.

56. See John 14:12; 17:20-21; 20:29. See further Godfrey Nicholson, *Death as Departure: The Ascent-Descent Schema in the Gospel of John*. SBLMS, 63 (Chico: Scholars, 1983) pp. 135-159.

prophet has no honor in his own country" (John 4:44).[57] This traditional Jesuanic logion is attested by the Synoptic tradition as well by the Gnostic Gospel of Thomas.[58] Luke, in fact, compares the logion to another proverb (*tēn parabolēn*), "heal yourself" (Luke 4:23). The Gospel language reflects the wisdom of the wandering sage whose message often falls on the deaf ears of friends and acquaintances despite its being warmly received by others. Within the context of the Fourth Gospel the saying highlights the fact that Jesus was not received by his own.[59] This reality stands in contrast to the reception that his massage had received among the Samaritans.

The proverb of John 4:44 is the focal point of a group of verses which serve as a transition to the narrative of the cure of the royal official's son (John 4:46-54). This fact requires that one recall that within the perspective of the Fourth Gospel it is Judea,[60] not Galilee, which is Jesus' "own country." Galilee symbolizes those who receive the revelation of Jesus, whereas Judea symbolizes those who reject it.[61] In Galilee, the royal official not only welcomes Jesus (see v. 45) but begs for his ministration (v. 47). In Galilee Jesus is warmly received. This situation contrasts sharply with that of Judea where Jesus is not received by the Jews even though he stands as a prophet in their midst. The proverb of John 4:44 has, therefore, a marked christological focus.

The Johannine usage of the proverb would, however, seem to call for further reflection because of the two levels on which the

57. Lindars notes that "John has inserted a proverbial saying of Jesus which does not seem to fit." See B. Lindars, *John*, p. 200.

58. Matt 13:57; Mark 6:4; Luke 4:24; *Gos. Thom.* 31 ("Jesus said: No prophet is acceptable in his village; no physician works cures on those who know him").

59. See John 1:11.

60. Thus even Origen, *In Joannem* 13,54.

61. See Robert T. Fortna, "Theological Use of Locale in the Fourth Gospel," in M.H. Shepherd, Jr. and E.C. Hobbs, eds., *Gospel Studies in Honor of Sherman E. Johnson, Anglican Theological Review*, Supplementary Series, 3 (1974) 58-59; and Jouette M. Bassler, "The Galileans: A Neglected Factor in Johannine Community Research," *CBQ* 43 (1981) 243-257.

Johannine account must be read. On the second level the Galileans symbolize the Johannine community which accepts Jesus as a prophetic figure and his message as God's revelation, whereas the Judeans (the "Jews") symbolize those who have not accepted the community's message about Jesus. On this second level, the proverb suggests that the message of the Johannine community has not been accepted by those to whom they are related.

John 5:19-20a

From a manifestly christological perspective the proverb which opens up to the most profound Johannine insights may well be found in John 5:19-20a, "The Son can do nothing of his own accord, but only what he sees the Father doing, for whatever he does the Son does likewise. For the Father loves the Son, and shows him all that he himself is doing." Charles Dodd has described the proverb as a hidden parable whose proper locale is the culture of the village and its artisans.[62] The use of the definite article before both "father" and "son" (*ho patēr, ton huion*) shows that the saying admits of universal application. Traditionally it spoke of any father and any son. The adage enunciated the

62. See C.H. Dodd, "A Hidden Parable in the Fourth Gospel," in *More New Testament Studies* (Manchester: University Press, 1968) pp. 30-40; *Historical Tradition*, p. 386, n. 22; and "The Portrait of Jesus in John and in the Synoptics," in W.R. Farmer, C.F.D. Moule, R.R. Niebuhr, eds., *Christian History and Interpretation*. J. Knox *Festschrift* (Cambridge: University Press, 1967) pp. 183-187, esp. pp. 185-187. Similarly, Paul Gächter, "Zur Form von Joh. 5,19-30," in J. Blinzler, O. Kuss, F. Mussner, eds., *Neutestamentliche Aufsätze: Festschrift für Prof. Josef Schmid zum 70. Geburtstag* (Regensburg: Pustet, 1963) pp. 65-68, esp. p. 67. Barnabas Lindars (*John*, p. 221), Raymond E. Brown (*John. I-XII*, p. 218), and F.F. Bruce (*John*, p. 128) concur with this opinion. Schnackenburg, however, demurs because of the use of the introductory *lemma*, "Truly, truly I say to you." See R. Schnackenburg, *John*, 2, p. 102 and p. 462, n. 33.

Dodd suggests that the structure of the saying (cf. Luke 8:16) consists of two general categorical clauses forming an antithesis, followed by an explanatory clause:

A. (Negation) A son learning his trade can do nothing but what he sees his father doing.

B. (Affirmation) What he sees his father doing, the son does likewise.

C. (Explanation) For the father shows him all that he is doing.

wisdom of the ages in a society where trade skills are hereditary, handed down from generation to generation. The Synoptic Gospels attest not only that Jesus himself was a carpenter (Mark 6:3) but also that he was the son of a carpenter (Matt 13:35).

In a world where a son was effectively apprenticed to his father, the son learned the father's trade from observation, imitation, and, eventually, cooperation. The wise man could then observe that the son sees what the father does and does likewise (John 5:19b). The father was, however, hardly a passive participant in the handing down of the traditional trade. For a father to teach his son a trade was an integral part of his paternal love. Indeed Jewish rabbis spoke not only of the responsibility of a father to teach his son the traditions of their people but also of the responsibility of a father to teach his son a trade, lest he teach him "to become a thief."

The evangelist is well aware that he is handing down a traditional logion as he writes the saying contained in vv. 19 and 20 for he has prefixed his remarks with the solemn introductory formula, "Amen, amen I say to you." The *lemma* bears the Johannine trademark; it indicates that the evangelist is passing along a saying acknowledged within the Johannine community as a logion traditionally ascribed to Jesus. The saying has been incorporated into the broad Johannine context of a sabbath discussion (John 5:9b-47) which has been appended to Jesus' poolside cure of the paralytic (John 5:1-9a).

As the evangelist unfolds his discourse, he moves from a discussion of sabbath day works to a consideration of the unique relationship which exists between Jesus and the Father. The sabbath context provides opportunity for a recalling of the priestly tradition of creation in which God is present as a divine artisan constructing and furbishing the world for human habitation prior to resting on the sabbath day (Gen 1:1-2:4a). This Jewish tradition which anthropomorphically portrayed God as an artisan provided the framework for the metaphorical application of the proverb of the apprenticed son to the relationship between Jesus and the Father. As applied by the evangelist the proverb intimates not only that Jesus is the Son of the Father but also that there exists a dynamic relationship between them: The Father loves the son; the Son does the works of His Father.

John 9:4

Discussion of the works of Jesus provides another opportunity for the evangelist to introduce a proverb into his Gospel at 9:4, "We must work the works of him who sent me, while it is day; night comes, when no one can work." The reference to persons in this verse is quite striking: we ... him ... me ... no one.[63] The latter reference ("no one," *oudeis*) suggests that at the origin of the saying attributed to Jesus lies a saying with general applicability. "Night comes, when no one can work" expresses a prudential point of view. Dodd[64] has suggested that Jesus' saying reflects a rabbinic aphorism utilized, among others, by Rabbi Tarphon who was a contemporary of the evangelist. "The day is short and there is much work to be done; the workers are lazy and the reward is great and the master of the house is urgent"[65] was the proverbial saying. Used by Tarphon, the adage was applied to the study of the Torah. Day represented the span of a human life within which the Torah could be studied and night represented death when study of the Torah was no longer possible.

It may be that the context of the proverb's application by Tarphon is no more consistent with the original formulation than is the Johannine application. The proverb speaks generally of the

63. Schnackenburg also finds the juxtaposition of the singular and plural numbers exceptional. See R. Schnackenburg, *John*, 2, p. 241.

64. See C.H. Dodd, *Historical Tradition*, p. 186. For Lindars the saying is "a piece of proverbial wisdom" (*John*, p. 342). Dodd's observations have been favorably referenced by Brown (*John. I-XII*, p. 372).

65. Mishnah, *Pirke Aboth*, 2:14-15. As further rabbinic parallels, Strack and Billerbeck cite a statement in the Babylonian Talmud attributed to Rabbi Simeon ben Eleazar (ca. 190), "Work as long as you can, while it is still possible for you and there is still strength in you," and a statement attributed to the daughter of Rabbi Chisda (d. 309) who spoke to her father to the effect that "there comes the night when no one can work." See Str-B, 2, p. 529.

day as the opportune time for work.[66] Its common-sense meaning is paralleled by the old Latin adage, *carpe diem*.[67] There was a time for the works of the Father to be done and that time was the time of the presence of Jesus. His work had a necessary and urgent quality. Such was the primary inference that the evangelist drew from his use of proverb.

Yet there was another inference to be drawn as well, one suggested by the evangelist's interchange of "we" and "me." The use of the first person plural suggests that the evangelist believed that the proverb was likewise applicable to the disciples of Jesus. Later the evangelist would write: "He who believes in me will also do the works that I do; and greater works than these will he do, because I go to the Father" (John 14:12). In the absence of Jesus the disciples are to do the works of the Father, indeed works even greater than those of Jesus himself. As applied to the community of the Beloved Disciple, the proverb echoed in John 9:4 reflects that there is an appropriate time in which the disciples are to do the works of the Father. That time is the time of Jesus' absence. It was also necessary for them to work, since there will be a time when it is too late. That time is symbolized by night. Thus the use of the plural suggests the urgency with which the disciples were to do the works of the Father.

John 11:9-10

The contrast between day and night is the point of yet another proverb used by the evangelist. This one is found in John 11:9-10: "Are there not twelve hours in the day? If anyone walks in the day he does not stumble, because he sees the light of this world. But if any one walks in the night, he stumbles, because the light is not in him." Some authors have suggested that the evangelist has composed this section of the Lazarus story according to the model of John 9:3-5, using another proverb.

66. Compare Paul's "acceptable time" in 2 Cor 6:2, where the apostle makes use of Isa 42:6 to speak of the time appropriate for his mission.
67. Horace, *Odes* I, XI, 8.

That the evangelist is making use of a proverb as he enters into his account of Jesus' encounter with Lazarus is clear. The twice-repeated generalized subject, "any one" (*tis*), and the balanced contrast between the two elements of the saying are clear signs that proverbial material has been used by the evangelist.

Yet the signs are equally clear that the evangelist has indeed altered the proverb, and that he has used it to his own advantage. Appended to the first part of the proverb is the explanatory statement "because he sees the light of this world." By and large explanations are not part of proverbial sayings. Proverbs function as axioms which need no explanation other than one's own experience. From the standpoint of rhetorical analysis statements with explanations, epithymemes, belong to logical discourse; proverbs, which appeal to experience, typically belong to a hortatory or judgmental discourse.[68] Moreover, "the light of this world" reflects Johannine language which more than once speaks of Jesus as the light of the world.[69] If the addition of an explanatory statement to the first part of the proverb seems to come from a Johannine source, the explanation of the second part of the contrast also seems somewhat inappropriate for a traditional aphorism.[70]

Indeed the explanation proved to be somewhat enigmatic to some of the scribes who were charged with copying the Johannine text. According to the original transcription, the fifth century Codex Bezae Cantabrigiensis (D) read "If any one walks in the night, he stumbles, because the light is not in it" (*en autē*). A corrector emended the manuscript to make it conformable with the vast majority of the ancient manuscripts which read "... because the light is not in him." The phraseology is strange indeed. The determination of its precise significance still puzzles

68. In Greek rhetoric, *logos* describes the mode of logical discourse; *pathos*, the mode of appealing to the emotions or self-interest of the hearer(s).

69. See John 8:12 and 9:4-5. In John 11:9-10, Schnackenburg speaks of "the light of the world" as metaphorical (*John*, 2, p. 325).

70. Similarly, Lindars who speaks of the "addition of the causal clauses" (*John*, p. 390).

modern commentators.[71] Bultmann has conjectured that the original saying ran something like "Whoever walks by day does not stumble; but if anyone walks by night, he stumbles."[72] He seems to have been on the right track.

A saying loosely parallel to the logion of John 11:19-10 and likewise developing the contrast between light and darkness is found among the secret saying of Jesus in the Gnostic Gospel of Thomas: "There is light within a man of light and it illumines the whole world; when it does not shine, there is darkness." John's development of the proverbial contrast is somewhat different. It preserves a Jewish ring in that the Jews distinguished day from night, according twelve hours to each.[73] The application of the proverb within the Johannine narrative suggests at one level that it is appropriate that Jesus perform his works while time remains, i.e., while there is still daylight. Nonetheless, the addition of the problematic "in him" (*en autō*) at the end of v. 10 and the resonant "light of this world" in v. 9 suggests, as Lightfoot has stated, "that the purpose of the apparently simple words in verses 9 and 10 is to teach spiritual truth."[74]

This suggestion leads us to the complex history of the Lazarus story. The complexity of the history and the length of the story (John 11:1-12:8) excuse us from entering into the matter in detail in an essay such as this. One can only suggest that the use of the parable, in a more or less traditional form, bespoke the appropriateness of the time of the miracle worked by Jesus.[75] The expanded proverb reflects the fact that the miracle story has been so reworked in the Johannine tradition that it has become a dramatic christological statement, proclaiming that Jesus is the

71. A situation somewhat akin to that of John 3:8.
72. See R. Bultmann, *John*, p. 399.
73. An "hour" was simply the twelfth part of the day, such than an hour at the summer solstice was approximately twenty minutes longer than an hour at the winter solstice. See Str-B, 2, p. 543.
74. R.H. Lightfoot, *St. John's Gospel: A Commentary* (Oxford: University Press, 1960) p. 220.
75. The force of the proverb would have been similar to that of the proverb in John 9:4.

resurrection and the life.[76] The expanded proverb suggests that the one who is to be revealed as the resurrection and the life is the one who has been previously revealed as the light of the world. As one has life because of Jesus, so one sees because of him.

Conclusion

The story-teller who compiled the epilogue of the Fourth Gospel and added it to the Gospel which was familiar to him was well aware of the significance of proverbs[77] in the teaching of the Johannine school. The use of proverbs such as these confirm that the Johannine community was composed of Jewish Christians.[78] In the Fourth Gospel it is typically Jesus who cites proverbs,[79] thereby reinforcing the view that he is a teacher. This estimation of Jesus was traditional in the Jewish Christian community which emerged as the community of the Beloved Disciple.

Yet, as the community's tradition developed, its christology transcended the relatively low christology of Jesus-rabbi.[80] Accordingly, the traditional proverbs were emended so as to bear some of the key insights of the Johannine community. Thus, as presently formulated, the proverbs in the Gospel of John speak of the unique relationship between Jesus and the Father, a relationship which is functional in that Jesus is the one who can do the Father's works. Indeed it was necessary and urgent that he do so

76. See John 11:24.
77. In addition to the sayings that have been examined, other common-sense logia appear in John 7:4; 12:24; and 16:21. These have the common characteristic of generic utterance, yet they do not appear to me to be so isolateable from their Johannine context as to be identifiable as traditional sayings of popular wisdom. Hence they have not been considered in the present study. Cf. John 15:11 (see below, p. 246, n. 111).
78. Note, in this regard, the parallels with various rabbinic aphorisms, and the Jewish quality of many of the proverbs.
79. Even the proverb of John 4:35 is placed on the lips of Jesus, as are the generic utterances found in John 12:24 and 16:21. An exception to this general state of affairs would be the attribution of the logion in John 2:10 to the chief steward of the feast.
80. See Raymond E. Brown, *Community*, pp. 25-58.

because his hour was the time for the works of the Father to be done.

The expanded proverbs give us further insight into the community's understanding of Jesus in that they indicate that what he had come to do effected a radical relativization of the Father's previous works. Through the expanded and applied proverbs the community came to appreciate that Jesus was not only the resurrection and the life but also the light of the world, who made it possible for his disciples to see, in faith.

The nature of the proverb is such that its applicability transcends a particular set of historical circumstances. For the Johannine community which saw the story of Jesus intertwined with its own story, and vice-versa, the proverbs attributed to Jesus spoke also to its own situation. In proverbs attributed to Jesus, the community found a warrant for its own mission, specifically its mission to the Samaritans. The traditional proverbs provided occasion for reflection on the incomprehensibility of the Spirit's action and allowed the community to perceive that its own rejection was not dissimilar to the rejection of Jesus himself.

In sum, for the members of ther community of the Beloved Disciple proverbs, the dicta of common-sense wisdom, were the bearers of profound truth.

8. THE OLDEST COMMENTARY ON THE FOURTH GOSPEL

In recent years there has been a veritable flood of articles and books devoted to the interpretation of the Fourth Gospel. On an average, approximately fifty significant books appear each year. They have been written to help today's Christians understand that Gospel whose author has been generally identified by the tradition of the Church as the "theologian" among the evangelists. Undoubtedly the work of redaction criticism is making us increasingly aware that each of the evangelists is a theologian in his own right; nevertheless, even the most severe critic of the Gospels must admit that the Fourth Gospel offers a singular and rich insight into the Gospel message. Its author well deserves the title of "theologian."

Today's Commentaries on John

Contemporary scholarship on the Gospel of John has made us well aware that the evangelist did not write his unique account of the ministry of Jesus of Nazareth in a literary or theological vacuum. More than ever before we have come to realize that the Fourth Gospel, like the Synoptics, is the product of the living oral tradition of the Church. This is so true that each of the scenes that comprise the Gospel may well be considered a little homily.

Proper to the Johannine homiletic tradition was the tendency to single out one of the disciples of Jesus as the hero or heroine of the narrative in order to illustrate one or another aspect of faith in Jesus, the Christ. Thus the evangelist singles out Mary Magdalene from among the Galilean women to teach that the resurrection of Jesus is to be understood as his ascension to the Father (John 20:1-2, 11-18; cf. Matt 28:1-10). In similar fashion, the evangelist has chosen Thomas from among the disciples to make his readers realize that even the disciples were at first not convinced that Jesus had indeed risen from the dead (John 20:24-29; cf. Mark 16:14). By so concentrating his narrative upon one of Jesus' disciples, the evangelist is able to give a dramatic twist to the narrative; yet at the same time he shows how much his narrative has been shaped by the homiletic tradition of which he is the heir.

Besides pointing to the influence of a living oral tradition upon the development of the Fourth Gospel, today's critical scholars generally concur in acknowledging that the Fourth Gospel was written for a group of Jewish Christians who continued to be engaged in some sort of ongoing dialogue with the Jews. This situation explains the great importance the Fourth Gospel attaches to Jewish feasts (e.g., the Feast of Tabernacles in ch. 8) and institutions (e.g., the Temple in 2:13-22), as well as its references to excommunication from the synagogue (9:22) and its discussion on the meaning of the Scripture (8:42).

This group of Jewish Christians was somewhat sectarian. Today we might well say that the Gospel of John emanated from a group of charismatic Christians who continued to be influenced by their Jewish heritage. Consequently, we are able to point to several similarities between the thought and language patterns of the Fourth Gospel and the group of sectarian Jews, generally identified as the Essenes, who produced the so-called Dead Sea Scrolls. The "sectarian" provenance of the Fourth Gospel is further reflected in the unique Johannine formulation of the love commandment, "love one another" (13:34, 35; 15:12; etc.). The Fourth Gospel's repeated reference to the Holy Spirit and the use of the imagery of living water to signify the Spirit (e.g., 7:38-39) show that the group of sectarian Christians were so aware of the presence of the Spirit in the life of Jesus and of his Church that it is not inappropriate to describe the Johannine church as a charismatic church.

Further consensus has been reached among scholars when they almost unanimously agree that the present redaction of the Gospel of John is the product of a long tradition in which various stages of oral and literary development can be discerned. Scholars disagree among themselves as to precisely which part of the Fourth Gospel owes its composition to a particular stage in the oral and literary development, but they generally agree with one another that the Fourth Gospel must be seen as the end product of an ongoing oral tradition and a complex process of literary development in which the author made use of various written sources.

When the Gospel had been substantially completed (20:30-31), an epilogue (ch. 21) and a prologue (1:1-18) were added to the Johannine Gospel. Accordingly, the prologue to the Fourth Gospel ought to be considered as the oldest commentary on the most recent Gospel. The author responsible for the addition of the first eighteen verses of John to the Gospel has given us an authoritative and canonical commentary on the Gospel itself. At a very early stage of the Church's history, he has let his readers — among whom we must number ourselves — know how the Fourth Gospel is to be interpreted. A careful reading of the prologue, therefore, allows us to know how the Fourth Gospel ought to be interpreted.

It is not possible to give a full commentary on the prologue in the space of a study as short as the present essay. Nevertheless, the main points of the prologue can be exploited as providing a hermeneutical key for the interpretation of John's Gospel. Thus, we will focus on five key points that help us to understand the significance of Jesus of Nazareth, witnessed to by the Fourth Gospel, as this Gospel has been understood by its first commentator.

Jesus in Cosmic Perspective

First of all, the author of the prologue has made use of an early hymn as the basis of his interpretive text. The hymn bears remarkable similarity to other christological hymns found in the New Testament (e.g., Col 1:15-20). The use of a hymn whose horizon is creation and whose perspective is the reality of God himself (1:1) reveals that the author intended his readers to know that the Jesus of Nazareth whom the group of sectarian Christians esteemed as the Teacher par excellence (see 1:38) was not an obscure and inconsequential figure who lived at some previous time in the relatively unimportant provinces of Palestine. Rather, the author of the prologue is telling us that this very Jesus of Nazareth is to be understood within the most significant of contexts, that is, the entire created order and the reality of God himself. This fundamental insight is basic to whatever further specific remarks the author would share with his readers as to the relation of the Word to God (i.e., the Father) and the role of the Word in creation.

Jesus the Exegete

It is, nevertheless, the final words of this short commentary on the Gospel that are the most significant. They tell us what the Gospel is all about. They state that it is the mission of Jesus to make the Father known to men. The language of the Greek text of the prologue (1:18) affirms that Jesus is the exegete, that is, he is the one who reveals and interprets the Father for us. It is the author's understanding that Jesus is the revelation of the Father which provides occasion for his designation of Jesus as "the Word." Jesus is the one who speaks the words of God (3:34); he is the one who personally reveals the Father (14:19). Accordingly, Jesus can be appropriately designated as "the Word."

One might well ask whether such a designation of Jesus is appropriate. Certainly there were other claims made of being the authentic revelation of God, both within Judaism itself and outside Judaism. Did not the then developping Gnosticism claim that "knowledge" (*gnōsis*) was the way to know and experience God? The author of the prologue effectively counters the claims of all who assert that the revelation of God is mediated in some other fashion. There is but one authentically qualified exegete of the Father: the only Son who is in the bosom of the Father (1:18). Because he alone belongs to the divine sphere, he alone is capable of revealing the Father. Thus the claims of religions and religious movements other than Christianity are quietly set aside.

Jesus Compared with Moses

As the Christian group from which the Fourth Gospel emanated was in dialogue with the Jews, it seemed most imperative for the author of the prologue to set the relationship between Christianity and Judaism in clear perspective. Since the Gospel was demonstrably Christocentric, its earliest commentator chose to contrast Christ and Moses. His reflection was that the old dispensation was replaced by a new dispensation. The law was given through Moses; grace and truth were given through Jesus Christ. It is not that the author denies the value of Judaism nor the authenticity of the revelation given through Moses. No, the earlier revelation was indeed "grace;" now, however, grace has been substituted for grace—there is grace in place of grace (1:16). In the new order of grace, there is the revelation given through Jesus Christ, the Truth. The old order has been superseded.

In fact, our commentator's thought is rather subtle. He would have his understand that the relationship between the revelation of Jesus and Judaism is unique. The importance of the covenant is to be affirmed. Jesus brings this convenant to its fulfillment, precisely by replacing the law with his revelation, and Jewish institutions with his person. Paradoxically, the fulfillment of the covenant was its replacement by Jesus.

Jesus, A Historical Figure

If it was necessary for the author of the prologue to contrast Jesus with Moses in order that the readers of the Gospel might come to an understanding of the singular relationship between Christianity and Judaism, it was also necessary for him to affirm that Jesus was a historical figure. Nascent Gnosticism was redolent with myths of heavenly revealers. Some Christians were all too ready to assume that Jesus was but a heavenly revealer. Docetism was already beginning to emerge in the Christian Church. Thus our author took pains to affirm that Jesus was indeed true man—the Word had indeed become flesh. As such, Jesus was not a disincarnate reality, but a reality of the human and historical order to whom the Baptist could and did bear witness.

Again, the author of the prologue wanted his readers to know full well that the light of Jesus was a light to which God's human messengers must bear witness. The function of the Baptist was preeminently that of bearing witness to Jesus. Yet he was not to remain the only witness to Jesus. Indeed, the very disciples of Jesus for whom the Gospel is intended are also to be witnesses (15:27). The paradox (1:15) to which the Baptist, as the first and typical witness, and the disciples of Jesus were alike to bear testimony is that the divine Revealer was present in human form.

Jesus Savior

As the author of the prologue reflected on the Gospel he had at hand, and as he reflected on the interpretation he himself was giving to that Gospel, he was well aware that one might conclude that acceptance of the Gospel message was a matter of intellectual commitment. It was all too easy to assume that the coming of Jesus and the interpretation of the Gospel were but a concern of the mind, as if both the person and the message were a matter of a correct intellectual understanding of reality. Was John's Gospel but a true philosophy?

Lest the Gospel be misconstrued, its first commentator pointed out that Jesus came in order that men might become children of God. The coming of Jesus was unto knowledge, but that knowledge was unto salvation (17:3). The Gospel was written in order that we might believe, and that believing we might have life (20:31). It was to the reality that Jesus was and is Savior of the world (4:43) that the author of the prologue drew attention when he affirmed that we have all received of the fullness of Jesus Christ (1:16). His presence among us was the salvific reality par excellence.

Conclusion

The plethora of contemporary studies on the Johannine Gospel has contributed something to our understanding of the Gospel. Perhaps the most significant contribution of these latter-day commentators has been to draw our attention to the earliest commentary on the Gospel. It provides an early and authoritative clue to the meaning of the Gospel. At the risk of overly simplifying his prologue, it might well be said that the earliest commentator on the most recent Gospel would simply have us know that Jesus came to reveal the Father in order that we might live. That is what the Fourth Gospel is all about.

III. Signs and Faith

9. CANA (JOHN 2:1-12)—THE FIRST OF HIS SIGNS OR THE KEY TO HIS SIGNS?

A comparison of the Fourth Gospel's narrative material with that of the Synoptics quickly reveals that the Johannine accounts of Jesus' miracles are quite different from those of the Synoptics. Whereas miracle stories comprise almost fifty per cent of Mark's Gospel, the Fourth Gospel tells the tale of but seven or eight miracles[1] performed by Jesus. Whereas the miracles tend to be grouped together in the Synoptics' accounts, perhaps showing the earliest evangelists' dependence upon a still earlier aretalogy, the Fourth Gospel narrates the signs of Jesus as so many individual and unrelated events. Whereas the Synoptics' miracle stories are easily isolable from their immediate context, the Johannine miracle stories are frequently complemented by an extensive discourse.[2]

The difference between the miracles stories as narrated by the Synoptists and as narrated by John goes still further. It extends even to the selection of material and the basic characterization of the miracles themselves. Typically the Fourth Evangelist styles the miracles of Jesus as "signs" or "works," whereas the Syn-

---

1. The marriage at Cana (John 2:1-12), the cure of the royal official's son (John 4:46-54), the healing of the lame man (John 5:2-9), the multiplication of loaves (John 6:1-15), the healing of the man born blind (John 9:1-7), the raising of Lazarus (John 11:1-44), the miraculous catch of fish (John 21:1-11), and possibly the walking on water (John 6:16-21).

2. The discourse on the Son (John 5:10-47), the discourse on the bread of life (John 6:22-65), a dialogue with the Pharisees (John 3:8-48). In the account of the raising of Lazarus, elements of the discourse on the "resurrection and life" are intermingled with the narrative elements in John 11:1-44.

optics consider the miracles as acts of power, *dunameis*. The Synoptics offer a fair number of exorcisms among their miracle stories — indeed the exorcisms effected by Jesus are, in a general fashion, to be classified among the events in the earthly life of Jesus of Nazareth most easily certifiable as "historical" — yet John offers not a single story of an exorcism within the twenty-one chapters of his Gospel. This may well be due to his eschatological vision. Stories of exorcism seem more appropriate within the context of consequent eschatology than they do within the Johannine context of a realized eschatology. On the other hand, John tells the story of water turned into wine during a marriage feast at Cana in Galilee, a tale for which no real parallel exists in the Synoptic tradition.

In fact the story of water-become-wine stands out among the Gospel accounts of Jesus' nature miracles. Altogether there are seven such nature miracles narrated in the four Gospels: the stilling of the storm (Matt 8:23-27; Mark 4:35-41; Luke 8:22-25), the multiplication of loaves (Matt 14:13-21; 15:32-39; Mark 6:32-44; 8:1-10; Luke 9:10-17; John 6:1-15), Jesus walking on water (Matt 14:22-23; Mark 6:45-52; John 6:16-21), the cursing of the fig tree (Matt 21:18-20; Mark 11:12-14, 20-21), a miraculous catch of fish (Luke 5:1-11; John 21:1-11), the finding of the temple tax (Matt 17:24-27), and the Johannine tale of water-become-wine at Cana of Galilee (John 2:1-12). Each of these stories is problematic in its own way, yet a common theme seems to run through them all. It is that Jesus ministers to man in his need. An exception must, of course, be made for the story of the withered fig tree but that account as found in Matthew and Mark, may well be a narrative development of the parable found in Luke 13:6-9.

One form of ministering to man in need must, however, be distinguished from another form of ministering to man in need. It is one thing for Jesus to secure safety for those threatened by a serious storm or for him to provide food for those who are hungry; it is quite another thing for him to provide six times 20

to 30 gallons of wine (John 2:6),[2a] the approximative equivalent
of 640 to 960 bottles of wine, for guests at a wedding feast. Does
the provision of such an abundance of wine bespeak the Redeemer's
ministering to his people in need? Or does the author of the
Fourth Gospel have something else in mind as he tells the story
of water-become-wine?

To put the question into its proper context, the reader of the
gospels must be aware that Jesus' nature miracles are generally
told so as to illustrate a truth more profound than the simple fact
that the historical Jesus of Nazareth was a thaumaturge. Thus the
narrative of the multiplication of loaves (John 6:1-15 and par.) is
told in such wise as to be an instruction on the Eucharist.[3] The
Markan story of the stilling of the storm (Mark 4:35-41) has
become a lesson on discipleship according to the Matthean
version (Matt 8:23-27).[4] The miraculous catch of fish ultimately
becomes something of a dramatic parable insofar as it is narrated
by both Luke and John in order to highlight the function of Peter
in the early Church. In a word it may be said that the Gospel
accounts of Jesus' nature miracles are full of symbolism. This is
not to deny, nor is it to affirm without further examination, the
historical foundation on which a miracle story is grounded. It is
simply to state that in their present gospel context Jesus's nature
miracles are narrated with respect to their capacity to symbolize.
Should we expect anything different in John's account of the
water-become-wine? Not only because the tale of water-become-
wine is so singularly different by reason of its non-redemptive
character, but also because the Fourth Evangelist is so prone to
use symbolism in the development of his narrative, it would seem
that we might look principally to a symbolic function of the first

---

2a. Cf. J. Villescas, "John 2:6: The capacity of the six jars," *BT* 28 (1977) 447.

3. The eucharistic symbolism is more apparent in the Johannine narrative than
it is in the five synoptic accounts (Matt 14:13-21; 15:32-39; Mark 6:32-44; 8:1-
10; Luke 9:10-17). However there is no doubt that eucharistic symbolism also
shaped the Synoptics' accounts of the multiplication of loaves.

4. Cf. Heinz Joachim Held, "Matthew as Interpreter of the Miracle Stories," in
G. Bornkamm, G. Barth, H.J. Held, *Tradition and Interpretation in Matthew*
(London: SCM, 1963) pp. 165-300, pp. 200-299.

miracle of Cana if we are to understand the role which that miracle plays within the total context of the Johannine account. My claim is that the account of the water-become-wine is the key to the Johannine signs just as much as it is the first of Jesus' miracles.

To begin our reflection on the significance of the account, we might briefly touch upon three points which, I believe, represent something of the consensus opinion of current scholarship on the Cana story.[5] First of all, John 2:1-12 is characteristically Johannine. Secondly, the primary meaning of the pericope is christological. Thirdly, the account must be understood against an Old Testament background. To each of these thoughts we can turn our attention for just a moment.

John 2:1-12 is characteristically Johannine. Despite the fact that the story of the water-become-wine was taken over by the evangelist from his signs-source,[6] the present redaction of John 2:1-12 bears a distinctively Johannine stamp. Despite the singularity of its content, the Johannine account makes abundant use of typical Johannine vocabulary: *hōra* (hour), *Ioudaioi* (the Jews), *pisteuein* (to believe), *doxa* (doxa), *sēmeion* (sign), etc. In typical fashion, the evangelist has introduced into his account examples of Johannine symbolism: the "hour," "the mother of Jesus," "the wine." Elements of Johannine style and the use of typically Johannine literary techniques offer further evidence of the evangelist's redactional activity. We find his narrative introduced by an expression of time (v. 1), making use of dialogue throughout, employing the interrogation (v. 4), incorporating a "Johannine note" (vv. 6, 9) and adding both a "Johannine comment" (v. 11) and a transitional verse (v. 12). Finally we must take note of the

5. Cf. Raymond F. Collins, "Mary in the Fourth Gospel. A decade of Johannine Studies," *LS* 3 (1970-1971) 99-142, p. 117.

6. Cf. Rudolf Bultmann, *The Gospel of John. A Commentary* (Oxford: Basil Blackwell, 1971) p. 113; Robert T. Fortna, *The Gospel of Signs*. SNTSMS, 11 (Cambridge: University Press, 1970) pp. 29-38. A brief examination of recent literature on the issue is given by Gilbert Van Belle, *De Semeia-bron in het Vierde Evangelie. Onstaan en groei van een hypothese* (Louvain: University Press, 1975) pp. 59-65.

placement of the account at the beginning of Jesus' public ministry. This placement serves to guarantee the paradigmatic nature of the miracle story.

A second point of agreement among contemporary exegetes is that the primary meaning of the account is christological. The evangelist tells us as much in John 2:11: "This the first of his signs, Jesus did at Cana in Galilee, and manifested his glory, and his disciples believed in him." Nevertheless earlier generations of scholars were wont to exploit John 2:1-12 for its Marian[7] or sacramental[8] significance. Even Ceslaus Spicq,[9] who points to Mary's intercession as occasioning the miracle and draws from that intercession the notion that Mary is the *omnipotentia supplex*, considers that John 2:1-12 is of primary importance for the christology of the Fourth Gospel insofar as the miracle reveals Jesus' true nature and serves as a first indication that he is the Incarnate Word of God. Spicq is perhaps pressing the point too far. The christology of the story of water-become-wine would seem to be more functional than ontological. The Johannine account shows Jesus as the giver of the messianic gifts much more clearly than it points to him as the Incarnate Word.

A further point which merits the assent of most contemporary students of the Fourth Gospel is that John 2:1-12 must be

7. As examples, we can cite C.M. Henze, "Quid mihi et tibi, Mulier? Nondum venit hora mea (Io. 2,4)," *Marianum* 23 (1961) 471-479; M.B. Eyquem, "La foi de Marie et les noces de Cana," *Vie Spirituelle* 117 (1967) 169-181.

8. Among contemporary authors who make an exegesis of the passage in a sacramental sense are Oscar Cullmann, Mathias Rissi and André Feuillet. Cf. Oscar Cullmann, *Early Christian Worship*. SBT, 10 (London: SCM, 1953) 66-71; Mathias Rissi, "Die Hochzeit in Kana" (Joh. 2, 1-11), in F. Christ, ed., *Oikonomia. Heilsgeschichte als Thema der Theologie*. Cullmann *Festschrift* (Hamburg: Reich, 1967) pp. 76-92, esp. pp. 80-81, 91; André Feuillet, "The Hour of Jesus and the Sign of Cana," in *Johannine Studies* (Staten Island, NY: Alba House, 1964) pp. 19-37. The two principal commentaries on the Fourth Gospel written by Catholics in recent years, however, take issue with this position. Cf. Raymond E. Brown, *The Gospel According to John. I-XII*. AB, 29 (Garden City NY: Doubleday, 1966) pp. 109-110; Rudolf Schnackenberg, *The Gospel According to St. John*, 1 (New York: Herder, 1968) pp. 338-339.

9. Ceslaus Spicq, "Il primo miracolo di Gesù dovuto a sua Madre (Giov. 2,1-11)," *Sacra Doctrina* 18 (1973) 125-144.

studied in the light of its Old Testament background, which provides the key to the symbolism of the passage. As the significance of its biblical background is more firmly emphasized, Bultmann's theory that the essential motif of the story is borrowed from the Dionysius legend[10] is proportionately relativized. Similarly the emphasis on the shaping influence of Old Testament tradition allows Murtonen's thesis[11] to recede somewhat into the background. Murtonen claims that the story of Cana was told as the tale of a communal meal in which Jesus and his family played the important role. He contends that the original tale was told in Aramaic. Translated into Greek at the moment of its transition into the Hellenistic world, the Cana story was told in such a way that the activity became miraculous and Jesus became a *theios anēr*, a "divine man."

One further point needs to be considered briefly. That is the structure of the narrative. Verses 1-8 do not seem to correlate well with what follows. The initial narrative bears upon the quantity of wine (vv. 1-8), whereas Jesus' dialogue with the steward of the feast bears upon the quality of the wine (vv. 9-10). It is quite likely, then, that we are dealing with a composite narrative. A parable has been appended to a miracle story.[12] Moreover it would appear that the verses with which the narrative concludes, i.e., vv. 11-12, do not correlate well with one another. The "Johannine comment" in v. 11 is a fitting conclusion to the entire narrative. Undoubtedly it represents a Johannine adaptation of a tradition contained in the signs-

10. Cf. Rudolf Bultmann, *John,* pp. 118-119. C.H. Dodd also cites the pagan parallels to the Cana story. Cf. C.H. Dodd, *Historical Tradition in the Fourth Gospel* (Cambridge: University Press, 1963) pp. 224-225.

11. Cf. A. Murtonen, "'Wedding at Cana,' On Comparative Socio-Linguistic Background," *Milla wa-Milla* 14 (1974) 32-36.

12. Cf. Barnabas Lindars, "Two Parables in John," *NTS* 16 (1969-1970) 318-329. Lindars speaks of a "relic of an authentic parable of Jesus" (p. 319) and of a parable derived from traditions of the words of Jesus (p. 320). It is a Johannine creation rather than a traditional proverb incorporated into the narrative. Cf. R.F. Collins, "Mary," p. 125.

source.[13] The source mentioned the first of the signs (John 2:11a)[14] and the evangelist added the thought that Jesus manifested his glory and his disciples believed in him (John 2:11b-c). By reason of this first conclusion, v. 12 seems rather superfluous. It is also a little bit out of character insofar as it introduces the "brothers" of Jesus who have not thus far been cited in the Johannine narrative. Indeed they do not make another appearance until John 7:3. Certain textual difficulties have led some authors to the conclusion that at one stage of the tradition both John 2:2 and John 2:12 originally spoke of but Jesus and his brothers.[15] Subsequently, "disciples" would have been substituted for "brothers" in v. 2 and would have been added to the tradition in v. 12. Accordingly John 2:12 would have been the more primitive conclusion of the pericope, John 2:11b-c being added at a later stage in the development of the tradition. To sum up, the structure of the narrative is basically that of a miracle story (vv. 1-8) plus a parable (vv. 9-10) plus a late Johannine comment (v. 11(a)b-c) plus a transitional verse based on an earlier conclusion of the narrative (v. 12).

In point of fact the narrative seems to betray a certain evidence of tradition and redaction throughout. The miracle story (vv. 1-8) bears traces of the characteristics of oral tradition to which form critics so readily point. The account of the water-become-wine is narrated according to the traditional three-part schema characteristic of a miracle story: (1) the difficult situation (v. 3), (2) the stylized command (v. 7), and (3) an attestation of the effect of the miracle (v. 8 whose natural sequence has been replaced by the parable of vv. 9-10). The law of stage duality, so characteristic of the story teller's art, is maintained throughout the narrative. In four successive scenes only two characters occupy the narrator's

13. Cf. B. Lindars, "Two Parables," p. 322; R.T. Fortna, *Gospel of Signs*, pp. 34-37.

14. Cf. John 4:54.

15. Cf. Julius Wellhausen, *Das Evangelium Johannis* (Berlin: Reimer, 1908) pp. 13-14; Rudolf Bultmann, *John*, p. 114; Barnabas Lindars, *The Gospel of John*, New Century Bible (London: Oliphants, 1972) pp. 128, 132-133.

attention and thus appear "on stage." There is the mother of Jesus and Jesus himself (vv. 3-4), the mother and the servants (vv. 5-6), Jesus and the servants (vv. 7-8), the steward and the bridegroom (vv. 9-10). In the succession of these little scenes, we see the Johannine drama develop before our eyes. It is characteristic of John's technique of composition to create a dramatic effect by placing one little scene after another.[16] However the fourth little scene (vv. 9-10) disturbs the dramatic sequence in that neither of the two characters who, so to speak, appear on stage appeared in the immediately preceding scene. We have Jesus and his mother, the mother and the servants, the servants and Jesus, and then the steward and the bridegroom. The broken dramatic sequance might well be another indication that the material of vv. 9-10 has come from another source. It confirms our earlier suggestion that a parable has been appended to a miracle story.

The miracle is situated at a marriage in Cana of Galilee. As with other Gospel stories, the author's attention is on the wedding feast rather than the wedding itself. Here as elsewhere,[17] the bride is nowhere to be found. By locating the wedding feast at Cana in Galilee, the evangelist links this first of Jesus' signs with the second sign, the cure of the royal official's son which likewise took place at Cana in Galilee (John 4:46-54). By locating the wedding feast "on the third day" (v. 1), the evangelist completes the programmatic week with which he begins his Gospel.[17a] He begins his week with the double scrutiny of John the Witness (John 1:19-28), the next day there is the testimony of John (John 1:29-34), the next day the encounter between two unnamed disciples and Jesus as well as the meeting between Jesus and Peter (John 1:35-42), on the next day follows the finding of Philip and

16. Cf. J. Louis Martyn, *History and Theology in the Fourth Gospel* (New York: Harper and Row, 1968) pp. 3-16, 49-57.

17. Cf. Matt 22:1-14; 25:1-13.

17a. For another suggestion as to the significance at the "third day," cf. F. Manns, "Le troisième jour il y eut des noces à Cana," *Marianum* 80 (1978) 160-163.

Nathanael (John 1:43-51), and on the third day a wedding takes place in Cana of Galilee. The geographical setting is not integral to the significance of the miracle. Mention of Cana simply betrays the author's use of a source, the so-called signs-source, and adds a little verve and realism to the narrative. The temporal setting is, however, significant for an understanding of the miracle. The evangelist sets the narrative in the context of the "initial week" of the public ministry, a week which sets a tone for the entire Gospel narrative.

Invited to the wedding, Mary appears as the spokesperson who elucidates the situation. John does not call her by name. Rather here as in John 19:25-27, the evangelist refers to Mary as "the mother of Jesus." The expression is Johannine[18] and not without its significance.[19] Her announcement that "They have no wine" has been variously interpreted by the commentators.[20] Some see it as a request for a miracle; others observe that her words serve but to characterize the situation. In fact the ambiguous nature of Mary's announcement is but the first ambiguity in the conversation between her and Jesus. Jesus' response (v. 4) seems to indicate that he will not perform a miracle. Immediately there follows both the order given to the servants by the mother of Jesus and the performance of the miracle itself. The difficulty of interpreting the narrative at this point has given rise to an opinion among some exegetes to the effect that John 2:3b-4 is a later addition to the tradition of the miracle at Cana in Galilee.[21] When the text is read without these verses, v. 5 follows immediately upon v. 3a. There is logical consistency in a text which would then have read: "When the wine failed, his mother said to the servants ..." Without verses 3b-4, the difficulties inherent in a passage which has been described as "one of the thorniest problems

18. Cf. Joachim Jeremias, "Johanneische Literarkritik," *TBl* 20 (1941) 33-46, p. 35; Eugen Ruchstuhl, *Die Literarische Einheit des Johannesevangeliums*, Studia Friburgensia, N.S. 3 (Freiburg: Paulusverlag, 1951) p. 204.

19. Cf. E.J. Kilmartin, "The Mother of Jesus was there. (The Significance of Mary in John 2:3-5 and John 19:25-27)," *ScEccl* 15 (1963) 213-226, p. 214.

20. Cf. R.F. Collins, "Mary," pp. 122-123.

21. Thus R.T. Fortna, *Gospel of Signs*, pp. 30-32.

facing the interpreter"[22] disappear. We have a relatively simple story of a nature miracle. While it may well be useful to observe that vv. 3b-4 were added to the tradition of the water-made-wine story at a later date, it also behooves the commentator to interpret the text as it now stands. No amount of fanciful speculation or even of well-grounded hypothesizing can allow the exegete to forgo an explanation of the text as it lies before us.[23]

The meaning of the troublesome text hinges upon the interpretation of the question "O woman, what have you to do with me?" The interrogation is an important literary device employed in the composition of the Fourth Gospel.[24] In John 2:4, Mary's words hark back to a formula employed in the Septuagint to render the Hebrew expression *mah-li wālāk*. The Greek version, *ti emoi kai soi*, poses a real question whose real meaning is "what relationship between you and me is the determining one in the present circumstances?" Of itself the interrogative phrase simply poses the question of relationship; it is the circumstances of the question which determine the connotation of the expression.[25] When the question is posed in a hostile context or in unpleasant circumstances it is tantamount to "what have you got to do with me?," implying estrangement and a refusal of cooperation.[26] When the question is posed in situations of particular friendship and in a context of some intimacy, it is indicative of a bond which binds two people together.[27] Those who interpret the

22. E.L. Titus, *The Message of the Fourth Gospel* (New York: Abingdon, 1957) p. 229.

23. Cf. C.H. Dodd who writes, "I conceive it to be the duty of an interpreter at least to see what can be come with the document as it has come down to us before attempting to improve upon it... I shall assume as a provisional working hypothesis that the present order is not fortuitous, but deliberately devised by someone—even if he were only a scribe doing his best—and that the person in question (whether the author or another) had some design in mind, and was not necessarily irresponsible or unintelligent." C.H. Dodd, *The Historical Interpretation of the Fourth Gospel* (Cambridge: University Press, 1963) p. 290.

24. Cf. Albert Vanhoye, "Interrogation johannique et exégèse de Cana (Jean. 2,4)," *Bib* 55 (1974) 152-167; esp. pp. 157-158.

25. Cf. A. Vanhoye, "Interrogation," pp. 162-163.

26. Cf. Josh 22:24-25; 1 Kgs 17:18; 2 Kgs 3:13; 2 Sam 16:10; 19:23.

27. Cf. Jugd 11:12.

Johannine question as if it implied a refusal of Jesus to cooperate with his mother are troubled by a postponement of their exegetical problem. Jesus does not, in fact, refuse to perform the miracle; in fact the water does become wine. Those exegetes who interpret the question as an indication of a positive bond between Jesus and his mother locate the *crux interpretum* in "My hour has not yet come." What is the significance of the phrase if Jesus' relationship with his mother is such that his determination is to effect a miracle? In these circumstances, it seems preferable to let the text speak for itself without prejudgement as to its connotation. The question is a simple interrogation, "What is our relationship?," "What is the determining relationship in the present circumstances?"

Authors who take "What have you to do with me?" as a question which implies a refusal, find confirmation of their interpretation in the statement which follows it in John 2:4, namely, "My hour has not yet come." The question and affirmation point to some distance between Jesus and his mother. He will not heed even her implicit request for a miracle. How then can the fact of the miracle's being performed be explained? Those who opt for a Marian interpretation of the pericope have recourse to some theory of Mary's intercessory power.[28] Those who propose that John 2:3b-4 is an addition to the tradition have recourse to the notion that the seeming contradiction did not belong to an earlier strata of the tradition of the water-becomes-wine. Given Dodd's apropos reminder that it is the text which lies before us for which an explanation must be offered, it seems preferable to look in another direction for an understanding of "My hour has not yet come."[29]

---

28. Among others authors, the reader might refer to A. Brunner, "Was er sagen, das tut (Joh. 2:5)," *Geist und Leben* 34 (1961) 81-84, p. 84; S. Hartdegen, "The Marian Significance of Cana (John 2:1-11)," *Marian Studies* 11 (1960) 85-103; E.J. Kilmartin, "The Mother of Jesus," pp. 221-222; C. Spicq, "Il primo miraculo," A Vaccari, "Maria Virgo et nuptiae in Cana Galilaeae. Elementa eucharistica et ecclesiologica huius miraculi," *Maria et Ecclesia*, 8 (Rome: International Pontifical Marian Academy, 1960) pp. 53-63, esp. p. 59.

29. It may well be that John 2:3b-4 is a later addition to the tradition. It is,

In the Greek text of the manuscript tradition, there was no punctuation. Affirmations and interrogations were written in similar fashion. The context provided the clue as the meaning of the sentence. Is it not possible, therefore, to take "My hour has not yet come" as a question to be rendered "Has not my hour yet come?" (= "Isn't this my hour?"). Such an interpretation would go contrary to the punctuation offered by the editors of the most popular Greek editions[30] of the New Testament as well as by several commentators on the Fourth Gospel.[31] However there seem to be substantial reasons for interpreting "Hasn't my hour come?" as a question inviting a positive response.[32] First of all, some Patristic witness is in favor of interpreting the saying as an interrogation. Tatian's Diatesseron, Gregory of Nyssa, Theodore of Mopsuestia, and Ephraem, the Syrian deacon, so interpret the text. Secondly, in the New Testament when *oupō* ("not yet") follows a question it introduces a second question. Thirdly, although *oupō* is normally used in affirmations in the Fourth Gospel—whence the opinion of those who would render the statement "My hour has not yet come"—*oupō* is always used with a connecting participle. John 2:4 is the only example of John's use of *oupō* in a statement marked by asyndeton. Fourthly, a double question is characteristic of the Fourth Gospel's literary style.[33] Finally, a negative interrogation normally looks for a positive response. Thus, the reading of John 2:4c as a question seems to fit the context better than does the RSV's affirmation, "My hour has not yet come." Taken from this perspective, Jesus' double question to his mother may be thus

however, the presence of these troublesome verses in the present text of the narrative which must be explained.

30. *The Greek New Testament* edited by the United Bible Societies, and *Novum Testamentum Graece* edited by Kurt Aland, *et al*.

31. e.g. R.E. Brown, *John. I-XII*, p. 99; R. Schnackenburg, *John*, pp. 328-329.

32. My argumentation is similar to, but an expansion of, the argumentation advanced by Vanhoye ("Interrogation," pp. 159-160).

33. John 1:21; 3:4, 4:11-12, 27; 6:30, 42; 7:35, 41-42, 47; 8:46; 9:19, 26, 27; 11:56; 12:27, 34; 20:15.

paraphrased: "Woman, what is the nature of our relationship? Isn't this my hour?"

Phrased even in this fashion, Jesus' double question makes use of symbolic language. In particular, as I have noted earlier in this essay, we must pay attention to the pregnant meaning of two Johannine terms: "woman" and "hour." In context, the vocative *gunai* appears rather unusual. A Palestinian son, when addressing his mother, would normally use the Aramaic expression *imma* which would be equivalent to the Greek *kurie*. It is true that there is nothing disdainful or pejorative attaching to the word *gunai*, but it is also true that no biblical or classical text gives any indication that a son would address his mother as *gunai*, "women." Yet John uses the expression here, and again in 19:26, in Jesus' address to his mother. Might not his usage be an indication that Mary is to be seen in a perspective other than that of her maternal relationship with Jesus? In other words, should we not, by preference, consider that Mary has a symbolic function to play in the present narrative.[34] Is not her role a representative one rather than an individual one? Does not Mary symbolize those who faithfully await the fulfillment of the Messianic times?

That we must look to the fulfillment of the Messianic times is suggested by the other symbolic expression which the evangelist uses in v. 4, namely *hōra*, hour. In the fullest theological sense of the word, there is but one hour of Jesus in the Fourth Gospel. That is the hour of his crucifixion-glorification. Although there are a few Johannine uses of "hour" with a rather common, ordinary meaning, John normally uses the term in reference to the supreme act of Jesus' self-revelation on the cross. This is particularly true, when "hour" is qualified—by the article (John 12:23; 17:1), a demonstrative adjective (John 12:27 (2 ×); 19:27), or a demonstrative pronoun (John 7:30; 8:20, 31 and 2:4). The hour of Jesus is his hour *par excellence*, i.e., the hour of

---

34. Cf. Raymond F. Collins, "The Representative Figures of the Fourth Gospel" *DR* 94 (1976) 26-46, 118-132, pp. 120-122; in this volume, pp. 30-33.

his self-revelation and his glorification by the Father. A rapid comparison of John 2:4 with John 7:30 and 8:20 confirms that this is indeed the hour to which Jesus is making reference in the second question of John 2:4.

Commentators increasingly interpret the "hour" of John 2:4 in reference to the hour of Jesus' crucifixion-glorification, but many are inclined to find in this identification a further reason to suggest that *oupō ekei hē hōra mou* is to be rendered as an affirmation: "My hour (i.e., the hour of the crucifixion-glorification) has not yet come." The exegetical problem to which these authors respond by interpreting the second question as an affirmation can be otherwise responded to when the Cana narrative (John 2:1-12) is taken as a paradigmatic narrative rather than simply as the first in a sequence of narratives. The original miracle story (without vv. 3b-4) would have been the first in a sequence. By adding "the mother of Jesus said to him, 'They have no wine.' And Jesus said to her, 'O woman, what have you to do with me? Hasn't my hour come?,'" the evangelist provides his readers with a clue as to how the water-become-wine narrative is to be understood. For him the water-become-wine story is pregnant with the significance of all the signs of Jesus. The evangelist has put the entire gospel, and especially his account of the "signs" of Jesus, in a definite perspective. That perspective is the "hour" of Jesus. In the hour of Jesus' crucifixion-glorification a gift is given to those who faithfully await the Messianic times.

To view John 3b-4 as a interpretive Johannine addition to the tradition helps to elucidate the meaning of the entire pericope. First of all, we would note that Mary's "They have no wine" loses some of its superfluousness when vv. 3b-4 are viewed as an addition to the tradition. Rather than being redundant with v. 3a, her words establish the contrast between the time in which there is "no wine" and the hour of Jesus. A contrast between two times is also implied by v. 10 which, as we have suggested, is also an appendage to the original miracle story. Secondly, the thought that vv. 3b-4 are a Johannine addition to the tradition allows for an easier correlation with John 19:25-27. This is to say that the evangelist has added vv. 3b-4 to his tradition precisely so that the signs of Jesus might be interpreted in the light of the salvific and revelatory event par excellence, the crucifixion-exaltation of Jesus. The similarity of language between the passion scene in 19:25-27 and the interpretive addition in 2:3b-4 provides a clear indication that the evangelist wants his readers to think of the crucifixion-exaltation as they read the story of the water-become-wine. Finally, the notion that the evangelist has used an addition to the tradition in order to give a symbolic meaning to his text means that he has relegated the material content of his tradition to a place of lesser importance. It is not the quantity of wine which impressed him, and which ought to impress us. It is rather the significance which the evangelist has imposed on his tradition, whatever its origin, which must occupy the attention of the discerning reader of the Fourth Gospel.

What is it that the evangelist would have us understand in the light of the crucifixion-glorification — an ancient tale of a family wedding (even an ancient tale of Jesus attending a family wedding),[35] a communal banquet in which Jesus and his family played an important role, or an ancient myth quite common in the history of religions? To interpret the text with principal reference to one or another of these suggestions as to the origin of the Cana tradition is to overlook two significant details of the pericope. These are traditional motifs whose symbolic meaning could not have escaped the Johannine audience. First of all, the miracle of water-become-wine is situated within the context of a wedding feast: "There was a marriage at Cana in Galilee ... Jesus also was invited to the marriage ..." (vv. 1-2). Israel's biblical tradition had long used nuptial imagery in reference to the relationship between Yahweh and Israel.[36] The same imagery was

---

35. That such a tradition should have circulated in the early Johannine church is not unlikely in view of the Johannine characterization of Jesus as a rabbi (John 1:38, etc.). A rather familiar motif in the Talmudic and other rabbinic literature is that of the presence of a rabbi at a wedding.

36. Exod 34:10-16; Deut 5:2-10; Isa 54:5; Jer 2:2; 11:15; Ezek 16:8-13; Hos 1:2-9; 2:4-25.

used in the biblical tradition to connote the realization and beatitude of the messianic era.[37]

The Synoptic tradition has made use of this very tradition in the parable of the great supper which has become the parable of a marriage feast in Matthew's version of that story (Matt 22:1-14) taken over from the Q tradition,[38] as well as in Matthew's parable of the ten virgins (Matt 25:1-13). Each of these Matthean parables narrates the story of a wedding feast without mention of the presence of the bride. The Johannine story of water-become-wine at Cana in Galilee represents a Johannine version of the traditional nuptial imagery in order to describe the eschatological era, the era of salvation definitively accomplished. The traditional motif, as adapted by the Johannine tradition and applied to Jesus, recurs again in John 3:29, where Jesus is described as a bridegroom.[39] In neither of these Johannine uses of the traditional motif is the bride specifically mentioned. Another late New testament author to make use of the Jesus-bridegroom motif is the author of the letter to the Ephesians. He has incorporated the so-called "Romance of Christ"[40] into his text at Eph 5:25-27 and has there identified the Church as the bride of Christ. Given this widespread indication of New Testament use of traditional nuptial imagery in order to describe the eschatological era, it is difficult to escape the conclusion that John is also making use of this imagery in 2:1-12 and that it is the eschatological messianic era as such upon which he is offering his reflections.[41]

The second traditional symbolic motif which occurs in the Cana story is that of the wine. The mother of Jesus' poignant

37. Isa 54:4-5; 62:5; Hos 2:4-25; Jer 3:29.

38. Cf. Luke 14:15-24.

39. The shifting of the characterization of the Cana account (cf. *infra*) suggests that the theme of Jesus-bridegroom is not far removed from the present redaction of John 2:1-12.

40. Cf. Markus Barth. *Ephesians. 4-6. AB*, 34A (Garden City, NY: Doubleday, 1974) p. 624.

41. Lindars styles this eschatological era, "the new order which is inaugurated by the coming of Jesus." Cf. B. Lindars, "Two Parables," p. 318; *John*, p. 133.

announcement in v. 3: "They have no wine" already points in the
direction of the element which will become the focal point in the
narrative. In similar fashion the words of the steward in v. 10
draw the reader's attention to the wine. Wine is, however, a
traditional symbol. The prophetic tradition had used wine to
symbolize the messianic blessings.[42] Israel's wisdom and apocalytic
traditions utilized the same imagery. Wine was among God's gifts
to man.[43] An abundance of wine symbolized the abundance,
indeed extravagance, of God's gift to man. Thus the apocalyptic
tradition particularly utilized wine imagery to denote the abundance
of Yahweh's blessings upon his people in the eschatological-
messianic era.[44] Within this perspective it is clear that the Johannine narrative shows that Jesus is the one who provides the gifts
of the messianic era. It is probably unnecessary to attempt to be
more specific and see in the wine, as some authors do, a symbol
of the joy of the messianic times, or the gift of the Spirit, or the
sacrament of the eucharist. Further examination of the pericope
may well point to one or another of these gifts as principal
among the gifts of the messianic era but a general interpretation
of the wine as a symbol of the blessings of the messianic era[45]
seems to represent best the idea that the evangelist is trying to
convey to his readers.

From the context it is clear that it is only Jesus who can
provide the gift which an expectant people, symbolized by Mary,
awaits. The ancient miracle story of John's tradition serves to
contrast Jesus' gift with the water which the stewards draw.[46] In
the dialogue with the Samaritan (John 4:1-15) the evangelist
again contrasts water which is drawn (John 4:7, 11, 15) with the
gift of God, the living water which Jesus alone can give (John

---

42. Cf. Amos 9:13; Hos 2:24; Joel 4:18; Isa 25:6; 29:17; Jer 31:5.

43. Cf. Ps 104:15.

44. *Enoch* 10:19; *Apoc. Bar.* 29:5; *Sib.Or.* 2:317-318; 3:620-624; 744-745.

45. In the ancient blessing of Jacob the gift of wine is characteristic of the
Messiah from Judah. Cf. Gen 49:11-12.

46. The use of the verb *antleō* ("to draw," vv. 8,9) indicates that the narrative
speaks of fresh, running water. Cf. F.S. Parnham, "The Miracle of Cana," *EvQ* 42
(1970) 107-109.

4:10). In John 7:37-39 the evangelist returns to the gift of the living water. An adapted use of Isa 58:11[47] allows him to affirm once again that the living water is Jesus' gift to those who believe in him. Then, in John 7:37-39, however, the evangelist specifies in a sort of typical Johannine note that the gift of living water is, in fact, the gift of the Spirit. Moreover he notes that the Spirit is not given until Jesus is glorified, i.e., until the hour of Jesus exaltation-glorification has been accomplished.

In his description of the Cana miracle the evangelist does not specify[48] so accurately the gift which Jesus gives in his "hour" (v. 4). The gift is simply described as wine, symbolic of the gifts of messianic times. It is, as we have already noted, wine which serves as the focal point of the narrative. Jesus is the one who gives the wine to those who are without wine (v. 4). Instead of commenting on the quantity of wine which Jesus offers to the woman, the evangelist comments upon its reality as wine and its quality. At the risk of mixing metaphors, John comments upon the fact that wine has been given to replace water with the notion that good wine has replaced poor wine. The contrast is underscored,[49] even though the imagery has been changed. This contrast points to one of the underlying motifs of the Johannine account. In v. 6 the evangelist had noted that "Six stone jars were

47. John 7:37 is not an exact citation of Isa 58:11, the reference given in the text of the United Bible Societies' *The Greek New Testament*. Most probably John 7:37 is a conflated or general reference to an Old Testament text. For a discussion of the issue, cf. F.-M. Braun, *Jean le Théologien*, 2. EBib (Paris: Gabalda, 1964) pp. 15-21, esp. pp. 16-17.

48. I concur wholeheartedly with Schnackenburg's suggestion that: "One would be well-advised, ... not to look for any special symbolic meaning, and to see under the many images of water (vf. 4:10, 14; 7:37f.; 6:35b), bread, wine, of Christ as shepherd, vine, etc., the comprehensive gift of divine life or the Holy Spirit, as promised constantly by the Johannine Jesus (3:16, 18, 36; 5:24; 6:40 etc.). Eschatological salvation is always present in Christ, whatever the form under which it is bestowed." R. Schnackenburg, *John*, 1, p. 339. Cf. also R. Bultmann, *John*, p. 120.

49. The contrast is also implied in the "new wine into old wineskins" tradition of Mark 2:22 (par. Matt 9:17; Luke 5:37-38). It is explicitly found in an additional saying of Luke 5:39, "And no one after drinking old wine desires new; for he says, 'The old wine is good.'"

standing there, for the Jewish rites of purification, each holding twenty or thirty gallons." The Greek text literally reads "two or three measures (*metrētas duo ē treis*)." The "measure", *metrē*, is undoubtedly the Hebrew *bat*, a unit of approximately nine gallons (35 liters). The jars are specifically identified as "stone" jars (*lithinai hudriai*), precisely because jars of porous material would easily incur contamination. They would consequently be unsuitable as vessels to be used in purification rites. In contrast, vessels made of stone do not contract ritual contamination.[50] The qualification of the jars as stone vessels should, therefore, render John's comment about their being placed there "for the Jewish rites of purification" superfluous were it not for the fact that John wanted explicitly to contrast the gift of Jesus with the running waters used in the Jewish rites of purification. In sum, from the standpoint of Johannine symbolism, the water-become-wine symbolizes the replacement of Jewish rites of purification,[51] by the gifts of the messianic era which Jesus has brought.

In this fashion the evangelist has presented his Cana account in such a way as to proclaim a theme which runs throughout the Book of Signs (John 1:1-12), namely, that Jesus has come to replace the institutions of Judaism.[52] The temple is replaced by the risen body of Jesus (John 2:13-22). The rabbinate is replaced by the only teacher who came from heaven (John 3:1-15). The account of Jesus and the Samaritan announces that worship in spirit and truth (John 4:23) replaces both Samaritan worship on

50. In the Mishnah, the Tractates *Yadaim* ("Hands") and *Kelim* ("Vessels") speak of stone vessels. Cf. *Miyad* 1:2; *Kelim* 10:1. Stone vessels are also cited in the Babylonian Talmud *b. Sabb.* 96a) and in Maimonides' commentary on *Kelim* 10:1. Additional references are provided by H.L. Strack and Paul Billerbeck in *Kommentar zum Neuen Testament aus Talmud und Midrash*, 2 (Munich: Beck, 1965) 406-407.

51. The inadequacy of these rites is indicated by the evangelists notation that there were six stone jars. Six, i.e., seven (the number of perfection) minus one, is a symbol of imperfection.

52. Cf. Raymond E. Brown, *John. I-XII*, p. lxx, who writes that the outline of John 1-12 "shows the importance of the theme of Jesus' replacement of Jewish institutions." With specific reference to John 2:1-11 one might consult D. Toussaint, "The Significance of the First Sign in John's Gospel," *BSac* 134 (1977) 45-51.

Mount Gerizim and Jewish worship in Jerusalem. The sabbath rest gives way to the work of Jesus (John 5:9, 17; cf. 9:14). The manna come down from heaven is replaced by the bread of life. The lights of the feast of the Dedication give way to him who is the light of the world (John 9:5). Even the allegory of the sheepfold (John 10) might refer back to the temple[53] rendered virtually useless by the coming of Jesus.

The author of the prologue enunciated this all pervasive theme of the Fourth Gospel in vv. 16-17: "grace in place of grace."[54] For the law was given through Moses; "grace and truth came through Jesus Christ." The words of the prologue serve as something of a commentary upon the body of the Gospel. They provide a hermeneutical key for the chapters which follow. Although the prologue was probably added to the Gospel at a later stage of the tradition by a hand which is most likely not that of the evangelist himself, the words of vv. 16-17 make us realize that the replacement of the institutions of Judaism was considered to be one of the principal themes of the fourth evangelist by one of its earliest commentators. "Grace in place of grace" enunciates the theme; the story of water-become-wine serves as the first dramatic presentation of the theme. In this respect the Cana story is programmatic for the entire Gospel.

In v. 10, the steward functions as a spokesperson to contrast the wine of the messianic era with that which the people had previously enjoyed. He does not state that they had nothing—in this respect the mother's interpretative comment in v. 3, "They have no wine" appears almost to be an overstatement of the

53. Cf. A.J. Simonis, *Die Hirtenrede im Johannesevangelium.* AnBib, 29 (Rome: Pontifical Biblical Institute, 1967).

54. My translation, "grace in place of grace" renders the Greek *charin anti charitos.* Exegetes differ among themselves as to the sense of the preposition *anti.* Many of the Fathers (Origen, Cyril of Alexandria, Chrysostom, etc.) as well as some modern commentators (M.-E. Boismard, R.E. Brown) take the preposition as indication of a substitution. With them, I have chosen the "grace in place of grace" translation. Other commentators take the preposition either as an indication of the accumulation of grace ("grace upon grace" - e.g. R. Bultmann, C.K. Barrett) or as an indication of the correspondence between two orders ("grace corresponding to grace" - e.g. J.H. Bernard, J.A.T. Robinson).

case—but that the wine which had been previously drunk was of poorer quality than that given by Jesus. He is contrasting the old era of God's gifts to his people, the era of the Jewish dispensation, with the new era of Jesus' messianic gifts to the people, effected in the hour of his glorification. The quality of the gifts is contrasted. That given by Jesus is specified as "good," it is the gift of the eschatological era, the gift appropriate to the time of the realization of Israel's hopes.

The contrast between the two eras made explicit by v. 10 helps explain another feature of our account. From the standpoint of a structural analysis of the text, P. Geoltrain[55] has noticed that there is a shifting in the characterization of the account. The mother of Jesus gives way to the steward, who also fulfils the role of spokesperson. The servants give way to the disciples, who believe in Jesus. Even Jesus himself gives way to the bridegroom.[56] The contrast between the two eras, that of eschatological salvation and that of the previous and now superceded dispensation, suggest further reflection on the mother of Jesus. Her symbolic role in vv. 3b-4 looks to John 19:25-27, the scene at the foot of the cross in which the "mother of Jesus" also appears.

An analysis of the scene leads to the conclusion that vv. 26-27 were not originally linked with John 19:25.[57] Examination of the style and vocabulary of the entire little scene leads to the further conclusion that the Jesus-mother-disciple scene of vv. 26-27 has been constructed by the evangelist himself. It is, however, these very verses which show a great affinity with the Cana story by reason of their perspective (the hour of Jesus' crucifixion-glorification), their characterization (Jesus, his mother, the disciple[s]), and their vocabulary (the vocative *gunai*, etc.). In the scene at the foot of the cross which he has constructed, John has used a

55. P. Geoltrain, "Les noces à Cana. Jean 2, 1-12. Analyse des structures narratives" *Foi et Vie* 73 (1974) 83-90.

56. Cf. John 3:29.

57. Cf. Anton Dauer, "Das Wort des Gekreuzigten an seine Mutter und den 'Junger, den er liebte.' Eine traditions-geschichtliche und theologische Untersuchung zu Joh., 19-25-27," *BZ* 11 (1967) 222-239; 12 (1968) 80-93. A brief summary is contained in my article, "Mary," pp. 110-111.

characteristic revelation formula[58] in the narration of Jesus' words to his mother. The use of the formula implies that Jesus' words have a meaning other than that of a simple expression of a dying son's concern for his mother who is about to be left alone.[59] The words are those of Jesus, enthroned as Messiah and king upon the cross. In the hour of his exaltation, a new relationship is established between the Messiah and the mother of Jesus. Within the perspective of the final times, the dominant relationship is no longer the family one. The one who had waited in faithful expectation is united to the one who is the faithful disciple par excellence, the one whom Jesus loved. The little scene at the foot of the cross represents the birth of the Church. Mary symbolizes the one, perhaps the eschatological daughter of Zion, who faithfully awaits the messianic times and now, at the hour of Jesus' glorification, is introduced into the community of faithful believers and witnesses to whom the messianic blessings are entrusted through the glorification of Jesus.

The account of the marriage at Cana in Galilee, looks to this scene at the foot of the cross. The dialogue of the Johannine insertion at 2:3b-4 raises the question of the relationship between Jesus and his mother. The response to the question is suggested by the Cana account; it is made explicit in the scene at the foot of the cross. In fact the Johannine Cana account is not the only New Testament narrative to raise the question of the relationship between Jesus and his mother (and brethren). Shortly after his account of Jesus' choice of the twelve (Mark 3:13-19), Mark narrates a pronouncement story which bears upon Jesus' family relationship (Mark 3:31-35).[60] The significant logion with which the narrative reaches its climax, "Whoever does the will of God is my brother, and sister, and mother" (Mark 3:35), relativizes merely biological relationships. In the order of eschatological salvation it is not family ties which count. Rather the significant

58. Cf. M. de Goedt, "Un schème de révélation dans le quatrième évangile," NTS 8 (1962) 142-150.
59. Cf. R.F. Collins, "Mary," pp. 129-131.
60. Par. Matt 12:46-50; Luke 8:19-21.

factor is something of a different order, represented by Mark's
"whoever does the will of God."

Undoubtedly the issue of Jesus' family relationship was a
matter of concern for the early Church. It might be suggested
that some of Jesus' relatives used their position to seek a position
of some prominence in the Church. Within this perspective we
can better appreciate the Synoptists' attempts to re-evaluate his
biological relationship in terms of the realities of the new era of
salvation.[61] That seems to have been a particular concern of
Luke, who not only reproduces the Markan account of Jesus'
true kindred at Luke 8:19-21, but adds to his Gospel two
additional accounts taken from his own tradition which have a
purpose similar to that of Mark 3:13-19. The account of Jesus in
the temple (Luke 2:41-52), with which Luke concludes his
diptych of infancy stories, offers "Did you not know that I must
be in my father's house?" (Luke 2:49) as the saying of Jesus to
which the pronouncement story points as to its climax. Even
before the reader of Luke's Gospel begins to read the account of
the public ministry, he knows that Jesus has transcended merely
physical and biological relationships. Almost as a reminder, lest
the perspective of this transcendence of relationship be lost, Luke
unexpectedly narrates (Luke 11:27-28) the words of a women in
the crowd: "Blessed is the womb that bore you, and the breasts
that you sucked." Jesus' response puts the mother-son relationship in a different light: "Blessed rather are those who hear the
word of God and keep it." The response echoes the logion with
which Luke concludes his account of the pericope of Jesus' true
kindred: "My mother and my brothers are those who hear the
word of God and do it" (Luke 8:21). Luke, it has often been
noted, is the Synoptic author whose account most closely re-
sembles the Johannine account of Jesus' public ministry. Given
Luke's concern for the proper understanding of Jesus' biological
relationships, one might well expect that John would also have
something to say about the matter. It would appear that the last

61. John 8:34-59 also takes up the question of the significance of biological
relationship for the new order of salvation.

evangelist did indeed have something to say about Jesus' physical relationships. Yet he says what he has to say in his own fashion. He says that the biological relationship between Jesus and his mother is not as important as the attitude of faithful expectation of the messianic gifts. It is that attitude which is symbolized in the role which John assigns to Mary in 2:1-12 and 19:25-27.

By reason of the dialogical insertion at 2:3b-4, the Cana account is dominated by the perspective of Jesus' hour. That hour is the hour of Jesus' glorification. It is because the Cana incident, as reworked by John, points to the hour of Jesus' crucifixion that the evangelist can say that Jesus manifested his glory and his disciples believed in him (v. 11). At first reading it is strange that the evangelist should say that Jesus manifested his glory at Cana in Galilee. Although he frequently makes mention of a belief related to signs, the evangelist does not associate belief with the manifestation of Jesus' glory in his accounting of any other sign performed by Jesus. Indeed he normally reserves the notion of "glory" to those passages which explicitly look to Jesus' crucifixion, the hour of Jesus' exaltation-glorification.[62] The strangeness which initially disturbs the one who reads the account of water-become-wine disappears when account is taken of the programmatic nature of the account of the marriage at Cana.

The account has not been written into the Johannine account so much to provide a description of a particular miracle as it has been written to say that all the signs of Jesus must be seen in the light of the hour of Jesus. That is the hour of Jesus' supreme manifestation and self-revelation. It is the moment of the crucifixion-glorification whose significance is central to the believer's faith. The moment of Jesus' glorification is the moment when the eschatological era dawns and Israel's hopes are fulfilled. It is the moment when the institutions of Judaism and Jesus' biological relationships are transcended. It is the moment when the Messiah, enthroned in glory, gives to those who wait upon him in faith the gifts which he alone can give. This may not have been the

62. Cf. especially John 13:30-32.

message of an ancient miracle story whose origins are now somewhat obscured. It is, however, the message of the Johannine account of the water-become-wine at a marriage feast in Cana of Galilee — a narrative which provides a most important key for understanding the signs of Jesus.

10. MIRACLES AND FAITH

Introduction

The author of the Fourth Gospel concludes his account of the water become wine at Cana in Galilee with a typical Johannine note: "This, the first of his signs, Jesus did at Cana in Galilee, and manifested his glory; and his disciples believed in him" (John 2:11). This is one[1] of many parenthetical comments with which the evangelist has spiced his narrative. His comments and notes serve to interpret old traditions for a new generation of readers.

The evangelist has made the comment of John 2:11 apropos a tradition that had been handed down.[2] In a gospel that is rather carefully structured, the comment has been appended to the first miracle story which the reader encounters—a miracle story that the evangelist has highlighted by characterizing it as "the first of his signs." His remark appears in the last of the canonical gospels to have been written (ca. 96 A.D.).[3] For these reasons, John 2:11 is a fitting starting point for a reflection on the miracles of Jesus and faith.

Jesus' Signs

The author of the Fourth Gospel typically characterizes the miracles of Jesus as "signs" (*sēmeia*).[4] He is the only New

1. Cf. Gilbert Van Belle, *Les parenthèses dans l'évangile de Jean: Aperçu historique et classification. Texte grec de Jean.* Studiorum Novi Testamenti Auxilia, 11 (Louvain: University Press, 1985) pp. 67, 108, 111.

2. Even though the story of the wedding in Cana does not appear in the Synoptic gospels, there are ample reasons to suggest that it is not a *creatio ex nihilo* on the part of the evangelist.

3. Pace the efforts of the late John A.T. Robinson to date the Fourth Gospel at a much earlier time. See J.A.T. Robinson, *Redating the New Testament* (London: SCM, 1976); *The Priority of John* (London: SCM, 1985).

4. John 2:11, 18, 23; 3:2; 4:48, 54; 6:2, 14, 26, 30; 7:31; 9:16; 10:41; 11:47; 12:18, 37; 20:30.

Testament author to do so. Yet it is not often realized that the
Jesus of the Fourth Gospel does not often speak about his own
miracles as "signs."

Sign language

On only two occasions does the word sign-*sēmeion* appear on
the lips of Jesus in the Fourth Gospel. The first occasion is when
Jesus addressed the royal official who had come to ask for the
cure of his moribund son. Jesus addressed a challenge to the
petitioner: "Unless you see signs and wonders you will not
believe" (John 4:48). The logion apparently links signs and belief
in a fashion akin to that suggested by the evangelist in John 2:11.

The second occasion on which the Johannine Jesus speaks of
signs is when he challenged the crowd gathered at Capernaum
after the feeding of the five thousand with the confrontational
utterance: "Truly, truly, I say to you, you seek me, not because
you saw signs, but because you ate your fill of loaves" (John
6:26).

Sometimes the Fourth Gospel's discourse about signs is to be
found on the lips of various characters who appear in the
Johannine drama. Generally, these are choral response on the
part of groups which are less than favorable to Jesus. Thus the
Jews (2:18; 6:30 cf. 6:41), some Pharisees (9:16), and the chief
priests and Pharisees (11:47) speak about the signs of Jesus.

An apparently exceptional case is the attribution of a statement
about Jesus' signs to Nicodemus (3:2). Nicodemus is, however, a
Pharisee and a leader of the Jews (3:1). In this capacity he
represents the entire group of Jewish leaders learned in the Law.[5]
As such, he projects the image of one who proves ultimately to be
less than fully open to Jesus.[6]

For the most part, however, the Fourth Gospel's mention of

5. Cf. Raymond F. Collins, "The Representative Figures of the Fourth
Gospel," *DR* 94 (1976) 27-46, 118-132, pp. 36-37; in this volume, pp. 14-16.
6. See my "Jesus' Conversation with Nicodemus," *TBT* 93 (1977) 1409-1418;
in this volume, pp. 56-67.

the signs of Jesus occurs in the Fourth Gospel's meta-narrative texts. The language of signs is introduced by way of a commentary on the events that have been described. Eight[7] of the gospel's seventeen explicit mentions of the signs of Jesus belong to this group. All but one of them are found in the first part of the gospel, John 1-12, a section of the gospel that Raymond Brown has appropriately described as "the book of signs."[8]

Source-Criticism

All eight of these reflective comments by the evangelist have been identified by various commentators on the gospel as parenthetical remarks.[9] That does not mean that they were all firsthand compositions by the author of the gospel.

Bultmann[10] long ago considered that John 12:27 and 20:30-31 constituted the two-part conclusion to one of the gospel's principal sources, the so-called Signs Source.[11] While proposing that 20:30-31 did indeed form the conclusion to the Signs-Source, Robert Fortna originally claimed that 12:37 was the result of the redactional work of the evangelist himself, but he has recently modified his position so as also to attribute 12:37 to the evangelist's principal source.[12]

7. John 2:11, 23; 4:54; 6:2, 14; 12:18, 37; 20:30.

8. See Raymond E. Brown, *The Gospel According to John. I-XII; Introduction, Translation and Notes.* AB, 29 (Garden City, NY: Doubleday, 1966).

9. See Van Belle's tables, pp. 63-104.

10. Since it is quite likely that the Fourth Gospel existed in different editions (see the commentaries of Brown, Schnackenburg, *et al.*), it is somewhat simplistic to speak of "the author of the gospel," as if he were a single person. The scope of the present essay neither allows for nor requires a discussion of the rather complex issue of the authorship of the Fourth Gospel.

11. R. Bultmann, *The Gospel of John: A Commentary* (Oxford: Basil Blackwell, 1971; German original, 1941) p. 698, n. 2. See also Dwight Moody Smith, *The Composition and Order of the Fourth Gospel: Bultmann's Literary Theory* (New Haven: Yale University, 1965) p. 44.

12. For a discussion of Bultmann's position and his earlier views, see Robert T. Fortna, *The Gospel of Signs.* SNTSMS, 11 (Cambridge: University Press, 1970) pp. 197-199. The more recent opinion is to be found in R.T. Fortna, *The Fourth Gospel and Its Predecessor: From Narrative Source to Present Gospel* (Philadelphia: Fortress, 1988) p. 137, where he states that 12:37 came from the source but

On the other hand, M.-E. Boismard has proposed that 12:37 belonged to the evangelist's first draft of his gospel (Boismard's John II-A), rather than to his source (Boismard's hypothetical Document C), while 20:30-31 was composed for the second draft of the gospel (John II-B) under the influence of 12:37.[13]

Source critical questions are hardly extraneous to a study of faith and miracles. Boismard opined that the early strata of the Fourth Gospel (Document C, John II-A) promoted an apologetic view of the miracles of Jesus, that is, the idea that miracles lead to faith. This point of view is radically different from that of the Synoptics which portray Jesus working miracles for those who have faith.[14] The viewpoint expressed in his sources was ultimately rejected by the evangelist when he wrote the final draft of the gospel. By the time of his final composition of the text, the evangelist would have departed from the opinion that miracles are a prelude to faith. In the final writing of his gospel, the evangelist advanced the view that true faith is based on the word of Jesus.[15] According to Boismard, there has, therefore, been a development in the Johannine comunity's understanding of the relationship between faith and miracles.

Source-critical issues are also pertinent to an adequate understanding of the miracle stories of the Synoptic gospels. Stories of miracles and discussions about them form a considerable portion of the contents of Mark's gospel. Many of these miracle stories reappear in the gospels of Matthew and Luke. According to the classic two-source theory of Synoptic composition, Mark is the source of Matthew and Luke.[16] From this perspective, the

was added to the written gospel only when the signs and passion narratives were combined.

13. Cf. M.-E. Boismard - A. Lamouille, *Synopse des quatre évangiles*, 3: *L'évangile de Jean* (Paris: Cerf, 1977) pp. 327, 474-475.

14. See Matt 8:23-27, where the exhortation to faith (v. 26) clearly precedes the miracle.

15. See M.-E. Boismard, "Foi et miracles dans l'évangile de Jean," *ETL* 58 (1982) 357-364.

16. See, in this regard, my *Introduction to the New Testament* (Garden City, NY: Doubleday-London: SCM, 1983) 50-52, 115-133.

miracle stories of Matthew and Luke represent editorial re-
writings of the tales that are told by Mark.

There is also a substantial scholarly opinion which hold that
the first of the evangelists had some limited written sources.
Among them, there might well have been collections of miracle
stories,[17] technically known as aretalogies (from the Greek *aretē*,
prowess).[18] It is, however, also clear that Mark had an ulterior
purpose in narrating the account of the miracles which he has
taken over from his sources.[19]

The source critical issues to which reference have been made
are not easy to resolve. Moreover, the limited length and focused
scope of the present essay neither allows nor calls for their
resolution. They have been mentioned, however, since they
clearly attest that the literary tradition of Jesus' miracles merits
extensive study.

At the very least, the conclusions of that study would point to
the fact that each of the evangelists had his own way of dealing
with the tradition of Jesus' miracles. It would also clearly confirm
that no one of the evangelists was interested in Jesus' miracles
for miracles' sake. Rather each of the evangelists wrote about the
miracles of Jesus, because those miracles pointed to something
else—a fact vividly illustrated by the fourth gospel's use of sign
language (*sēmeion*) to characterize the miracles of Jesus.

History of Tradition

If the literary history of Jesus' miracles is complex, the history
of the process of the transmission of those stories is equally, if not
even more, complex. The written gospels provide some clues as to
the complexity of the process. In this way they allow scholars to
differentiate various stages in the history of the transmission.

17. See, for example, P.J. Achtemeier, "Toward the Isolation of Pre-Marcan
Miracle Catenae," *JBL* 83 (1970) 265-291; "The Origin and Function of the Pre-
Marcan Miracle Catenae," *JBL* 91 (1972) 198-221.

18. Cf. H.C. Kee, "Aretalogies and Gospel," *JBL* 92 (1973) 402-422.

19. See my "Los Milagros en el Evangelio de Marcos," *Actualidad Pastoral* 132
(1980) 51-64.

Once again, the purpose and limitations of the present essay do not allow for a consideration of these issues, not even as far as the history of a single miracle story is concerned.[20]

From the history of the transmission of the various miracle stories in the gospels, it is obvious that tales about Jesus' miracles were narrated by early Christians in the form of miracle stories, with its particular constraints and possibilities. The most characteristic feature of the form of a miracle story is its three-part structure: presentation, ritual, and verification, that is, the circumstances in which the miracle was worked, the actual working of the miracle, and the proof that the miracle was effective. This format allowed the tradition of Jesus' miracles to be handed down in the form of miracle stories.

The history of transmission of Jesus' miracle stories also indicates that it is quite unlikely that any one of the extant gospels offers a verbatim report of any single miracle worked by Jesus. The conditions of the oral transmission of the stories were such that they had to be modified, precisely in order that they be retained and transmitted.

Jesus' miracles

That Jesus actually did work miracles during the period of his public ministry lies, nonetheless, beyond any doubt. Even the most skeptic of biblical critics have to admit that the tradition of Jesus, the miracle worker, must be considered an authentic piece of early Christian tradition. The tradition easily satisfies the criterion of multiple attestation and the law of dual exclusion.

As far as the former is concerned, mention is made of Jesus' miracles in all four gospels, in various sources utilized by the evangelists, and in various literary forms (miracle stories, controversies, etc.). As far as the latter is concerned, it need only be said that the Jews did not generally expect the Messiah to be a wonder-worker. From the Christian standpoint, it must be re-

20. As an example, one might refer to my study of Mark 7:31-37 in "Jesus' Ministry to the Deaf and Dumb," *Melita Theologica* 35 (1984) 12-36, pp. 26-30.

called that Jesus' miracles did not really prove anything about
him, as both the ad hominem argument preserved in the Q
tradition (Luke 11:19 = Matt 12:27) and the Johannine statement about those who did not believe (John 12:37) clearly attest.
Moreover Mark 3:21 seems to suggest that memebers of Jesus'
own family were not very comfortable with Jesus' activity as an
exorcist.[21]

An evangelist's choice

The Fourth Gospel does not once even mention Jesus' activity
as an exorcist. Now, it is unlikely that the tradition behind the
Fourth Gospel was totally ignorant about the tradition of Jesus
as exorcist. However, the particular weltanschauung of the Fourth
Gospel and the choice among the stories of Jesus' miracles (John
20:30-31)[22] that the evangelist decided to make led to the writing
of an exorcism-free Fourth Gospel.[23]

What then are the miracle stories found in the fourth gospel?
Most scholars identify seven[24] of them: the water become wine at
Cana (John 2:1-12),[25] the cure of the royal official's son (John
4:46-54), the healing of the lame man (John 5:2-9), the feeding of
the five thousand (John 6:1-15), the walking on water (John 6:16-
21), the healing of the blind man (John 9:1-7), and the raising of

21. That Jesus' own family was so embarrassed apparently was an em-
barrassment for the church, leading neither Matthew nor Luke to reproduce Mark
3:21 in their respective gospels. It is one of the relatively few verses in Mark that
has been taken over by neither of the later Synoptics.

22. See also John 3:2, where mention is made of Jesus' "signs," even though
the only miracle story which has hitherto appeared in the Fourth Gospel is John
2:1-12, the story of the water become wine.

23. A plausible case can also be made to the effect that in the process of the
oral tradition, the stories of exorcisms, following familiar Semitic patterns,
gradually were transformed into stories of miracles, following more Hellenistic
patterns. Once again, a full discussion of that issue and of its relevance to the
development of the Johannine tradition would take us far beyond the possibilities
of the present essay.

24. The evangelist's predilection for groups of seven is well known.

25. This is a unique case of a miracle story. Cf. my "Cana (John 2:1-12) - The
First of his Signs or the Key to his Signs?" *ITQ* 47 (1980) 79-95; in this volume,
pp. 158-182.

Lazarus (John 11:1-12:8). To these may be added the story of the miraculous catch of fish (John 21:1-11), which appears in the epilogue to the Fourth Gospel.

Of these seven stories, only three have clear parallels in the Synoptic gospels, and one of them, the story of Jesus' walking on the water, may not even be a miracle story as such.[26] While the story of the miraculous catch of fish has a parallel in Luke 5:1-11, the only miracle stories found in the body of the Fourth Gospel with parallels in the Synoptics are the feeding of the five thousand (with parallels in all three Synoptics; Matt 14:13-21; Mark 6:32-44; Luke 9:10b-17), and the cure of the royal official's son (with a parallel apparently deriving from Q; Luke 7:1-10 = Matt 8:5-13).

On the other hand, the Synoptics do tell of Jesus' raising people from the dead (Matt 9:18-19, 23-26; Mark 5:22-24, 34-43; Luke 8:40-42, 49-56; Luke 7:11-17). In addition, the healings of John 5 and 7 are quite similar to the stories of Jesus' cures of various people which are narrated here and there throughout the Synoptic gospels.

Taken as a group, the New Testament accounts of Jesus' healing miracles are remarkably sober compared to those found in Hellenistic literature. Indeed, they are quite restrained when compared to the stories told about Jesus, the boy wonder worker, in the apocryphal *Infancy Gospel of Thomas* (mid-second century).

A Reflection

Now that the terrain has been properly plowed, at least insofar as areas for more in-depth research have been identified, we might turn to the "sign language" of the fourth gospel and ask about the relationship between miracles and faith. At the outset it

---

26. Its literary form, identified as an epiphany, specifically a sea-rescue epiphany, by John P. Heil, is quite different from the other types of gospel miracles. Cf. J.P. Heil, *Jesus Walking on the Sea: Meaning and Gospel Functions of Matt. 14:22-33, Mark 6:45-52 and John 6:15b-21.* AnBib, 87 (Rome: Biblical Institute Press, 1981).

must be stated that we cannot enter into a discussion of Jesus' own appreciation of the miracles[27] nor can we expatiate on the relationship between Jesus' activity and the notion of "miracle" developed for an apologetic reasons during the scientific age.[28] None of the gospels claim that Jesus' wonderful deeds were "miracles," in the critical-apologetic sense of the term.[29]

What must be considered in the present essay is how the Fourth Gospel perceives the relationship between the signs of Jesus and the "belief" which the evangelist specifically relates to the signs of Jesus in John 2:11, 23; 6:14, 30; 7:31; 12:37; and 20:30 (implicitly in John 3:2; 4:54; and 6:14).

In the evangelist's vision of things, it is clear that only Jesus can do a sign.[30] On the other hand, the evangelist surely knew that other people were capable of working prodigies. He himself intimates that the man who had been a paralytic for thirty-eight years would have been cured by the miraculous effects of the waters of the pool at Bethzatha, if only he had someone to help him enter the pool at the proper time (John 5:7).[31] Various exorcists were at work in first century Palestine, during Jesus' own lifetime,[32] and their is no reason to doubt that their exorcisms were effective. In the Hellenistic world, the cure of a blind

27. See the discussions found in E.P. Sanders, *Jesus and Judaism* (London: SCM, 1985) pp. 133-144, 157-173, etc.

28. Cf. Colin Brown, *Miracles and the Critical Mind* (Grand Rapids, MI: Eerdmans, 1984).

29. The distinction between natural and supernatural as well as the idea that nature has its proper laws, independent of God, would have been foreign to the evangelists.

30. The verb "to do" (*poieō*) is typically used with the noun *sēmeion* (see John 2:11, 23; 3:2; 4:54; 6:2, 14, 30; 7:31; 9:16; 10:41; 11:47; 12:18, 37; 20:30, i.e., in reference to fourteen of the seventeen occurrences of *sēmeion*). Jesus is always the subject of the verb, except in 10:41 where it is stated that "John did no sign," - a confirmation that it is only Jesus who does signs.

31. Some Greek manuscripts, most of them relatively late, attribute the curative powers of the waters not to the water itself but to an angel's intervention. See John 5:4 in majuscules A, D, and L and the minuscules of the Ferrar family.

32. Cf. Luke 11:19 = Matt 12:27. One might also take into account the stories told about rabbis in various Jewish sources.

man was effected by the Emperor Vespasian[33] in a way that
recalls Jesus' restoration of sight to a blind man (John 9). In sum,
there were many wonder-workers; but only Jesus could do a sign.

From the fact that the evangelist has made a choice from
among the signs which he could have described,[34] it is obvious
that the evangelist has no interest in describing as many signs as
he can. A greater number of signs will not convince those who do
not believe, because, of themselves, the signs do not lead to faith:
"Though he had done many signs before them, yet they did not
believe in him" (John 12:37).

It is likewise clear that the author of the Fourth Gospel was not
particularly interested is accentuating the "wonder" element of
the signs.[35] Apart from John 4:48, the evangelist did not use the
traditional biblical terminology, "signs and wonders" (*sēmeia kai
terata*),[36] as a description of Jesus' miracles. Neither did the
evangelist characterize Jesus' miracles as "acts of power" (*dunameis*), as do the Synoptists.[37] Moreover, in comparison with
other ancient miracle stories, his narrative accounts of Jesus'
signs are relatively sober. They hardly accentuate Jesus' power as
a wonder worker.

Indeed, in his account of the first of signs, the evangelist
presents the steward as a commentator who reflects upon the
quality of the wine provided by Jesus, rather than upon its
tremendous quantity[38] (John 2:10). In his account of Jesus' cure
of the lame man, Jesus is described as providing the paralytic

33. See M.-E. Boismard, "Foi et miracles," p. 363, for the historical sources
and a discussion of the event.

34. Cf. John 20:30; 3:2.

35. In 1 Cor 12:1-11, Paul indicates that the extraordinariness of a phenomenon is not necessarily an indication that it comes from God (v. 2). On the
other hand, in 1 Cor 12:28, he indicates that some very ordinary ministries
(helpers, administrators) are from God.

36. Cf. Matt 24:24; Mark 13:22; Acts 2:22, 43; 4:30; 5:12; 6:8; 7:36; 14:3;
15:12; Rom 15:19; 2 Cor 12:12; 2 Thess 2:9; Heb 2:4. The hendiadys is
traditional biblical language, cf. Exod 7:3.

37. Cf. Matt 7:22; 11:20, 21, 23; 13:54, 58; 14:2; etc.

38. The equivalent of some 640 to 960 bottles of wine.

with a benefit which might have accrued to him from another source, if only he had a bit of assistance (John 5:7).

Therefore, it was neither the quantity of Jesus' signs nor their extraordinary character that led the evangelist to incorporate an account of Jesus' signs into his gospel. Yet an account of these was provided specifically in order "that you may believe that Jesus is the Christ, the Son of God, and that believing you may have life in his name" (John 20:31). The evangelist is well aware that signs are related to faith and wants his readers to know that Jesus' signs are related to their faith.

A merely physical perception of a deed performed by Jesus is not a sufficient reason for calling what Jesus did a "sign." At least some among the five thousand fed by Jesus did not see the sign which he had done (John 6:26), even though they had benefited from what he had done. Sign language is the language of faith. To call Jesus' works "signs," is to interpret them with the insight that is proper to faith.

Events which are appropriately termed "signs" can lead to belief. They are "acts of credence,"[39] one's credentials. Some might ask that these credentials be produced. Thus, the Jews ask Jesus to show his credentials, by doing a sign (John 2:18; 6:30). There is a kind of faith that stems from the perception of these credentials. From his knowledge of Jesus' signs, Nicodemus affirms that Jesus is a teacher come from God" (John 3:2). Even the Christ will do signs, in order to establish his credentials (John 7:31).[40] When a person presents proper credentials, but for some reason appears not to be duly accredited, one can only wonder. Hence, some of the Pharisees asked, "How can a man who is a sinner do such signs?" (John 9:16).

Signs attract interest (John 12:18), but of themselves they prove nothing. They do not convince; they call for a decision. There is faith, and there is faith. Those who believed in Jesus

39. In this sense they are analogous to letters of credence.
40. This is manifestly a Christian formulation (cf. Matt 11:2). In the popular expectation the Christ, i.e., the royal Messiah, was not expected to be a wonder-worker.

because of his signs did not necessarily believe that he was the Christ, the Son of God (John 7:31). Belief in Jesus because of his signs cannot be equated with belief in Jesus, the Christ.

Those who have faith in Jesus merely on the basis of the signs which he has done do not have that life-giving faith which is real faith according to the vision presented in the Fourth Gospel. The chief priests and the Pharisees knew of the signs of Jesus. Their knowledge of these signs called for them to make a decision (John 11:47), but the signs did not lead them to true faith since they proved to be chiefly responsible for the death of Jesus.

Signs open up the possibility of real faith and call for a decision. The fact that those who are unfavorable to Jesus discuss his signs (John 2:18; 6:30; 9:16; 11:47) shows that Jesus' signs constitute a crisis, a moment of decision. The case of Nicodemus (John 3:1-15) tragically portrays the story of a man whose awareness of Jesus' signs leads him to Jesus, but who, in the end, is found wanting because he does not understand. Signs brought this nocturnal figure to Jesus, the rabbi, but they did not suffice to allow him to see Jesus, the light of the world. Faith on the basis of mere signs is insufficient faith.

On the other hand, those who are open to what the Father was doing in and through Jesus allow the works of Jesus to reveal who he truly is. Those who have faith allow the signs of Jesus to be revelatory, albeit not demonstrative. Thus, those who had truly appreciated the sign of Jesus' feeding the five thousand could see in Jesus the prophet who was to come, that is, the prophet like Moses (cf. Deut 15:15, 18). In like manner, the believers for whom the Fourth Gospel were written allow the stories of Jesus' signs to manifest for them that Jesus is the Christ, the Son of God. It is the insight of faith, at the invitation of Jesus and as the gift of the Father, which allows Jesus' deeds to be perceived as signs.

That Jesus' signs open up to belief in this full sense is paradigmatically enunciated by the evangelist when he tells the story of the water become wine at Cana in Galilee. This is the first of Jesus' signs. It is not first in the sense that it is numerically the first, with the implication that others will subsequently follow. It is rather the first in the sense that it is the paradigm of all Jesus' signs.

All of Jesus' signs derive their real meaning from the reality of his hour (John 3:4), that is, the supreme moment of his passion-revelation-glorification. The signs proclaim to those who truly appreciate them as sign, who perceive their real meaning with the insight that comes with faith, that something new and different is present because of Jesus (John 2:10). Signs open up for those who believe the vision of Jesus' true glory (John 2:11).[41]

In some ways the signs of Jesus are analogous to the parables attributed to Jesus in the Synoptic gospels. In one and the other instance, we have an activity of Jesus (in deed or word) that is enigmatic and ambivalent. No more than the merely physical hearing of a parable brings a person to true faith does the physical perception of Jesus' signs bring a person to true faith.

In this regard it is enlightening that Isa 6:9-10, used by the Synoptic tradition[42] as a scriptural warrant to make sense of an unbelieving reaction to Jesus' parables, is used in the Fourth Gospel as a scriptural reflection who do not believe in Jesus even though signs had been done in their presence (John 12:38-40). It is possible to see Jesus' signs without really "seeing" them.

Signs, like parables, are critical: they call for a decision in faith. Ultimately they separate believers from non-believers. For the one who adheres to Jesus in faith, the signs are a manifestation of who Jesus is.

Application and an Unfinished Conclusion

What purpose has this extended reflection on enigmatically simple matters to serve in the context of contemporary African Christianity?[43] What lessons are to be learned? What challenges arise?

41. Cf. John 1:14.
42. Cf. Matt 13:13-15; Mark 4:12; Luke 8:10 (comp. Acts 28:26).
43. John S. Mbiti, with due acknowledgment of the work of K. Enang,

First of all, it is clear that the early Christians quickly realized that faith in Jesus the wonder-worker was not an adequate faith. There were other wonder-workers in Jesus' day, just as there are many workers of wonders in our times. Faith which sees in Jesus merely the worker of authentic "miracles," is a faith which attributes to Jesus significant status, but not the unique status that he enjoys in Christian tradition as the Son of God.

Secondly, stories about Jesus' miracles are some of the earliest stories told in the gatherings of Christians. They were told and retold. They were living stories, which, from the very first moments of the Christian experience, were adapted to the context in which they were told. Only in this way did the stories come alive and lead people to faith.

In similar fashion, if a story of Jesus' miracles is to lead people to faith and confirm them in their faith, the story needs to be retold within a contemporary context, that is, the real life situation in Africa today. Resignification[44] and actualization are characteristic of the story which is relevant and life-giving.

Thirdly, if aretalogies did indeed exist during the first years of the Christian experience, the memory of them was preserved only because people of Christian faith quickly assimilated them into a broader context, that of the gospel with its varying focus on the death and resurrection of Jesus.

When the early Christian authors told the story of Jesus' miracles, they did not accentuate the wondrous aspect. Emphasis upon the prodigious for prodigy's sake would only have served to place Jesus in the ranks of wonder-workers. Thus, the evangelists used the miracle stories to point to something else, for instance, the authority of Jesus as teacher, the nature of discipleship, or the revelation of Jesus.

suggests that the stories of Jesus' exorcisms and cures have an important influence on the development of the independent churches in Africa. See J.S. Mbiti, *Bible and Theology in African Context* (London: Oxford University, 1986) pp. 112-113, 153, etc.

44. See James A. Sanders, "The Bible as Canon," *Christian Century* 98 (1981) 1250-1255, pp. 1252-1253.

The wonder aroused by the miracles is just a first step on the road to authentic faith and discipleship.

Finally, the understanding of Jesus for which the story of Jesus' miracles provides an opening must be expressed in the christological formulations best suited to each community.

From the story of Jesus' miracles Mark[45] opened up the world of Jesus, the authoritative teacher and proclaimer of the end times. From the story of Jesus' miracles, Matthew opened up the vision of Jesus the Christ. From the story of Jesus' miracles, Luke showed Jesus to be the prophet and son of God *par excellence*. From the story of Jesus' miracles, the fourth evangelist manifested Jesus as the Christ and Son of God.

From the story of Jesus' miracles, those who proclaim the gospel anew today...

45. Some dimensions of the insights derived from the presentation of miracles in the different gospels are offered by Colin Brown in *That You May Believe: Miracles and Faith. Then and Now* (Grand Rapids, MI: Eerdmans, 1985) pp. 110-150.

IV. Coming and Going

11. "HE CAME TO DWELL AMONG US" (John 1:14)

There was a time when the most popular exegesis of John 1:14 placed considerable emphasis upon the etymology of the verb *skēnoun*, "to dwell in a tent." The allusion to nomadic life contained in the term made it a natural and effective symbol of the temporary presence of the enfleshed Word among His own. Many of the older commentaries explicated the verse in this way. So, too, do some of the more recent commentaries, as well as the dictionary of Arndt-Gingrich.[1]

Most of the recent commentaries, however, view this interpretation as somewhat inadequate. This type of exegesis ascribes to the verb *skēnoun* a connotation which it has in both classical Greek and the Greek of the Septuagint, but which it does not have in New Testament usage. Thus the preponderance of modern commentators on John 1:14, instead of drawing our attention to the etymology of the term, point to the sacral character of the language of the text. To the Jewish mind, and the Christian reader of the Fourth Gospel, the use of the term *skēnoun* recalls the presence of God with His people throughout the long history of his dealings with them.

Far from being a banal reference to the short-lived presence of the Word among His own, the expression "He came to dwell among us" is pregnant with theological significance. It situates the presence of the enfleshed Word in the world within the broad

1. Cf. C.K. Barrett, *The Gospel According to St. John: An Introduction with Commentary and Notes on the Greek Text* (London: SPCK, 1955) p. 138; E.C. Hoskyns, *The Fourth Gospel* (London: Faber and Faber, 1947) p. 147; W. Arndt - F. Gingrich, *A Greek-English Lectionary of the New Testament and Other Early Christian Literature* (Cambridge: University Press, 1957) p. 762.

context of salvation history by means of sacerdotal-liturgical imagery. Its implications can be elaborated upon by means of the priestly traditions embodied in the Old Testament. Nonetheless, while John 1:14 is full of meaning in itself, it ought not to be separated from the body of the Gospel since it serves as a programmatic statement of one of the major themes of the Fourth Gospel.

"Dwelling" in Salvation History

The coupling of the verb "to dwell" with the notion of "glory," a favorite Johannine theme, indicates the direction in which the theological significance of John 1:14 can be sought. At the time of the Exodus, Moses was ordered to make a tent, the Tabernacle, which would serve as dwelling place of Yahweh among his people: "Let them make me a sanctuary, that I may dwell in their midst" (Exod 25:8). When the tabernacle had been constructed, duly erected and properly appointed, the ark of the convenant was carried into it (Exod 40:21). Then, on the day of its inauguration, the glory of Yahweh filled the Tabernacle so that not even Moses could enter into it: "Then the cloud covered the tent of meeting, and the glory of the Lord filled the Tabernacle" (Exod 40:34). By this manifestation of His glory, Yahweh wishes to show that He was taking possession of His Tabernacle. He had come to dwell among His own people in a tent, not totally dissimilar so those in which they dwelled. Thus Yahweh's glory in the Tabernacle was a sign of his divine presence among the nomadic Israelites during the period of their deliverance.

Once the Israelites had conquered Canaan, Yahweh gave a new command to the appointed leader of his people. As a tent had been his dwelling place among a nomadic people, a permanent structure was to be his dwelling place in a nation established on its own territory, his own land. Thus Yahweh spoke to David through the prophet Nathan: "I have not dwelt in a house since the day I brought up the people of Israel from Egypt to this day, but I have been moving about in a tent for my dwelling. In all places where I have moved with all the people of Israel, did I speak a word with any of the judges of Israel, whom I commanded to shepherd my people Israel, saying, 'Why have you not built me a house of cedar?'" (2 Sam 7:6-7). In fulfillment of Yahweh's promise (2 Sam 7:13), Solomon built the Temple as the new dwelling place of Yahweh among his people (1 Kgs 6:13). When the Temple was completed and properly furnished, the glory of Yahweh filled the Temple so that the priests could no longer fulfill their duties within it: "And when the priests came out of the holy place, a cloud filled the house of the Lord, so that the priests could not stand to minister because of the cloud; for the glory of the Lord filled the house of the Lord" (1 Kgs 8:10-11). The motif is similar to that associated with Yahweh's presence in the Tabernacle.

Against this Old Testament background, John 1:14 implies that the Word made flesh is the new localization of God's presence among men. It is no longer a house made of human hands, neither Tabernacle nor Temple, that is the localized presence of God on earth. Rather the enfleshed Word has succeeded and replaced both Tabernacle and Temple as the glorified sign of the divine presence among men.

Beyond this, John 1:14 has an eschatological connotation. According to Old Testament tradition, Yahweh's dwelling among his people was a sign of his covenantal love. Were Israel to become unfaithful to the covenant, this gracious benefaction would be withdrawn. Thus Ezekiel who had a vision of Yahweh's glory filling the temple (Ezek 8:4; 9:3; 10:3-4) also saw the glory of Yahweh leave the Temple defiled by Israel's sins (Ezek 10:18-19). For the era of the new covenant, there was promised a new Temple which would be the place of Yahweh's throne where he would dwell forever among his people: "As the glory of the Lord entered the temple by the gate facing east, the Spirit lifted me up, and brought me into the inner court; and behold, the glory of the Lord filled the temple" (Ezek 43:4-5).

The notion of this mode of the divine presence was central to the eschatology of the Old Testament and later Judaism. In the post-exilic period the prophets encouraged the rebuilding of the Temple, for it was necessary that Yahweh dwell again among his people. "Go up to the hills and bring wood and build the house, that I may take pleasure in it and that I may appear in my glory, says the Lord. You have looked for much, and, lo, it came to little; ... Why? says the Lord of hosts. Because of my house that lies in ruins, while you busy yourselves each with his own house. ... And the Lord stirred up the spirit of Zerubbabel the son of Shealtiel, governor of Juda, and the spirit of Joshua the son of Jehozadak, the high priest, and the spirit of all the remnant of the people; and they came and worked on the house of the Lord of hosts, their God" (Hag 1:8-9, 14).

Indeed, the expectation of the renewed tented presence of Yahweh among his people became a keynote of the eschatological hope of Israel. Thus Joel writes of the future restoration of Jerusalem: "So you shall know that I am the Lord your God who dwell (*ho kataskēnōn*) in Zion, my holy mountain" (Joel 3:17). In much the same vein the prophet Zechariah proclaimed: "Shout aloud and rejoice, daughter of Zion; I am coming, I will make my dwelling (*kataskēnōsō*) among you, says the Lord" (Zech 2:14 [LXX]).[2] In brief, the renewed tenting of Yahweh among his people is a characteristic feature of the eschatological era. Thus when John writes that "He came to dwell among us, and we saw his glory," he has equivalently stated that the eschatological era has dawned with the enfleshment of the Word.

These themes which form the Old Testament background of John 1:14 were developed in different manners within Judaism. On the one hand, apocalyptic thought looked to the establishment of a new Temple in which God would dwell with his people in the eternal age to come.[3] This train of thought was adapted by the Johannine church, in which the Book of Revelation was composed shortly before the Fourth Gospel. In his Christian

2. Cf. Zech 8:3.
3. Cf. *Apoc. Mos.* 29:4-10 (Lat.); D. Barthélemy - J.T. Milik, *Qumran Cave I. Discoveries in the Judaean Desert* (Oxford: Clarendon, 1955) pp. 134-135.

apocalypse, the visionary uses the verb *skēnoun*, "to dwell," to describe God's presence among his redeemed people: He who sits on the throne will dwell (*skēnōsei*) with them (Rev 7:15). Having seen the new Jerusalem, the prophet "heard a loud voice from the throne saying, 'Behold, the dwelling (*hē skēne*) of God is with men. He will dwell (*skēnosei*) with them, and they shall be his people, and God himself will be with them'" (Rev 21:3).

On the other hand, the rabbinic strain of Judaic orthodoxy developed a theology of the *shekinah* after the destruction of the Temple. In an era when the temple, now destroyed, could no longer function as a sign of Yahweh's presence among his own, the *shekinah* was construed as God's presence among his people. The *shekinah* represented the reality of the divine presence among those who had come together to study the Torah or to pray. As such, the *shekinah* was a rabbinic equivalent of the divine name, almost a periphrasis for Yahweh himself.

Thus, in a fashion similar to that of his contemporaries still within Judaism, the author of the Fourth Gospel drew from the biblical theme of Yahweh's "dwelling" among men to articulate dimensions of his faith. In John 1:14 he presents the enfleshed presence of the Word as the new mode of the divine presence among God's people. Even in its newness, it implies God's fidelity to his sworn covenant whose lasting validity is attested by his tented presence among men. For the author of the Fourth Gospel, however, there is more than mere fidelity to the covenant of old which is implied in his affirmation of the Word's presence among men. In John's perspective, Yahweh's Old Testament presence in Tabernacle and Temple is less a reality in itself than it is a sign of the reality to come. Yahweh's tented presence in the Old Testament is a waiting which will be fully realized in the Word's tenting among his own people. Even though John does not explicitly describe Jesus as the *alēthinē skēnē*, the "true tent," his thought is that the Word is indeed the true Tabernacle. His tented presence is the fulfillment of the Old Testament prophecies which foretold the tented dwelling of God among his people in messianic times. The affirmation of the tented presence of the divine Word in John 1:14 is a proclamation of that divine presence among men which is characteristic of the final days. The Word's presence among men is an anticipation of the eschatological presence of God among his people who perceive his glory and dwell in eternal life. In a word, John 1:14 is a first statement of the realized eschatology of the Fourth Gospel.

God's Dwelling in the Priestly Tradition

If its Old Testament background and the eschatological expectations of the Jewish people shed considerable light upon John 1:14, the context of the verse is not without significance. For some time scholars have recognized the points of contact between the prologue of the Fourth Gospel and the Old Testament's Wisdom literature.[4] Some commentators have even drawn our attention to a sapiential tradition that Wisdom sought to pitch its tent in Israel.[5] Yet, while most commentaries note that the opening verse of the prologue harks back to Gen 1:1, they fail to note that all of the prologue's allusions to the Genesis story of creation are to the priestly version of the narrative (Gen 1:1-2:4a). Thus they fail to draw our attention to the specifically priestly dimensions of the Old Testament tradition as a key to the understanding of the prologue's biblical allusions.

On the other hand, not a few authors have pointed to the priestly and liturgical influences on the body of the Fourth Gospel. Its chronological setting within the liturgical calendar, its description of the Beloved Disciple's access to high priestly circles (John 18:15-18), and Papias' enigmatic reference to "John the Presbyter" all point to some sacerdotal influence on the composition of the Gospel. Interest in the priestly provenance of the Gospel has been whetted further still in recent years because of

4. Cf. J. Rendel Harris, *The Origin of the Prologue to St. John's Gospel* (Cambridge: University Press, 1917); C.H. Dodd, *The Interpretation of the Fourth Gospel* (Cambridge: University Press, 1953) pp. 274-275; etc.

5. Cf. Sir 24:8.

the manifold points of similarity between the Fourth Gospel and the "priestly circles" of sectarian Judaism.

Whence, it seems to me, we can draw from the Old Testament's Priestly tradition on the "tented" presence of Yahweh among his people to elucidate further the meaning of John 1:14. These traditions point to the tent as the place of revelation, as the resolution of the problem of the presence of the Transcendent, as covenant-related, as centre of unity, and as place of worship.

As a matter of fact, "tenting" expressed by means of the Hebrew verb *sakan*, usually rendered by the verb *kataskēnoun* in the LXX, has become almost a technical term within the priestly tradition to describe Yahweh's presence among his people. The Priestly tradition always uses *sakan* in this sense, and never uses the verb in any other sense. Conversely, the priestly tradition uses the verb *yasab* to speak of men "dwelling" and never uses this term in reference to any manifestation of Yahweh's presence among his people on earth. The Priestly tradition, moreover, uses the theme of the tent to describe Yahweh's abiding presence within Israel, whereas the earlier Elohist tradition draws upon this theme to indicate that Yahweh has paid a visit to his people.

The oldest tradition had stressed the role of the Tabernacle in oracles. The tent of meeting, the *'ohel mo'ed*, is the place where Yahweh meets with Moses and speaks with him. Anyone who wanted to consult with Yahweh went to the Tent, but only Moses entered. Still today the tradition of a portable tent which can be set up and serve as a tent of oracles in a camp of nomads is preserved by some Bedouin tribes. The Old Testament's priestly tradition also looked to the Tabernacle as the tent of revelation. "It shall be a continual burnt offering throughout your generations at the door of the tent of meeting before the Lord, where I will meet with you, to speak there to you. There I will meet with the people of Israel, and it shall be sanctified by my glory" (Exod 29:42-43).[6] For the priestly author, the *'ohel mo'ed* is the place of Yahweh's revelation to his people. The Tabernacle is the locus of

6. Cf. Exod 25:22; 30:36.

Yahweh's self-revelation. There God speaks; there his word is conveyed to his people.[7]

In the Fourth Gospel, the enfleshed Word is likewise the locus of God's self-revelation to man. Indeed, the Word is called the *Logos* because he is the one who reveals the Father. He is the bearer of the word of God and is himself the Word of God. That Jesus is the Revealer is most forcefully expressed in the Fourth Gospel's celebrated "I am" formula. This revelation formula characterizes Jesus as the self-revealer, as the one who reveals and who is at the same time the object of his own revelation. This notion is foreshadowed in the prologue which calls Jesus the *Logos*, the Word of God.

Since the notion that Jesus is the Revealer is most significant in Johannine thought, it may well be the notion that the Tabernacle is the locus of God's self-revelation which led to the introduction of the Word's "tenting" into the prologue. It has already been noted that the function of the Tabernacle was eventually taken over by the Temple. This is no less true of the oracular function. The Temple is the place where oracles are given and God's word conveyed. Thus it is not altogether surprising that in the Fourth Gospel the temple (*hieron*) is the place where Jesus teaches.[8] John's temple is the place where the Word of God is given to men. John 1:14 adumbrates the notion by pointing to the Word himself as the tabernacled presence of God. It is in him that the revelatory Word of God for man is personally present. Jesus is himself the locus of divine revelation, the tent of meeting—the tent of testimony. He is, in a word, the true Tabernacle, the real Temple. This concept concurs with the basic perspective of the prologue which presents Jesus under the formal aspect of the one who reveals.

There is yet another aspect of the Old Testament's priestly understanding of the tented presence of Yahweh which throws light upon John 1:14. In the history of Israel there always existed

7. Cf. Exod 25-26; 36-40.
8. John 7:14; 8:2, 20; 10:23; 18:20.

a tension between the absolute otherness and supreme freedom of Yahweh and his presence among his people. Israel's totally other, free and all-powerful God could not be confined to any earthly sanctuary. Yet the very existence of the covenant which Yahweh had made with Israel required his presence among his people. The priestly authors also struggled with the problems of Yahweh's immanence and transcendence. For them the ideas of Tabernacle and Temple in which Yahweh dwelled and which He filled with his glory both assured Israel of his active presence within the nation and avoided too crude a notion of the presence of Yahweh. First, for the nomads in the desert, and then for the inhabitants of Jerusalem a happy solution to the problem of the divine transcendence and the divine immanence had been found.

The paradox of the divine transcendence and the divine presence is also a problem for which the author of the prologue had to find a solution. The prologue is run through with the tension between the verb "to be" (ēn) and the verb "to become" (egeneto), the one used of the divine, the other of the creaturely. The author's first mention of the Word affirmed his presence in the divine sphere (John 1:1); his second mention of the Word pointed to his participation in weak and mortal humanity (John 1:14). For the Johannine author, the notion of the divine tenting among us, already rich with pertinent Old Testament resonance, was a happy solution to the paradox of the divine Word present among men. The very construction of John 1:14, in which the verb skēnoun unites two contrasting notions, the enfleshment of the Word and the glory of the only God, indicates how well the divine tenting was a convenient idiom for expressing the presence of the Transcendent in the world of creation.

Moreover, the tenting idiom could also serve to allude to the relationship between the Word and the covenant. While the Tabernacle is sometimes called the 'ohel or the miskan by the authors of the priestly tradition, they seem to be more comfortable with the designation 'ohel mo'ed, an epithet which means "the tent of meeting." This designation harks back to the amphictyony,[9] when Yahweh was considered to be the head of the covenant assembly. The expression thus implicitly recalls the history of the covenant which Yahweh had established with his people, Israel. What is implicit in the expression is sometimes explicitated by the association of covenant themes with the Tabernacle.[10] This Old Testament, and priestly, tradition is continued by the author of the Fourth Gospel. Mention of the tented presence of the Word is followed by the proclamation that he is "full of grace and truth" (*plērēs charitos kai alētheias*). The binomial, slightly adapted by John, is a typical Old Testament expression of covenant-minded disposition, of Yahweh's fidelity to the covenant oath which he had sworn. Thus the enfleshment of the Word as the new mode of the divine presence among men is construed not only as an indication of God's eternal fidelity to the covenant itself. The covenant itself is brought to its consummation in the new tabernacled presence of God among his people.

This mention of the convenant and the ancient amphyctiony draws our attention to the unity of the people as a covenant motif. The members of the amphyctiony were formed into one people by the covenant which was established. In the priestly tradition, however, the unity of the people is no less a motif in the description of the Tabernacle and Temple. The sanctuary is viewed as the central and unifying factor of Israelite life. The architectural symmetry of the Tabernacle,[11] centred about the holy of holies, was a symbol of the unity of the people. So, too, was the fact that the tribes were stationed on all four sides of

9. Cf. F. Cross, "The Priestly Tabernacle," p. 224, in G.E. Wright and D.N. Freedman, eds., *The Biblical Archaeologist Reader*, 1 (Garden City, NY: Anchor, 1961) pp. 201-228.

10. Cf. Lev 26:12, 1 Kgs 8:8-9, etc.

11. Cf. Exod 25-27; 37-38. The meaning of the priestly author's symmetrical plan was essentially the same as that of Exod 40-48 with this difference that Ezechiel projected his plan into the future whereas the priestly author thought of a past execution of the plan.

the Tabernacle.[12] According to the latter prophets and some documents of Jewish Apocalyptic,[13] the eschatological Temple was also expected to function as the center of unity of the new people of God. As the center of the people of God, there can only be one Temple. Little wonder, then, that the prologue is quick to proclaim that the new Tabernacle is "the only Son."[14] The notion that Jesus is the unifying center of the new people of God will be further developed in the body of the Gospel, particularly in John 12:32.

Mention of the covenant also recalls that the covenant is the bond by which God has linked himself to his people in faithful loyalty and according to which He has addressed his commandments to his people as covenant prescriptions. It is particularly within the Deuteronomic tradition that these covenant stipulations are described as "commandments" (*entolai*). Nonetheless any idea that the covenant is consummated should entail as a correlative the notion that the commandments themselves have also been superceded. Within the context of Johannine theology, when the time has come for the old Temple to be replaced, Jesus announces a new commandment: "A new commandment I give to you, that you love one another; even as I have loved you, that you also love one another" (John 13:34).[15]

Finally, it ought to be noted that the Priestly tradition connects the Tabernacle with worship in the desert, just as the Temple itself would later be considered the privileged place for the worship of Yahweh. Indeed, the term *mo'ed*, originally meaning "meeting," came to designate an assembly that had come together to celebrate a feast. Some Old Testament texts even use the term as a metonym for feasts, especially for the great feasts of the

12. Cf. Num 2.

13. Isa 56:6-8; 60:4-7; 66:18-21; Zech 14:16-19; 1 En 90:33; *Sib. Or.* 3:702-718; 773-776; 808; 5:426-433; etc.

14. There is a dual problem affecting the expression: (i) the state of the Greek textual tradition and (ii) the interpretation of *monogenēs*. The matter is treated in the standard commentaries and by D. Moody, "God's Only Son, The Translation of John 3:16 in the Revised Standard Version" *JBL* 72 (1953) 213-219.

15. Cf. John 15:12.

Israelite nation. In this sense, *mo'ed* is used alongside the "new moons," "sabbaths" and the "great feasts" of Israel. Thus, as the *'ohel mo'ed*, the tent of meeting, the Tabernacle was the locus for festal celebration. The Tabernacle was the tent for feasts.

The Johannine tradition, which proclaims Jesus as the tabernacled presence of God, also shows that Jesus is the fulfillment of the Old Testament cultus. Successively John writes that the feast of Tabernacles, the Dedication, and the Passover are consummated in Jesus. In him the great feasts of the Israelite nation find a new meaning and are fulfilled. As he is the new Tabernacle and the replacement of the Temple, Jesus must necessarily be the locus of the new worship of the Father. This theme will be developed in the body of the Fourth Gospel, but it is already germinally present in John 1:14, whose full significance can only be appreciated in the light of the Old Testament's priestly tradition and the theology of the Fourth Gospel.

A Keynote of Johannine Throught

That Jesus is the replacement of the Temple is, in fact, one of the principal themes of the Fourth Gospel. Hence our attention should dwell briefly upon the principal passages (viz., 1:51; 2:13-25; 4:21-24; 10:7-9; 11:48-50; and 12:41)[16] which explicate the theme keynoted in John 1:14.

Since the time of Augustine, exegetes have recognized the connection between Jesus' enigmatic statement to Nathanael (John 1:51) and Jacob's vision at Bethel (Gen 12:8; 13:3-4). There Jacob had his vision (Gen 18:10-22). There the Israelites had consulted the Lord (Judg 20:18, 26; 21:2-5; 1 Sam 10:3). In short, Bethel was, according to ancient tradition, the place of Israel's primitive sanctuary, the locus of an ancient theophany, and the place of divine revelation.

According to the Fourth Gospel, however, it is in Jesus that true worship of the Father takes place (John 4:21-24). In Jesus

16. Cf. also John 7:37-38; 19:34.

man is enabled to see the Father (John 14:9) and perceive his glory (John 1:14; 2:11; 5:41; etc.). In Jesus the Word of God is conveyed to man (John 1:1; etc.). The functions which had primitively accrued to Bethel have finally been fulfilled in Jesus. Thus Jesus has taken the place of Bethel of old. Not only has Jesus replaced the Tabernacle (John 1:14); he has also superceded Israel's most ancient sanctuary. As Jesus is the true tabernacle, so he is the real Bethel, the authentic "dwelling place of God." In a word, Bethel was the prototype, Jesus the reality.

John 2:13-25 contains the Johannine description of the cleansing of the temple and Jesus' prophetic statement: "Destroy this temple (*naon*),[17] and in three days I will raise it up" (John 2:19). The Synoptic traditions allude to both the incident and the saying, but John has departed from the traditional order so that he can highlight the theological significance of the incident as a dramatic statement of one of the major themes of his gospel: the replacement of Jewish institutions.

The prophetic logion itself is best understood against the background of a notion that was already current in Judaism before the destruction of the Temple in 70 A.D.[18] No matter how magnificent the Temple was, it was only a material reality and so could not serve as the definitive dwelling place of God on earth. During the general renovation of all things, the Temple must disappear in order that it be replaced by the perfect sanctuary— the one not made by human hands, the one which does not properly belong to the created order. The actual destruction of the Temple by the Roman armies served to reinforce this tra-

17. In the New Testament *naos* is not generally distinguished from *hieron*. If a distinction is to be made, *naos* must refer to the central sanctuary, *hieron* to the Temple and its precincts. In John 2:13-25, the Temple cleansed by Jesus is cited as *hieron* or "my Father's house." The designation *naos* is first introduced into the narrative in Jesus' logion (v. 19). Subsequently it appears in the context of the commentary of the Jews (v. 20) and John's own commentary (v. 21). These three verses contain the only use of *naos* in the Fourth Gospel.

18. Cf. M. Simon, "Retour du Christ et reconstruction du Temple dans la pensée chrétienne primitive," in *Aux Sources de la tradition chrétienne*. M. Goguel *Festschrift* (Neuchâtel: Delachaux & Niestlé, 1950) pp. 251-252.

dition and strengthened the eschatological-apocalyptic expectations that were current in first century Palestine. Thus, in itself, Jesus' proclamation of the disappearance of the Temple was a prophetic utterance, consistent with the expectations of the times. What was striking in his proclamation was the suggestion[19] that the Jews themselves would destroy the Temple, God's dwelling place among his people. Not even Jeremiah who had foretold the destruction of the sanctuary of God as a punishment for Israel's sins (Jer 7:11-15) had dared to make such a statement.

Even more striking was Jesus' claim that he would raise up the sanctuary in three days. This aspect of his prophetic utterance took on new meaning in the light of Jesus' death and resurrection. The essentially christological import of the prophetic utterance is understood by the author's explanatory addition in John 2:21. Already, however, the prophetic logion itself implied that the new locus of the divine presence would be an improvement over the old. To "raise again" is not merely to replace. It is to do something different, to change the floor plan, to make improvements, etc. Yet the significance of the utterance goes beyond this to a Jewish tradition that the restoration of the Temple is one of the chief offices of the Messiah.[20] As Messiah, Jesus will raise up the new Temple. Thus John 2:19 is one of the clearest affirmations of messianic claims by the Johannine Jesus.

According to John's explanation, the new Temple to be raised by the Messiah, Jesus, was the temple of his body. Already some Old Testament texts had suggested that Yahweh himself had become the Temple.[21] The resurrected Lord would take the place of Yahweh himself as the Temple. There is little wonder, then, that the Johannine tradition proclaims that there will be no Temple in the new Jerusalem since "its temple is the Lord God

19. Of the various versions of the logion preserved in the New Testament, John 2:19 is the only one which attributed the responsibility for the destruction of the Temple to the Jews. I would consider John's version as the most authentic rendering of the saying.

20. Cf. *Ps. Sol.* 17:32-34; *Sib. Or.* 5:424-425.

21. Ezek 10:18; 11:15-16; cf. Jer 17:12-13; Isa 8:14.

the Almighty and the Lamb" (Rev 21:22).[22] This passage, along
with John 2:19, 21, is the clearest Johannine reference to the idea
that the resurrected Jesus is himself the new Temple.

Implicit in John 2:19-21 is, therefore, an affirmation of Jesus'
divinity[23] as well as an affirmation of his messianic claims. These
and other implications of the passage are not spelled out by John,
but they are apparent to those who insert John 2:19-21 into the
mainstream of Old and New Testament tradition. What the
passage further implies is that Jesus is the new place in which
occurs the encounter between God and man. In him God and
human nature are joined in one. In him the cult at Jerusalem has
been fulfilled and superseded. With him and in him the time of
the worship of God in spirit and in truth has dawned. In him the
Church[24] is the new assembly of God in which Jew and Gentile
are but one people before the Lord. Jesus is the house of God; he
is the place where God is to be adored.

Thus the implications of John 2:13-25 go far beyond the
purification of the cultus at Jerusalem. The author of the Fourth
Gospel generally avoids an explication of these implications, but
does develop one of them within the context of the conversation
between Jesus and the Samaritan woman (John 4:19-24). From
the Johannine dialogue it appears that it is the manner in which
men are to worship the Father rather than the place where
worship is to be offered which is the focal point of interest. Those
who worship must worship in spirit and in truth (v. 24). Here the
"spirit" can only mean the Spirit of God which Jesus is to give as
living water. The "truth" is the revelation which Jesus has given.
It is the Spirit which Jesus gives and the truth which is Jesus

22. Passages such as Rev 7:15-17; 11:19 and 16:17 do, however, speak of a
heavenly temple. This discrepancy is not entirely unexpected in a book of
apocalyptic writing, yet in this instance it may be due to the author's use of
sources in the composition of Revelation.

23. That the Tabernacle-Temple theme points to the divinity of Jesus is already
apparent from the first introduction of the theme at John 1:14.

24. This Pauline concept is not found in the Fourth Gospel. Nonetheless
John's association of the Temple theme and the resurrected body of Jesus attests
to traditional material out of which the Pauline notion developped.

himself which makes possible true worship of the Father. Not only has Jesus replaced the Temple; he also animates the worship which replaces the Temple cultus.

Although the emphasis of the dialogue lies on the manner in which true worship is offered to the Father, there underlies the notion that neither Mount Gerizim nor Jerusalem will subsist as places for authentic worship of the Father. The Samaritan temple on Gerizim had been destroyed under John Hyrcanus. Jesus had reiterated the prophetic utterance that the Temple at Jerusalem would be destroyed. Divisive worship in competing sanctuaries would come to an end. Worshipping communities comprised of "you" and "us" would be no more. The hour was coming when there would be but one true cult, the worship that takes place in and through Jesus himself.

The perspective of the conversation is that of eschatological promise. The Jews hoped that in the days to come all would worship on Zion. The Samaritans believed that all would worship on the mountain that was sacred to them.[25] Their respective beliefs were but different articulations of a common eschatological hope characterized by a vision of a single worshipping community comprising all the righteous. Jesus reiterated the promise, but announced that it would be realized neither on Zion nor on Gerizim. It was to be realized in himself who would enable all men to worship in Spirit and in truth.

The theme of Jesus as the new Temple is even more subtly developed in the second part of the Book of Signs (John 1:19-12:50). According to John 10:7,[26] Jesus proclaimed "I am the door of the sheepfold—sheep." The Greek text does not read "the door of the sheepfold," but *hē thura tōn probatōn*, the "door of the sheep," i.e., the gate for the sheep. The image is not so much that of a gate which gives a third party access to the sheep, but the gate through which the sheep themselves pass. Com-

---

25. Cf. J. MacDonald, *The Theology of the Samaritans*, NTL (London: SCM, 1964) pp. 385-386.
26. Cf. John 10:9.

mentators who appreciate this meaning of the text have usually
identified the gate to which Jesus makes reference in this solemn
proclamation with the gate of heaven.[27] Even this would seem to
be inadequate since it is hardly likely that the sheep go in and out
through the gate of heaven (vv. 3, 9). Entrance into heaven ought
to be one-way.

Thus I am inclined to look to the little parable (John 10:1-6)
which precedes the double reference to Jesus as the "door" as
providing the key to its meaning. There the sheepfold appears as
a means of protection in the night. The door has the function of
assuring this protection. The door also is the means by which the
sheep come in and out. The door is the way to the pasture as well
as the means of protection. In other words, the gate is the means
by which salvation is assured. In the Old Testament this notion is
associated with Jerusalem or the Temple, as well as with the gate
of the Temple used metonymously of the Temple itself. Ps 118:20
refers to the gate of the Lord, through which victors shall make
their entry. The psalm refers to the gate of the Temple as a *pulē*.
John has preferred the use of the term *thura*. This more generic
term is better adapted to the pastoral imagery of the Johannine
parable. It is, nonetheless, a term used in the Old Testament in
reference to the entrance to the Tabernacle (Exod 29:4; 33:9).

Thus John 10:7, 9 is a double affirmation that Jesus has taken
over the function of the gate of the Temple. He is the means by
which the sheep find protection and pasture. He is the source of
their salvation. Thus John 10:7, 9 might well be translated "I am
the place of salvation for the sheep."[28] By the use of metonymy,
Jesus has proclaimed that he is the new Temple. Comparison of
these verses with the preceding parable and the subsequent ex-
patiation reveals that Jesus is the only gate for the sheep. There is
only one flock which belongs to him. The point is clear. Jesus, as

27. Cf. C.K. Barrett, *St. John*, pp. 307-308; J. Marsh, *The Gospel of St. John*,
Pelican Gospel Commentaries (Harmonsworth: Penguin, 1968) p. 400, etc.

28. Cf. A.J. Simonis, *Die Hirtenrede im Johannes-Evangelium. Versuch einer
Analyse von Johannes 10,1-18 nach Entstehung. Hintergrund und Inhalt*. AnBib, 29
(Rome: Pontifical Biblical Institute, 1967) p. 206.

the gate, is the means by which the sheep are gathered into one. Jesus is the new collection point for salvation. The theme of the Temple as a unifying center has recurred.

In the perspective of the Fourth Gospel neither the theme of unity nor that of Jesus as the new Temple can be dissociated from the thought of Jesus' death and resurrection. Thus even the mentonymous reference to Jesus as the new Temple calls for mention of his laying down his life and receiving it back (vv. 11, 15, 17, 18). In fact, it is the risen Jesus who is the door for the sheep. No longer is the Temple the source of salvation. It is Jesus himself who is the true door, that is, the gate of the true Temple, the locus of salvation. With the death and resurrection of Jesus the Old Temple will have become useless.

Ironically it is the chief priests and the Pharisees who introduce the thought of the irrelevancy of the Temple by reflecting about its destruction: "If we leave him alone like this the whole populace will believe in him. Then the Romans will come and sweep away our temple (*ton topon*) and our nation" (John 11:48). Both Old and New Testament tradition indicate that it is the temple which is "the place" (*ho topos*) *par excellence*.[29] The Pharisees and the high priests were ready to sacrifice one man in order to preserve their hegemony over the Temple and their privileged status as the people of Yahweh. In fact, the death of Jesus was decreed. Then, by way of supreme irony, what the Jews had sought to avoid actually befell them. The Temple was destroyed by the Romans. The effective universalization of Jesus' mission was brought about by his death-exaltation (John 12:24, 32). With his death came the end of the privileged position of the Jews. The exalted Lord would draw all men to himself. By his death the scattered children of Israel were gathered into the unity of the true Israel. The irony of it all is that it was the Pharisees and priests who linked the death of Jesus with the destruction of their beloved Temple.

With John 12:41, the Johannine Tabernacle-Temple theme is

29. Cf. 2 Macc 5:19; Jer 7:14; Neh 4:7; Matt 24:15; Acts 6:13, 14; 7:8; 21:28.

brought to a close.[30] Isaiah's vision of the heavenly Temple allows him to perceive the glory of the Lord, which John explicates as the glory of Jesus. According to this piece of Johannine theology, Isaiah had no more difficulty in appreciating the divinity of Jesus than did Abraham (John 8:56). His vision of the heavenly Temple is a vision of the glory of the Lord which dwells within it—the glory of Jesus himself. To see the Heavenly Temple is to perceive the glory of Jesus.

With this affirmation, John's thought has come full-cycle. He had begun by announcing that Jesus was the true Tabernacle, come to dwell among us (John 1:14), and endowed with the glory as of the only Son of the Father. In the history of salvation, the Tabernacle had given way to the Temple as the locus of God's presence among men. According to John's theology, not even the Temple could be the definitive locus of God's presence among men. At most it was a prototype and foreshadowing of the true Tabernacle, the true Temple, Jesus himself. He is the eschatological mode of God's presence among men, the locus of revelation and the place of salvation. In him all men can contemplate the glory of the Lord.

---

30. I.e., apart from the problematic reference in John 19:34.

12. "A NEW COMMANDMENT I GIVE TO YOU, THAT YOU LOVE ONE ANOTHER..." (JOHN 13:34)

By way of conclusion to an examination of the love ethic in the Johannine writings in the important monograph which he consecrated to the moral teaching of the New Testament, Rudolf Schnackenburg wrote that "St. John is not a only a loyal guardian of Christ's inheritance preserving his spirit but also a disciple of the Lord illumined by the Holy Spirit, giving added profundity to the commandment of love and raising it to be the ruling principle of Christian morality throughout all ages."[1] Schnackenburg's enthusiastic praise of the Johannine endeavor is undoubtedly shared by most believers and teachers of morality who stand within the Christian tradition. It is, nonetheless, an enthusiasm which some contemporary exegetes refuse to share. Many of them see in the Johannine formulation of the love commandment, not so much a new profundity as a restriction of the commandment in view of the so-called sectarianism of the Fourth Gospel. Illustrative of this other position is the opinion offered by the Tübingen exegete, Ernst Käsemann. Käsemann claims that the Fourth Gospel was intended for a Johannine conventicle whose thought-patterns were decidedly gnostic. In view of this gnostic sectarianism, Käsemann proffers the opinion that "the object of Christian love for John is only what belongs to the community under the Word, or what is elected to belong to it, that is, the brotherhood of Jesus."[2]

This dichotomy of opinion is sufficient to indicate that the meaning of the Johannine "new commandment" is not as easy to ascertain as a first reading of the Gospel might suggest. In point of fact, the interpretation of John 13:34 raises a series of ex-

1. Rudolf Schnackenburg, *The Moral Teaching of the New Testament* (New York: Herder, 1969) pp. 328-329.

2. Ernst Käsemann, *The Testament of Jesus. A Study of John in the Light of Chapter 17*. NTL (Philadelphia: Westminster, 1968) p. 65.

egetical questions for which a response must be found if the Johannine version of Christ's command to love is to be understood fully. These questions are of a literary, linguistic, and theological nature.

From the standpoint of a literary consideration of John 13:34 the exegete must direct his attention to the appearance of the verse within the Johannine farewell discourse (John 13:31-14:31). Although the discourse apparently concludes at 14:31, it is followed by other farewell discourse material (John 15-16) which also includes the love commandment: John 15:12 and John 15:17. According to Raymond Brown, these verses are "related to and perhaps a duplicate of" 13:34.[3] In these passages, however, the commandment is not styled "a new commandment." This expression recurs in the New Testament only in 1 John 2:7-8 and 2 John 5. Given the rarity of the expression, some authors conclude that it is to 1 John 2:7-8 that we must go if we are to understand the meaning of the "new commandment" in John 13:34. This quickly brings one to a thorny aspect of the Johannine problem, namely the relationship between the Johannine epistles and the Fourth Gospel. When literary considerations are brought to bear upon the Gospel, considered as it were in isolation from other elements of the Johannine corpus, attention must be directed to the relationship between John 13:34-35 and the footwashing scene (John 13:1-20) as well as to the relationship between the love command of John 15:12, 17 and the parable of the true vine (John 15:1-11).

From the standpoint of a linguistic analysis of the text, two questions call for careful consideration. First of all, in what sense can the Johannine love command be styled a "new" commandment? Apparently the qualification was traditional within Johannine circles. Nevertheless it seems to have been problematic for the author of 1 John who writes, "Beloved, I am writing you no new commandment, but an old commandment which you had from the beginning; the old commandment is the word which you

3. Raymond E. Brown, *The Gospel According to John. XIII-XXI.* AB, 29A (Garden City, NY: Doubleday, 1970) p. 681.

have heard. Yet I am writing you a new commandment" (1 John 2:7-8a). The author of the Fourth Gospel used the adjective *kainos* (new) but twice in his Gospel, namely in John 13:34 and again in 19:41. There the term is used with an obviously different meaning (the "new tomb"). Why, then, does the author use this adjective in John 13:34? The Fourth Gospel clearly stands within the Judeo-Christian tradition. Within Judaism the love command was at least as old as Lev 19:18; within Christianity the love command was at least as old as the Synoptic traditions reflected in the discussion on the greatest commandment in the Law (Mark 12:28-34 and par.) and those lying behind the Sermon on the Mount (Matt 5:43-48; Luke 6:27-28, 32-36). Why, then, is the Johannine formulation of the love command designated a "new commandment?"

In addition, attention must be directed to the very use of the term *entolē* ("commandment") in John's formulation of the Jesuanic logion. John uses the term in a sense different from that of the Synoptics. There *entolē* characteristically refers to the commandments of the Torah. As John uses the term, however, *entolē* refers to the commandments which the Father has addressed to the Son. It is also used of the commandments which Jesus addresses to his disciples. Does the use of the term imply an order issued from without? What is the relationship between the commandments (plural) of Jesus and his commandment (singular)?

From the standpoint of an analysis of the text which I would call theological because it has reference to the meaning of the Scripture as the "ruling principle of Christian morality," there are again two major issues to be raised. First of all, there is the matter of the object of love.[4] According to the Johannine version

4. It is commonly noted that the Gospel of John, unlike the Synoptics (Mark 12:28-34 and par.), unlike 1 John as well (1 John 4:10, 20 (2 ×), 21; 5:2), does not refer to God as the direct object of the disciples' love. Cf., for example, André Feuillet, "La morale chrétienne d'après saint Jean," *Esprit et Vie* 83 (1973) 665-670, pp. 669-670; K. Ottoson, "The Love of God in St. John Chrysostom's Commentary on the Fourth Gospel," *Church Quarterly Review* 166 (1965) 315-323, p. 317. The problematic entailed by John's omission of God as the object of love will not be my concern in the present essay.

of the command, the disciples are to love "one another." The
Synoptics characteristically speak of love of one's "neighbor" or
love of one's "enemy." Albeit it from radically different perspectives,
authors as different as William Wrede, Ethelbert Stauffer, Hugh
Montefiore, Archbishop Bernard, Brown, and Käsemann indicate
that the Johannine command has a scope more restricted than
that of the Synoptics.[5] Is there truly a difference between the
Johannine and Synoptic traditions?[6] If so, does this difference
reflect an impoverishment or an intensification of the Johannine
tradition as seen against that of the Synoptics? This question has
been raised with renewed earnestness in recent years because of
interest in the possible Gnostic background of the Fourth Gospel
as well in the comparison of John and the Qumran writings.

A second point to be considered is the christological import of
the "new commandment." The issue is all the more important in
that there exists an ever-growing consensus which holds that the
christological and eschatological character of the New Testament
ethic constitutes the hallmark of this ethic. Specifically the issue
of the christological import of the Johannine new commandment
must be raised in view of the christological insertion at John
13:34, "as I have loved you."[7] A similar insertion is not to be
found in the Synoptic or Pauline versions of the love command.
Granted the Johannine formulation of the insertion, some discussion
must be had as to the nature of the christological reference. Is

5. Stauffer, for example, comments: "It is not love for one's fellow man which
Jesus proclaimed, with which the Johannine corpus is concerned: it is the love of
the Christian brother and fellow-believer." Even C.H. Dodd noted that "Probably...the early church narrowed the concept of neighbour until it was equivalent
to church member." Cf. E. Stauffer, *Die Botschaft Jesu, damals und heute*. Dalp-
Taschenbücher, 333 (Bern: Franke, 1959) p. 47; C.H. Dodd, *Gospel and Law; The
Relation of Faith and Ethics in Early Christianity* (Cambridge: University Press,
1953) p. 42.

6. Ludwig Berg has relegated, in effect, this discussion to a relatively secondary
place by stressing that the emphasis of the love commandment is on the spontaneity
of love, "that man should *be loving*," rather than on the object of love, "that man
should love *someone*." He finds a confirmation of his opinion in the exemplarity of
God's love. Cf. L. Berg, "Das neutestamentliche Liebesgebet-Prinzip der Sittlich-
keit," *TTZ* 83 (1974) 129-145, esp. pp. 134-136.

7. Cf. John 15:12.

Christ the exemplar of fraternal love or is he the source of
fraternel love? Should we perhaps speak of both at once and of
even more? Such are but some of the issues to which the
remainder of this essay will be devoted as it seeks to shed some
light on John 13:34: "A new commandment I give to you, that
you love one another; even as I have loved you, that you also
love one another."

The Farewell Discourse

It is now commonly asserted that John 13:31-16:33 is written
according to the literary genre of the farewell discourse.[8]
Approximately fifty speeches ascribed to famous men in anticipation
of their deaths have been preserved for us in biblical and extra-
biblical sources. A most striking example of the genre is to be
found in the speeches of the *Testaments of the Twelve Patriarchs*.
Farewell discourses typically contain exhortations to keep the
commandments of God, especially the commandment to love one
another, and thus manifest the unity of the brethren. Indeed, in
an unpublished dissertation, John F. Randall[9] has demonstrated
that *agapē* (charity) is one of the most commonplace words in the
whole literature. Love is sometimes expressed in service. Love
serves as a sign for the nations. Joseph is the example or image of
fraternal love. Randall's study thus points to fraternal charity as
a characteristic trait of the farewell discourse genre. Consequently
the appearance of the exhortation to fraternal charity in the
farewell discourses of the Fourth Gospel is to be expected. In
effect, the presence of the love motif in the Johannine farewell

8. Among the characteristic traits of the farewell discourse found in John are
the use of direct style ("I-you") and the characteristic expression, "little children"
(John 13:33. Cf. *T. Gad* 4:1-2; 6:1; *T. Rub.* 1:3, 4:5; *T. Iss.* 5:1; 6:1). Cf. Noël
Lazure, "Louange au Fils de l'homme et commandement nouveau. Jean 13, 31-
33a. 34-35," *AsSeig* 26 (1973) 73-80, p. 74. For a brief exposition of the literary
genre, one might consult R.E. Brown, *John. XIII-XXI*, pp. 597-603.

9. Cf. John F. Randall, *The Theme of Unity in John XVII:20-23*, Louvain,
doctoral dissertation, 1962, pp. 63-83.

discourses is not as striking as is the specificity with which John casts his presentation of the love command.

That the exhortation to fraternel love is integral to the Johannine farewell discourses has been confirmed by André Feuillet's comparative structural analysis of John and 1 John.[10] Feuillet notes that whereas "light" and "life" are the key words of the first part of the Gospel, *agapē* (love) and *agapan* (to love) are the key words which characterize the second part of John. Of the thirty-six appearances of these two words[11] in the Fourth Gospel, thirty-one are found in the farewell discourses, where the verb is employed twenty-five times and the noun appears some six times. The verse which occupies our attention not only contains three of the verbal uses of *agapan*; it also makes use of a characteristic Johannine expression, the *kathōs*-relationship formula, in a way which is restricted to the farewell discourses and the "high priestly prayer" which is appended to them.[12]

While a consideration of the literary genre of the farewell discourse and the use of agapeic vocabulary in John 13:31-16:33 confirm one another in the assertion that the theme of love is integral to John's farewell discourse, we may not overlook the fact that the extant text of John 13-17 gives evidence of having developed over a long period of time before reaching its present form.[13] The problematic "Rise, let us go hence" of John 14:31 as well as the many parallels between John 13-14 and 15-16 have led many authors to consider that the Johannine farewell discourse contains two editions of the same discourse or considerable

10. André Feuillet, "The Structure of First John. Comparison with the Fourth Gospel. The Pattern of Christian Life," *BTB* 3 (1973) 194-216.

11. For some general considerations on Johannine "love" vocabulary, cf. Ceslaus Spicq, *Agape in the New Testament*, 3 (St. Louis: Herder, 1966).

12. The usage of the formula to compare the relationship between Jesus and his disciples with that among the disciples is restricted to John 13:15, 34; 15:12; 17:14, 16. De Dinechin considers this to be a third (of four) type of *Kathōs*-relationship, which he calls "*agape* as similitude." Cf. Oliver de Dinechin, "ΚΑΘΩΣ: La similtude dans l'évangile selon saint Jean," *RSR* 58 (1970) 195-236, pp. 208-209.

13. Cf. J.M. Reese, "Literary Structure of John 13:31-14:31; 16:5-6, 16-33," *CBQ* 34 (1972) 321-331, p. 321.

secondary material (John 15-17) which has been added to an earlier text by a later redactor, a disciple of the evangelist.[14] Indeed Zimmermann has suggested that John 13-14 and 15-16 constitute two discourses.[15]

In any event the commandment of love, found at 13:34 and 15:12, is one of the duplicative elements which have led the majority[16] of Johannine commentators to conclude that the present text of John 13-17 is a composite whose present format results from a later redaction of the Johannine text. Within this perspective it has been suggested that the exhortation to love one another (John 13:34-35) is out of place in its present context and may well have been inserted into the farewell discourse from some other tradition of Jesuanic logia.[17] Analysis of John 13:31-38 reveals that the pericope has a structural pattern which recurs some six times in John 13-17.[18] The structural pattern consists of three elements: a revelation by Jesus, a question by his interlocutors who speak on a superficial level, and a response by Jesus to clarify his original revelation. Since the love commandment (vv. 34-35) is not alluded to within the context, it must be considered as an addition to the pattern.[19] Thus, the pericope

14. Thus, in various ways, A. Merx, P. Gächter, C.H. Dodd, C.K. Barrett, A. Wikenhauser, R. Schnackenburg, M.-E. Boismard, etc. A brief discussion of the issue is offered by R.E. Brown, *John. XIII-XXI*, pp. 582-586. George Johnston divides John 13-16 into three speeches, 13:31-14:31, 15:1-16:4a, 16:4b-33, without, however, accepting a duplicate version theory. Cf. George Johnston, *The Spirit-Paraclete in the Gospel of John*. SNTSMS, 12 (Cambridge: University Press, 1970) pp. 72, 168.

15. Cf. Heinrich Zimmermann, "Struktur und Aussageabsicht der johanneischen Abschiedsieden (Jo. 13-17)," *BibLeb* 8 (1967) 279-290. Zimmermann (p. 289) even cites the change of locale, indicated at John 14:31, as support for his theory.

16. Cf. Jürgen Becker, "Die Abschiedsreden Jesu in Johannesevangelium," *ZNW* 616 (1970) 215-246, p. 218.

17. Cf. J. Becker, "Die Abschiedsreden," p. 220. Becker cites Heitmüller, Wellhausen, Hirsch, and Richter.

18. Cf. J.M. Reese, "Literary Structure."

19. Cf. J.M. Reese, "Literary Structure," pp. 323-324. Schnackenburg agrees that vv. 34-35 are a redactional insertion. In favor of his opinion he cites seven arguments including the link between vv. 33 and 36 and the fact that John 14 does not dwell on the love commandment. Cf. R. Schnackenburg, *Das Johannesevangelium, 3. Kommentar zu Kap. 13-21*, HTKNT 4/3 (Freiburg: Herder, 1975)

within which the love commandment occurs, John 13:31-38, must be considered as a composite text with its own history. In this composite text the love commandment is situated within a frame of reference which has the departure of Jesus as its theme. By means of the sandwich technique,[20] a redactor has highlighted the love commandment as the legacy of the departing Jesus for the community which he has left behind.

By identifying six instances of the revelation-question-clarification pattern in John 13:31-14:31 and 16:4-33, Reese has called into question the broadly held theory that John 14 and John 16 are duplicate discourses. While accepting John 15:1-16:4 as a later insertion,[21] he has raised many questions, not the least of which is the unity of the present redaction of the farewell discourse. In an independent study,[22] Günter Reim has identified 15:18-16:4 as the later insertion and cites the changed situation of the community—namely, one of persecution—as its Sitz-im-Leben. Thus any attempt to explicate the farewell discourse in its present unity must take into account that the composite text is both a reflection upon the disciples' relationship to Jesus in his absence and a reflection upon the disciples' relationship to the world in its persecution. This is, of course, the point of Zimmermann's article, which so emphasizes the differences between John 13-14 and 15-16 as to conclude that they constitute two discourses, the first (13-14) expressing the significance of Jesus' departure and its bearing upon the situation of the Church while Jesus is with the Father, whereas the second (15-16) bears on the significance of Jesus' union with the disciples and their situation in the world.

---

p. 59. Bultmann suggests that vv. 34-35 are the evangelist's insertion into his "revelation discourse" source. Cf. R. Bultmann, *The Gospel According to John* (Oxford: Blackwell, 1971) pp. 523-524. Heinz Becker, however, allows for the trace of sources in 13:31-38 but concludes that the pericope is largely the composition of the Evangelist. Cf. H. Becker, *Die Reden des Johannesevangelium und der Stil der gnostischen Offenbarungsrede*. FRALNT, 50 (Göttingen: Vandenhoeck und Ruprecht, 1956) p. 94.

20. Cf. N. Lazure, "Louange," p. 73.

21. J.M. Reese, "Literary Structure," p. 323.

22. G. Reim, "Probleme des Abschiedsreden," *BZ* 20 (1976) 117-122, p. 117.

Despite the differences, we must note that the present text constitutes a unity[23] in which it is possible to discern an emphasis on the modality of Jesus' presence in his absence in the first part, and an emphasis on the recognition of the world in the second part. Within this unified body of material the evangelist and/or redactor have interspersed their version of traditions which are otherwise formulated in the Synoptic Gospels.[24]

When now we look to the Johannine formulation of the love commandment within the context of the farewell discourses, it is apparent that the author would have his readers understand the love commandment in specific reference to the passion-glorification of Jesus. The *oun*[25] ("therefore") of 13:31 indicates that the entire pericope, consisting of vv. 31-38, must be considered in the light of the passion. If Bultmann's suggestion to the effect that the *arti* ("now") of v. 33 relates in fact to the love commandment of v. 34,[26] then clearly the hour of the Son of Man gives urgency to the commandment itself. Now that he is about to depart in the hour of his exaltation-glorification, the Son of Man gives the new commandment of love to his disciples as his legacy and challenge.

---

23. Cf. John L. Boyle, "The Last Discourse (John 13,31-16,33) and Prayer (John 17): Some Observations on Their Unity and Development," *Bib* 56 (1975) 210-222.

24. In these five chapters (John 13-17) John has gathered together his version of material which the Synoptics have dispersed throughout. We might cite the mission logia (Mark 6:7-11 and par.), the instruction on life in the Christian community (Mark 9:35-40), the warning about persecution and the promise of divine assistance (Mark 13:9-13), the prediction of the Passion (Mark 13:26-27), the prediction of Judas' betrayal, Peter's denial, and the disciples' scattering (Mark 14:18-21, 26-31). Lagrange was in fact so impressed by some of these parallels that he considered John 15:1-17 to be the Johannine parallel of the Synoptics' mission discourse. We should also note the presence of the "Truly, truly, I say to you" formula—a formula which Lindars has identified as generally indicating a traditional logion. Cf. John 13:16,20,21; 14:12; 16:20,23 (with "you" in the plural); John 13:38 (with "you" in the singular). Cf. M.-J. Lagrange, *Saint Jean.* EBib (6th. ed.: Paris, Gabalda, 1936) p. 399; B. Lindars, *The Gospel of John,* New Century Bible (London: Oliphants, 1972) p. 48.

25. Cf. Francis J. Moloney, *The Johannine Son of Man,* Biblioteca de scienze religiose, 14 (Rome: LAS, 1976) p. 195; cf. p. 199.

26. Cf. R. Bultmann, *John,* p. 525, n. 2; R.E. Brown, *John. XIII-XXI,* p. 607; O. de Dinechin, "ΚΑΘΩΣ", p. 212.

In John 15, the love commandment (v. 12) is followed by a passage which explicitly cites the passion as an example of the love to be imitated by Jesus' disciples: "Greater love has no man than this, that a man lay down his life for his friends" (v. 13). Thus the reference to the passion is a consistent and specifically Johannine element[27] in the presentation of the new commandment.

From the literary point of view, both John 13:34-35 and 15:12, 17 are joined to a symbolic narrative. The new commandment of John 13 is linked to the footwashing scene (John 13:1-20).[28] The composition of the scene owes to Johannine redaction. Whether its refers essentially to the passion as a symbolic action or to baptism as a sacramental action remains, however, a moot question.[29] In any event, the present redaction of the scene offers Jesus' washing of his disciples' feet as a *hupodeigma*, an "example" (v. 15), to be followed by his disciples. The example shows that the love which the disciples are to imitate is the example of loving service, directed to one another. In its turn, the love commandment in John 15:12 has been linked to the parable of the vine and the branches (John 15:1-11).[30] Both the parable and the pericope which follows (15:9-17) are concerned with the fruitfulness of the word of Jesus. *Menein* ("abide") serves as the catch-word which links together the two inseparable pericopes. The catch-word demonstrably points to the intimate relationship among the Father's love for Jesus, Jesus' love for his disciples,

27. Cf. R. Thysman, "L'éthique de l'imitation du Christ dans le Nouveau Testament. Situation, notations et variations du thème," *ETL* 42 (1966) 138-175, pp. 173-174. Thysman speaks of the salvific deeds as grounding "imitation ethics."

28. Cf. Lucien Cerfaux, "La charité fraternelle et le retour du Christ (Jo., XIII, 33-38)," *ETL* 24 (1948) 321-332, rp. in *Receuil Lucien Cerfaux* II, 27-40, cf. p. 37; R. Percival Brown, "*entolē kainē* (St. John 13,38)," *Theology* 26 (1933) 184-193, pp. 184-185, 193; Jack Seynaeve, "La 'charité' chrétienne est-elle dépassée?", *Revue du clergé africain* 27 (1972) 389-413, pp. 393, 399.

29. Cf. Georg Richter, *Die Fusswaschung im Johannesevangelium. Geschichte ihrer Deutung*. Biblische Untersuchungen, 1 (Regensburg: Pustet, 1967) pp. 252-259. Cf. J.D.G. Dunn, "The Washing of the Disciples' Feet in John 13:1-20," *ZNW* 61 (1970) 247-252.

30. Cf. Piet van Boxel, "Glaube und Liebe. Die Aktualiteit des johanneischen Jüngermodells," *Geist und Leben* 48 (1975) 18-28, p. 25.

and the disciples' love for one another. The pericope concludes with the refrain, "This I command you, to love one another" (v. 17). Although this verse was undoubtedly added to the narrative at a relatively late stage of composition,[31] it truly belongs to the narrative as presently edited. Indeed a quick look at the text shows that the thought of vv. 16-17 picks up the thought of vv. 7-8, albeit in reverse order.[32] Thus, the discourse material added to each of the symbolic narratives offers significant reflections on the Johannine notion of love as well as on the symbolic narratives themselves.

These brief reflections on the context of the love commandment in the Fourth Gospel have served to show that the evangelist and his disciple-redactor have truly integrated the theme of mutual love into the farewell discourses. Behind the farewell discourses of John 13-17 lies the history of the composition of the Johannine text. The pericopes in which the love commandment appears show clear and considerable evidence of Johannine composition/redaction. As a result, the entirety of the farewell discourses is encompassed by the theme of love, which occurs at their outset (13:1) and their conclusion (17:26). The most obvious lesson to be learned from the author's redactional efforts is that he would have the love command understood in reference to Jesus' passion-glorification. It is the passion-glorification which imparts meaning to the love commandment; the love commandment is Jesus' legacy for his own to be fulfilled during the period of his absence. Such are but a few elements connoted by the rich Johannine formulation of the love commandment.

31. On the other hand, Dibelius argued that it was vv. 13-15 which do not fit well into the context. The linchpin of his thesis was that v. 13 offered an example of "heroic" love which is not otherwise characteristic of the thought of the fourth evangelist. Cf. Martin Dibelius, "Joh. 15,13. Eine Studie zum Traditionsproblem des Johannesevangeliums," in *Festgabe für Adolf Deissmann zum Geburtstag 7 November 1927* (Tübingen: Mohr, 1927) pp. 168-186.

32. Cf. P. van Boxel, "Glaube und Liebe," p. 25.

The Johannine Epistles

To speak of the love commandment as a "new commandment" is to speak the language of the Johannine school. The Johannine phraseology "new commandment" appears not only in John 13:34 but also in 1 John 2:7-8 and 2 John 5.[33] All three of these writings reflect a situation of tension within the Christian community. The tension present in the life situation of 1-2 John appears nevertheless to be more critical than that of the life situation of the farewell discourses.[34] It is to the situation of some crisis that John draws our attention when he writes of a commandment which is "no new commandment," the "old commandment," and yet "a new commandment" as he does in 1 John 2:7-8: "Beloved, I am writing you no new commandment, but an old commandment which you had from the beginning; the old commandment is the word which you have heard. Yet I am writing you a new commandment, which is true in him and in you, because the darkness is passing away and the true light is already shining." A similar assertion, but without the reversal of thought, is to be found in 2 John: "And now I beg you, lady, not as though I were writing you a new commandment, but the one we have had from the beginning, that we love one another."

The polemical aspects of each of these passages is clear enough. John affirms that the love commandment is not a new one

33. I cannot now consider the interrelationship among the five books in the Johannine corpus (John, 1,2,3 John, Rev) in full detail. As a working hypothesis, I would only suggest that the five books emanate from the same, somewhat closed, circle of Christians. This I find it useful to speak as does Culpepper of "the Johannine school." Nevertheless I am inclined to the view that no two of the writings which directly concern the present essay—John, 1 John, 2 John—derive from the same hand. Notwithstanding my acceptance of this view, and without therefore implying common authorship, it seems useful to maintain the traditional designation "John" as an indiscriminate signum to identify the authors of the respective texts. Cf. R. Alan Culpepper, *The Johannine School. An Evaluation of the Johannine-school Hypothesis Based on an Investigation of the Nature of Ancient Schools*. SBLDS, 26 (Missoula: Scholars, 1975).

34. Cf. David L. Mealand, "The Language of Mystical Union in the Johannine Writings," *DR* 95 (1977) 19-34, p. 32.

because his correspondents have heard it "from the beginning."
For John's correspondents, the love commandment cannot be
considered a new revelation. The love commandment was part of
their baptismal catechesis.[35] That is certainly the import of the
explanatory formula, "the old commandment is the word which
you heard" (v. 7).[36] For the recipients of the letter the commandment is not new, since they have received it as part of their
fundamental catechesis, from the very beginning of their faith in
Christ. Yet the author of the letter may well have intended to say
even more. He may have intended to affirm not only that the
recipients of the letter had received the love commandment along
with the initial proclamation of the Gospel *to them*, but also that
the love commandment is the commandment which Christianity
has had from the very beginning, that is, from the first moment of
the proclamation of the Gospel.[37] If this is indeed the case, then
John is both affirming his fidelity to the proclamation of the
primitive Gospel and indicating that the primitive (i.e., in Johannine terms, the "old") Gospel was actualized in the baptismal
catechesis of the recipients of the letter.

The contrast between the old and the new makes sense only if
we understand why the author takes pains to affirm that the love

35. Thus, Matthew Vallanickal. Cf. *The Divine Sonship of Christians in the
Johannine Writings*. AnBib, 72 (Rome: Pontifical Biblical Institute, 1978) p. 234.
Rudolf Schnackenburg speaks only of "the beginning of their Christian life"
whereas Bultmann speaks of "the point within history in which the Christian
proclamation was received by the believers." Cf. R. Schnackenburg, *Die Johannes-
briefe*, HTKNT 13/3 (2nd. ed.: Freiburg: Herder, 1963) p. 111; R. Bultmann, *The
Johannine Epistles*. Hermaneia (Philadelphia: Fortress, 1973) pp. 27, 111. For a
similar opinion, cf. Johannes Schneider, *Die Briefe des Jacobus, Petrus, Judas und
Johannes. Die katholische Briefe*. NTD, 10 (9th. ed.: Göttingen: Vandenhoeck und
Ruprecht, 1961) p. 150.

36. Cf. 1 John 2:7, 18, 24; 3:11; 4:3.

37. Cf. J. Schneider, *Die Briefe*, p. 191; R. Schnackenburg, *Die Briefe*, p. 311
(both in reference to 2 John 5). Cf. also H. Conzelmann, "Was von Anfang war,"
Neutestamentliche Studien für Rudolf Bultmann. BZNW, 21 (Berlin: Töpelmann,
1954) 194-202, esp. pp. 195-199; V. Furnish, *The Love Command in the New
Testament* (Nashville: Abingdon, 1972) p. 152. This opinion is also offered by
Alphonse Humbert. Cf. A. Humbert, "L'observance des commandments dans les
écrits johanniques," *Studia Moralia* I (1963) 187-219, p. 206.

commandment of Christian tradition is not new. His concern is undoubtedly occasioned by the Gnostics who are the trublesome opponents for the author of both letters. It is hardly likely that the Gnostics had proposed any "new commandments." What is more likely is that they exploited a "new Christian experience" in the Spirit at the expense of Christian tradition.[38] Within that perspective, the Gnostics considered such commandments as the love commandments to be an outmoded part of tradition. In contrast the Johannine authors suggest that what is new is later and lacks the necessary authority to be an authentic part of the Christian experience. In this sense the love commandment is certainly not new—for it is the commandment of Jesus himself.[39]

Nevertheless the commandment which is not new in one sense is indeed new in another sense. Thus we have the paradox of 1 John 2: 7-8:[40] the commandment which is not new, but old, is, in fact, new. It is clear that the author of 1 John knew the logion of John 13:34; most probably his readers knew the logion as well.[41] His reference to the past, made in the heat of controversy, has brought him to consider the newness of the commandment which he is proposing once again.[42] The commandment of love has been given for those who abide in the light by none other than the Lord himself. The commandment is new because it is the commandment for the new age. Thus the author of 1 John affirms that the newness of the commandment owes to the fact that its

38. Cf. A.E. Brooke who write that "the real force of the expression is to heighten the contrast of the 'newer' teaching which places knowledge higher than love." A.E. Brooke, *The Johannine Epistles*. ICC (Edinburgh: Clark, 1912) p. 35. Commenting on 2 John 5, Schnackenburg notes that the love commandment is formulated not only to insist on brotherly love but also to underscore the link with older tradition. Cf. R. Schnackenburg, *Die Briefe*, p. 311. Cf. also R. Bultmann, *The Johannine Epistles*, p. 27; J. Schneider, *Die Briefe*, p. 150.

39. In this respect Balz, Brooke, and others note that the Jesuanic commandment is also the commandment of God. Cf. Horst Balz, *Die Katholische Briefe*. NTD, 10 (11th ed.: Göttingen: Vandenhoeck und Ruprecht, 1973) p. 170; A.E. Brooke, *Johannine Epistles*, p. 35.

40. Cf. Marinus de Jonge, *De Brieven van Johannes*. De Prediking van het Nieuw Testament (Nijkerk: Callenbach, 1968) p. 82.

41. M. de Jonge, *ibid.*

42. Cf. the *palin* ("yet" (RSV), literally "again") in 1 John 2:8.

truth[43] derives from Christ himself ("truth in him" — v. 8), and that its fulfillment is pertinent to the lives of Christians ("and in you") who live in the new age. In effect the love commandment is new because it is the eschatological commandment, the commandment for the new age,[44] ethics for the final times.[45]

In this new age love for one another is proof of one's love for God.[46] If one does not have mutual love, then one is only a liar. He belongs to the realm of darkness, rather than to the realm of light. Thus the love commandment is much more than one among the other Christian commandments. It is even more than the most important commandment in the Christian moral code. It is the decisive commandment.[47] For the Johannine authors, the fulfillment of the love commandment is the sign of true knowledge of God and the sign of belonging to the community of light. The one who does not practice brotherly love can no more claim to have true knowledge of God than membership in the brotherhood; he has cut himself off from one and the other. Thus the commandment of mutual love is "new" precisely insofar as it is the hallmark of the new age. 1 John, therefore, insists with even more emphasis than is found in the Gospel, that love for the brethren is the distinctive sign of belonging to the Christian community. The exercise of brotherly love is the essential manifestation of the Christian life. The commandment of mutual love is part of the traditional and authoritative proclamation of the Gospel. As such it is paradoxically old and new at the same time.

43. Bultmann's comment is apropos. He writes: "*Alēthēs* therefore does not mean 'true' in the sense of 'correct,' but characterizes the 'new commandment' as something verifying itself as real. That it verifies itself as real in the congregation is also said in 3:14." R. Bultmann, *Johannine Epistles*, p. 27, n. 20.

44. Cf. H. Balz, *Die Katholische Briefe*, p. 171; R. Schnackenburg, *Die Johannesbriefe*, pp. 111-112; R. Bultmann, *The Johannine Epistles*, p. 27.

45. Cf. J. Becker, "Die Abschiedsreden."

46. Cf. R. Schnackenburg, *Die Johannesbriefe*, p. 111; David L. Mealand, "Language," p. 32. Vallanickal writes, "*agapē* in John becomes an objective reality, a form of existence, a concrete expression of the life of God in this world." Cf. M. Vallanickal, *Divine Sonship*, p. 314.

47. Cf. J. Schneider, *Die Briefe*, p. 151.

It pertains to the traditional kerygma, and proclaims an ethic pertinent to the time of waiting for the end.

We must note, nevertheless, that it is on the commandment as such, as a precept demanding observance in behavior,[48] that the author of 1 John insists in the first pericope of his epistle in which he dwells upon the theme of love which pervades the entire document.[49] Subsequently[50] he will cite (1 John 3:10-24) the example of Christ as a model for love among the brethren. The author calls for a concrete expression of love: a love of one's "brothers" in mutual service.[51] Still later in the epistle (1 John 4:7-21) he will turn his attention to God as the very source of love. Thus while he chooses to counter the Gnostics' deviant neglect of the practice of mutual love by referring to the Lord's promulgation of a commandment (1 John 2:8), his total understanding of love is that it is a necessary concomitant of union with God.

The Love Commandment

In his commentary on 1 John 2:7-8, Bultmann not only suggests that this pair of verses has been added to a source by the redactor of the epistle but that the use of "commandment" in the singular

48. We must note the practicality of the love commandment's demand. Mutual love is a matter of exercise, practice, action. Thus Schnackenburg, contrary to Brooke (p. 177) takes the *hina* clause of 2 John 5 as dependent on *erōtō* ("beg") rather than on *entolēn* ("commandment"). In effect the text should be understood as follows: "And now, lady, not as writing you a new commandment, but the one we have had from the beginning, I beg you to love one another." The practical aspect of the love ethic is also emphasized in 2 John 6, linked externally to v. 5 by the catchword "love" (*agapē*). To love one another is to "follow" (*peripatein*) love. The author uses *peripatein* (literally, "to walk"), the verb traditionally used of behavior in Jewish and Christian writings. Stress on the reality of love is also strongly emphasized at 1 John 4:7-10. Cf. R. Schnackenburg, *Die Johannesbriefe*, pp. 311-312; M. de Jonge, *De Brieven*, pp. 246-247.

49. Cf. A. Feuillet, "The Structure."

50. M. Vallanickal, *Divine Sonship*, p. 303.

51. Cf. Heinrich Schlier, "Die Bruderliebe nach dem Evangelium und den Briefen des Johannes," in A. Descamps and A. de Halleux, eds.., *Mélanges Béda Rigaux* (Gembloux: Duculot, 1970) 235-245, p. 243.

is a reference to a logion of the Lord.[52] Undoubtedly the use of "commandment" in 1 John 2:7 has a referential function, but that function should not obscure the even more important fact that "commandment" is a particularly significant Johannine concept. Indeed the Johannine corpus[53] has the highest preponderance of the use of "commandment" (*entolē*) and its cognate verb, "to command" (*entellesthai*) in the entire New Testament.[54] In John's Gospel the term is used once to denote a legal commandment or order issued by the Sanhedrin (11:57). Apart from that singular reference, the term is used either of the charge or mission given to Jesus by the Father (10:18; 12:49, 50; 14:31) or the commandment given by Jesus to his disciples (13:34; 14:15, 21; 15:10, 12).[55] In this latter sense, the terminology is restricted to the farewell discourses, where, indeed, it seems to have an imperative force.[56] It is questionable, however, whether it is the imperative force which predominates in the use of the terminology when it is applied to the "commandment" of the Father to the Son. In those passges, "commandment" seems rather to indicate the will of the Father directing the Son to the work of salvation and indicating to Him the means by which the salvation of men should be accomplished.[57] From this perspective, "commandment" seems to have a universal rather than a specific sense, and a salvific rather than an imperative sense. This suggests that the Johannine use of "commandment" has

52. Cf. R. Bultmann, *The Johannine Epistles*, p. 27.

53. The Book of Revelation offers an exception to the otherwise Johannine predilection for "commandment."

54. Cf. Noël Lazure, *Les valeurs morales de la théologie johannique (Évangile et épîtres)*. EBib (Paris: Gabalda, 1965) p. 31. *Entolē* ("commandment") appears ten times in John (10:18; 11:57; 12:49, 50; 13:34; 14:15, 21, 31; 15:10, 12), fourteen times in 1 John (2:3, 4, 7 [3 ×], 8; 3:22, 23 [2 ×], 24; 4:21; 5:2, 3 [2 ×]), and four times in 2 John (2 John 4, 5, 6 [2 ×]). It also appears in Rev 12:17; 14:12. *Entellesthai* ("to command") appears only in John 8:5; 14:31; 15:14, 17. It appears some twelve other times in the NT, including five times in Matthew.

55. Cf. William Hendriksen, *New Testament Commentary. Exposition of the Gospel According to John*, 2 (Grand Rapids: Baker, 1954) p. 252.

56. Cf. C. Spicq, *Agape*, 3, p. 49; *Théologie morale du Nouveau Testament*, 2, EBib (Paris: Gabalda, 1965) pp. 507-509.

57. Cf. N. Lazure, *Les valeurs morales*, p. 144.

some similarity with the LXX in which "commandment" (*entolē*)
is used as an expression for the will of God.

If, then, we look to the Old Testament in the hope that it will
shed some light on the Johannine notion of "commandment" we
find that it is principally to the Deuteronomic literature that we
must look.[58] Indeed, "the whole spirit of Deuteronomy is expressed by the term, 'commandment.'"[59] "Commandment" is a
relational term which can be understood only within the convenantal context. The "commandments" are the covenant obligations imposed by Yahweh and undertaken by Israel. Specifically one can look to the Decalogue as a synopsis of these
obligations. They represent the material content of the covenant
prescriptions. Yet the formal sense of the "commandments" is
something other than the material (ethical) content of the ten
commandments.

The *entolē* of the Septuagintal version of Deuteronomy corresponds to the Hebrew *miswa*, both terms having the basic sense
of "command." The emphasis lies on the fact of being commanded.
There is, thus, a relational element and a personal quality inherent in the connotation of the term. This personal quality
means that the commandment derives from moral authority,
rather than from forceful constraint or arbitrary demand. In most
instances of the use of *entolē* in Deuteronomy, the commandment
is of divine origin. Thus *entolē* generally indicates God's will. The
stress is on the Lawgiver who would lay claim to the service of
man in order that man be united to Himself. The commandment
is parallel to God's instruction (*nomos*, "the law") and thus is, at
least in some sense, a revelation of God Himself.[60] Thus the

58. Cf. Matthew J. O'Connell, "The Concept of Commandment in the Old
Testament," *TS* 21 (1960) 351-403, esp. pp. 351, 369.

59. J. van der Ploeg, "Studies in Hebrew Law," *CBQ* 12 (1950) 248-259, 416-
427, p. 258.

60. With van Boxel, we can note the similarity between "words" and
"commandments" (Exod 20:1; Deut 5:5, 22). Cf. P. van Boxel, "Glaube und
Liebe," p. 26. Something similar is to be found within the Johannine corpus (1
John 2:4-5). Cf. N. Lazure, *Les valeurs morales*, p. 138; H. Schlier, "Die
Bruderliebe," p. 241.

commandment is a convenantal reality,[61] a sign of Israel's special relationship with Yahweh. In context, therefore, the commandment is not only an expression of the divine will but is also, as Spicq notes,[62] both an instruction and a salvation device. The first and fundamental content of *entolē*, taken in its singular Deuteronomic sense, is the imperative of love.[63] All the other commandments depend on love. To love[64] is to keep God's commandments.[65] Finally, and most significantly, "the *entolē* ... becomes a mode of the presence of God to His people and an evidence of the dynamic and active quality of this presence."[66]

This Deuteronomic concept of commandment appears to have provided the model for the Johannine concept. In the first instance, the Johannine concept has an all-embracing sense which is linked to the history of salvation. This is particularly evident in those passages which speak of the commandment which the Father has given to Jesus. The material content of the "commandment" is Jesus' death (10:18)[67] or his revelation (12:49, 50). Thus the "commandment" has to do with the Father's will directing the revelatory and salvific mission of Jesus: "the Father who sent me has himself given me commandment what to say and what to speak. And I know that his commandment is eternal life" (12:49b-50a). Since the context raises the issue of the authority of Jesus' revelatory message and since the author

61. Thus O'Connell describes the commandment of Deuteronomy as "the creative and redemptive pattern, revealed by God, for Israel's existence as His holy people." M.J. O'Connell, "Commandment," p. 372.

62. Cf. C. Spicq, *Agape*, 3, p. 49.

63. Cf. M. O'Connell, "Commandment," p. 394; A. Lacomara, "Deuteronomy and the Farewell Discourse (John 13:31-16:33)," *CBQ* 36 (1974) 65-84, pp. 73-74; William L. Moran, "The Ancient Near Eastern Background of the Love of God in Deuteronomy," *CBQ* 25 (1963) 77-87, p. 78.

64. A specific formulation of the commandment of brotherly love is not found in Deuteronomy, as it is in Lev 19:18. G.E. Wright considers this to be an accidental phenomenon insofar as "the motive of brotherly love is so basic and prominent in the exposition of the law." Cf. G.E. Wright, *Deuteronomy*. Interpreter's Bible, 2 (New York: Abingdon, 1953) p. 401.

65. Cf. Deut 10:12; 11:1, 22; 19:9.

66. M.J. O'Connell, "Commandment," p. 394. Cf. pp. 382-383.

67. Here the RSV renders *entolē* as charge.

invokes the "poverty principle"[68] in response, it is clear that the commandment concept is one which includes its obligatory force. The idea of commandments as precepts to be fulfilled by Jesus is likewise present in 15:10: "I have kept my Father's commandments and abide in his love." In this case John speaks of commandments, in the plural, as he always does[69] when commandment is the object of the verb *tērein* (to keep).

A link to the history of salvation is no less present when the evangelist writes of the commandment which Jesus gives to his disciples. The constant reference to the passion, the comparison between Jesus and the disciples, and the situation of the love commandment within the farewell discourses provide the history of salvation framework for the love commandment. Indeed the situation of the love commandment within the farewell discourses provides another positive point of comparison between the Johannine and the Deuteronomic notions of commandment. Deuteronomy is one of the oldest examples of the farewell discourse genre. In its entirety it is presented as the address of the departing Moses to the nation of Israel.[70] There Moses is the mediator of the covenant and the lawgiver; now Jesus appears as the mediator of the covenant and the lawgiver.[71] In both cases

68. Cf. David M. Stanley, "Believe the Works," *The Way* 4 (1978) 272-286, p. 281.

69. John 14:15, 21; 15:10 (twice). These are, in fact, the only passages in the Gospel in which the plural is used. 1 John uses the plural seven times (2:3, 4; 3:22, 24; 5:2, 3 [twice]), five times with the verb *tērein*. Lazure claims that the distinction between the singular and the plural should be maintained. The singular has reference to a specific precept, whereas the plural refers to the total will of God. Cf. N. Lazure, *Les valeurs morales*, pp. 126-127.

70. Cf. Deut 1:1; 32:45; 33:1. Cf. A. Lacomara, "Deuteronomy," p. 84.

71. Cf. A., Lacomara, who writes: "Jesus is the first-person subject of the 'I-thou' form of address and hence, like Moses in Deuteronomy, he is not a mere herald of the law, he is a lawgiver: 'I give you a new commandment' (John 13:34; cf. 14:15; 15:12, 14). In the OT it is only in Deuteronomy that we find a parallel to this presentation of the law in the person of the mediator." A. Lacomara, "Deuteronomy," p. 67; A. Humbert, "L'observance," p. 202.

72. Bernard has gone beyond the evidence of the text in asserting apropos John 13:34 that, "He claimed to 'give commandments,' and so claimed to be equal to God." Cf. J.H. Bernard, *A Critical and Exegetical Commentary on the Gospel of St. John*, ICC (Edinburgh: Clark, 1929) p. 326.

the binding force of the precept is inherent in the notion of the commandment which is given.

Yet the commandment is not simply a precept to be obeyed. The new commandment is a commandment which Jesus gives to his disciples.[72] It is the gift of the departing Jesus. The use of the verb *didōnai*[73] by the evangelist serves to place the new commandment among the great realities of divine salvation with which John employs the powerful verb "to give": the Spirit (3:34; 14:16), the bread of life (6:11, 27, 31, 32 (2 ×), 33, 34, 37, 39, 51, 52, 65), the living water (4:10, 14, 15), peace (14:27), eternal life (10:28; 17:2), glory (17:22, 24), the power to become children of God (1:12) and the word of God (17:8, 14). These are the "gifts of God" (4:10) which Jesus gives to his own. The new commandment is no less a gift. It is the legacy which Jesus gives to those whom he is about to leave.

That legacy is not only commandment to be kept; it is also revelation to be treasured. Already in Deuteronomy, "commandment" had the sense of divine revelation and instruction. That sense is preserved in John's use of commandment which appears predominantly in a passage which serves as an instruction to the disciples by Jesus as to the meaning of his departure. The revelatory nature[74] of the Johannine commandment is highlighted by the parallelism between "word" and "commandment" in 14:21, 23. Jesus' commandment is the word which he entrusts to his disciples. It makes known to them God's plan for them.

In Deuteronomy, the commandment was also a mode of God's active and dynamic presence. In this respect it can be suggested that the love commandment is the modality of Jesus' presence[75]

73. Cf. A. Vanhoye, "L'œuvre du Christ, don du Père," *RSR* 48 (1960) 387-391.

74. Cf. N. Lazure, *Les valeurs morales*, pp. 130-131. That the commandment is Jesus' revelatory word is also indicated in 1 John where we find a parallelism between Jesus' commandments and his word in 2:4-5 and where the love commandment is styled "the message" (*aggelia*) in 3:11.

75. While noting that John has no symbol for love, P.S. Naumann has shown that in John "love is the presence of Christ." Cf. P.S. Naumann, "The Presence of Love in John's Gospel," *Worship* 39 (1965) 369-371. Cf. also C. Spicq, *Agape*, 3, p. 54.

with his disciples after his departure. Jesus' glorification involves his separation from his disciples and their attendant distress. The farewell discourses seek to express the meaning of his departure. In 13:34-35 it appears that the solution to the problem of Jesus' absence is the presence of love. Mutual love is the new mode of Jesus' presence among his disciples.[76] His presence constitutes the moral demand.

The "New Commandment"

The love commandàent is called a "new commandment" (*entolē kainē*) in John 13:34. Otherwise the commandments which Jesus addressed to his disciples are called "my commandments," with the pronomial adjective *emē* as in 14:15; 15:10, or the pronoun *mou* as in 14:21; 15:12. Outside of John 13:34, John employs the adjective *kainos* but once, i.e., in reference to the "new tomb" in which the body of Jesus was placed.[77] The love commandment appears elsewhere in the NT,[78] but is not called a new commandment except in 1 John 2:7-8 and 2 John 5. In a real sense, the love commandment is not a new commandment at all, as even the author of 1 John must admit.[79] Not only does the love commandment go back to Jesus but it was an integral part of the Torah[80] to such an extent that rabbinic legend ascribes to R. Hillel the summation of the entire Torah in the golden rule.[81]

Given this situation, one must ask why and in what sense did the Johannine school[82] interpret the love commandment as a new

---

76. While the verb *didōnai* occurs some eight times in John 17, it is relatively rarely used in the farewell discourses. However it does serve to indicate that peace (14:27), the Spirit (14:16), and the "new commandment" (13:34) are Jesus' gifts to his disciples. Certainly the gift of the Spirit is the answer to Jesus' absence; it is the new mode of his active presence. Something similar can also be said of the new commandment.

77. Cf. John 19:41.

78. Cf. Mark 12:31 and par.

79. Cf. 1 John 2:7-8 and *supra*, pp. 228-231.

80. Lev 19:18.

81. *M. 'Abot* 1:12.

82. That the love commandment is called a "new commandment" in John

commandment. The designation is certainly somewhat unusual and warrants reflection. Reflection is not absent from the writings on John. As a matter of fact, commentators on the Fourth Gospel are rather inclined to devote considerable attention to the expression. Thus Ceslaus Spicq indicates no less than eight reasons why the Johannine love commandment is styled a "new commandment."[83] (1) The new commandment places mutual love among the specific elements of the new economy of salvation, the new covenant replacing the old. (2) The innovation in the commandment is that love is given an unequaled place and made the object of a fundamental and quasi-unique precept. (3) In relation to Lev 19:18, love has a new object, determined by ties of faith, not blood ("one another" rather than "your neighbor"). (4) In reference to the Sermon on the Mount's love of enemies, the Lord at the Last Supper asked for reciprocal love which will constitute the Church as a society of loving and loved man. (5) The great innovation is the nature and mode of the new love insofar as the disciples' love is rooted in Christ. (6) Mutual love is not an additional rule of conduct nor is there given a new reason for loving; rather, love is gift as well as precept. (7) The mode and activity of love are changed insofar as praying and doing

13:34, 1 John 2:7-8, and 2 John 5 would seem to indicate that the epithet is common to the Johannine school. That the author of 1 John who wants to stress the relative antiquity of the love commandment nevertheless feels constrained to call the love commandment a "new commandment" would seem to indicate that the designation enjoyed the force of normative tradition within the Johannine school. Thus it is difficult to agree with the contention of Alphonse Humbert and Noël Lazure that the "new commandment" designation of John 13:34 indicates a literary dependence on 1 John 2:7-8. An argument in favor of the Humbert-Lazure position might be that vv. 34-35 are a relatively late addition in the redaction of John 13. However vv. 7-8 would also seem to warrant the judgment that they too are a traditional element inserted by a redactor into material taken from a source (thus, Bultmann). In any event 1 John seems to have been composed after John, in which case it is more likely that 1 John 2:7-8 and 2 John 5 depend on John 13:34-35 than vice versa. Cf. A. Humbert, "L'observance," pp. 205-206; O. Prunet, *La morale chrétienne d'après les écrits johanniques: évangile et épîtres* (Paris: PUF, 1957) p. 106; N. Lazure, *Les valeurs morales*, p. 229; R. Bultmann, *The Johannine Epistles*, p. 27.

83. Cf. C. Spicq, *Agape*, 3, pp. 53-54.

good give way to self-sacrifice, a love for the other which is greater than one's love for oneself.[84] (8) The love commandment constitutes the Church as truly as does the eucharist in that the eucharist is a memorial of his going, and love a sign of his the presence.

While an extensive enumerated list is somewhat overwhelming there is something to be said for each of the reflections offered by Spicq.[85] It would appear, nevertheless, that the most fundamental reason for calling the love commandment a "new commandment" is that it is the commandment for the final times. The dualism of the Johannine *Weltanschauung* is apparent in the Gospel, and is quite explicit in the very context in which the author of 1 John explains the new commandment.[86] There it appears that the love commandment is the commandment which obtains among those who exist in the light, whereas it is not kept by those who walk in the darkness. In the epistles as the Gospel, Johannine dualism is often expressed by antithetical images. This is in keeping with the realized eschatology[87] of the Johannine school. The Synoptists' espousal of consequent eschatology, on the other hand, generally provides for a contrast between the present age and the age to come. Within this perspective the realities of the age-to-come are often called "new."[88] In effect, "new" is equivalent to "eschatological" or "of the final times." The Johannine school has retained this sense of "new" when it speaks of the "new commandment." In John, however, the love commandment is not

84. Cf. also, E.C. Hoskyns, *The Fourth Gospel* (2nd ed.: London: Faber and Faber, 1956) p. 450; R. Schnackenburg, *Moral Teaching*, p. 324.

85. Surprisingly Joseph Bonsirven gives two reasons why "new" is an appropriate qualification of the Johannine love commandment. In the first instance he cites the universal extension of the commandment. Cf. J. Bonsirven, *Épîtres de saint Jean* (Paris: Beauchesne, 1935) p. 116.

86. 1 John 2:7-11.

87. The purpose of the present essay allows me this generalisation, à la C.H. Dodd, despite the consequent eschatology of John 5:25-29, etc.

88. New wineskins (Matt 9:17; Mark 2:22); new things (Matt 13:52); new covenant (Matt 26:28; Mark 14:24; Luke 22:20); new teaching (Mark 1:27); new cloth (Mark 2:21); new wine (Mark 2:22; Matt 9:17; Luke 5:37, 38); new garment (Luke 5:36 [3 ×]). Cf. Matt 26:29; Mark 14:25.

new from a temporal perspective; it is new only from the qualitative point of view. The love commandment as exposed by John derives its newness, i.e., its characteristic uniqueness, from the new eschatological world which Jesus brings.[89]

In its specifically Johannine interpretation,[90] the love commandment is new because it is an eschatological commandment but it is eschatological because it is a gift of the Johannine Jesus. At root then the Johannine love commandment is a new commandment because of its reference to Jesus. Yet John does not consider the love commandment a "new" commandment because he is citing a traditional Jesuanic logion (which, of course, he does); rather, the commandment is new because it is the final challenge and gift of the departing Jesus for his own. It is a reality of the post-resurrection era; it pertains to the times dominated by the apparent absence of the glorified Jesus. In this sense it is a rule for the new eschatological community. Yet it is more than a rule since it is Jesus' gift to the community of light created by the gift of his presence. Thus, with Schnackenburg, one can understand the commandment as new in the light of John's profound understanding of discipleship.[91] Thus, too, with Lazure we can understand the commandment as new because it is

89. Cf. Roy A. Harrisville, *The Concept of Newness in the New Testament* (Minneapolis: Augsburg, 1960) p. 93; R. Bultmann, *John*, pp. 526, 527; L. Cerfaux, "La charité fraternelle," pp. 38-39; V. Furnish, *The Love Command*, pp. 138, 151, etc. Bultmann writes, with characteristic—and correct—conciseness: "Jesus' command of love is 'new' even when it has been long-known, because it is the law of the eschatological community, for which the attribute 'new' denotes not an historical characteristic but its essential nature." (p. 527). Cf. E. Käsemann, *Testament*, pp. 67-70. Among other reflections, Käsemann states that "brotherly love is heavenly solidarity directed towards individual Christians" (p. 70).

90. The Synoptics formulation of the love commandment, i.e., as the great or first commandment(s), from among the 613 of the Torah is not endowed with the same eschatological qualification as is the Johannine formulation in which the commandment is given as Jesus' legacy to his disciples at the moment of his departure. Thus the Synoptists' love commandment could not be properly described as a "new commandment." Nonetheless Cerfaux has correctly exploited Matt 25:34-45 as an indication that charity is the normal occupation of the Christian who is waiting for the Parousia, i.e. who is in a state of eschatological anticipation. Cf. L. Cerfaux, "La charité fraternelle," p. 32.

91. Cf. R. Schnackenburg, *Moral Teaching*, p. 325.

qualified by "as I have loved you."[92] The absent-present Jesus and the disciples are the poles of the relationship which constitutes the newness of the Johannine love commandment.

The Johannine love commandment is "new," then, insofar as it is specifically Christian.[93] But is it new with the more or less explicit specificity of the new covenant so that the gift of presence which it entails is properly qualified as the Johannine analogue to the institution of the eucharist?[94] There are, in fact, substantial reasons for considering John 15:1-8 as a eucharistic text,[95] but it is in John 13 rather that John 15 that the love commandment is styled a "new commandment." The symbolic action (John 13:1-12) which serves as a prelude to that portion of the farewell discourse which presently contains the new commandment does not, however, appear to have a sacramental reference clearly in view.[96] Thus it would be difficult to argue for a specifically eucharistic sense of the Johannine love commandment.[97] This opinion is all the more probable in that John does not cite the new covenant formula of Jeremiah in reference to the new

92. Cf. N. Lazure, *Les valeurs morales*, p. 230.

93. Cf. L. Cerfaux, "La charité fraternelle," p. 38; N. Lazure, *Les valeurs morales*, p. 230; J. Seynaeve, "La charité chrétienne," p. 395; S. Cipriani, "Dio e amore. La dottrina della carità in San Giovanni," *Scuola Cattolica* 94 (1966) 214-231, p. 221.

94. Cf. Alfred Loisy, *Le quatrième évangile*, Paris, 1903, p. 736; G.H.C. MacGregor, *The Gospel of John*, MNTC (London: Hodder and Stoughton, 1928) p. 283.

95. Cf., for example, B. Sandvic, "Joh. 15 als Abendmahlstext," *TZ* 23 (1967) 323-328; R.E. Brown, *John. XIII-XXI*, pp. 672-674; D.J. Hawkins, "Orthodoxy and Heresy in John 10:1-21 and 15:1-17," *EvQ* 47 (1975) 208-213, p. 212.

96. Cf. J.G.G. Dunn, "The Washing,"; Georg Richter, "Die Fusswaschung Joh. 13,1-20," *MTZ* 16 (1965) 13-26.

97. In effect, the main arguments for the eucharistic interpretation of the Johannine new commandment seem to be its placement within the farewell discourse and its connotation as Christ's presence. These arguments seem weak and unnecessary to me, especially in view of John's treatment of the profound significance of the eucharist in John 6. This I would take issue with the position modestly suggested by Furnish (*The Love Command*, pp. 138-135), and advanced by R. Percival Brown ("*entolē kainē*," pp. 190-191), and André Feuillet, (*Le mystère de l'amour divin dans la théologie johannique.* EBib [Paris: Gabalda, 1972] p. 98).

commandment as do the Synoptics in their respective narrations of the institutions of the Eucharist.

On the other hand, there are sufficient parallels between the literary form and content of Deuteronomy and the literary form and content of John 13-17 to suggest a Deuteronomic model for the latter. In this case, the new commandment would indeed be a reality of the new covenant, even though John does not formally describe it as such. Indeed it is not only *a* reality of the new covenant; it is *the* reality of the new covenant[98] insofar as all the commandments are reduced to one[99] by the Johannine Jesus. Thus without citing the *berith*-formula itself and without making reference to Jeremiah's new covenant, John is able to establish the love commandment as the covenantal stipulation *par excellence* of the new covenant[100] and to indicate that the bond of union between the Father and the new people of God is constituted by the fulfillment of that obligation in covenant of which Jesus is the mediator.

"As I Have Loved You"

It is, in fact, the christological reference which constitutes the essential novelty of the Johannine new commandment.[101] John has inserted the love commandment in a literary framework which interprets it within the context of Jesus' great saving presence-absence, his glorification and return to the Father.

98. Thus Raymond Brown writes: "The newness of the commandment of love is really related to the theme of covenant at the Last Supper—the 'new commandment' of John XIII 34 is the basic stipulation of the 'new covenant' of Luke XXII 20." R.E. Brown, *John. XIII-XXI*, AB, 29A, p. 614.

99. Cf. A. Loisy, *Le quatrième évangile*, p. 769; J.H. Bernard, *John*, pp. 485-486; E.C. Hoskyns, *The Fourth Gospel*, p. 450; A. Feuillet, "La morale chrétienne d'après saint Jean," *Esprit et Vie* 83 (1973) 665-670, p. 669; "Le Temps de l'Église," p. 68; P. van Boxel, "Glaube und Liebe," p. 27; R. Schnackenburg, *Das Johannesevangelium*, p. 123; *Econtrario*, V. Furnish, *The Love Command*, p. 137. Cf. A.E. Brooke, *The Johannine Epistles*, p. 177.

100. Cf. J.L. Boyle, "The Last Discourse," pp. 210-211; A. Feuillet, *Le mystère*, p. 88.

101. Cf. R. Schnackenburg, *Das Johannesevangelium*, pp. 59-60.

Indeed, by his repetition of the "as I have loved you" formula in 13:34[102] John has drawn emphatic attention to the singular importance of the christological reference. Hence the crucial question for the interpreter becomes that of the significance of this christological reference. What is the meaning of "as I have loved you," stated and emphasized again?[103] What precisely is the sense of the *kathōs* in the expression? Does it mean "as" or "because"? Is Jesus' love for his own the exemplar, the motivation, the foundation, or the source of the disciples' love for one another?

To respond disjunctively is effectively to sap the Johannine formulation of the love commandment of its unique strength. When John writes that the disciples are to love "as I have loved you," he implies that Jesus is at once[104] the model, the reason, the ground, and the mediator of the disciples' love for one another. Thus we must look to various levels of meaning in the expression "as I have loved you" rather than opt for one or another meaning to the exclusion of all others.

Certainly one ought not to set aside, as readily as does Bultmann,[105] the fact that Jesus' love for his disciples is the model of their love for one another. In the present redaction of the text,

102. Cf. John 15:12.

103. With R.P. Brown we can note a "sub-final clause introduced by *hina* to define the content of a command or a request is extraordinarily frequent in the NT." The second *hina* clause reaffirms and amplifies the first, with which it is coordinated. Cf. R.P. Brown, *"entolē kainē,"* p. 189; L. Morris, *The Gospel According to John*, NICNT (Grand Rapids, MI: Eerdmans, 1971) p. 633, n. 73.

104. Fully a half-century ago, MacGregor already wrote that, "Jesus' love is to be at once the source and measure of theirs." Cf. G.H.C. MacGregor, *John*, p. 289. De Dinechin also points to a fuller understanding of the *kathōs* formula by citing the "three dimensions: logical, chronological, and unifying" of the relationship. Cf. O. de Dinechin, "ΚΑΘΩΣ," p. 210. Brown notes that "For John *kathōs* is not only comparative but also causative or constitutive, meaning 'inasmuch as.'" Cf. R.E. Brown, *John XIII-XXI*, p. 663.

105. Cf. R. Bultmann, *John*, p. 525. Undoubtedly Bultmann's rejection of the interpretations of Loisy and Schumann, the former suggesting that Jesus' love offers a model for the intensity of the disciples' love and the latter suggesting that Jesus' love offers a model for the manner of the disciples' love, owes to his exegetical apriori. An existential analysis of the text does not leave room for an exemplary role to be accorded to the love of the historical Jesus.

the footwashing scene (John 13:1-20) is clearly presented as an
example of Jesus' love for his disciples. It is situated within the
context of Jesus' love for his disciples unto the end (v. 1) and
terminates with a discussion on the exemplary character of Jesus'
action (vv. 13-20).[106] Within that discussion Jesus' action is
presented as "an example that you also should do" (v. 15). The
parallelism between v. 15, "For I have given you an example, that
you also should do as I have done to you,"[107] and v. 34, "A new
commandment I give to you, that you love one another, even as I
have loved you," is, moreover, such to link the commandment
with John's exposition of exemplary gesture.[108] The gesture not
only situates the commandment within the perspective of Jesus'
passion-glorification but serves notice that the fulfillment of the
commandment is effected in loving service.[109] Thus Cerfaux
noted that the footwashing is "the example, the symbol, and the
commandment of brotherly love."[110]

---

106. It must be granted that there is considerable discussion as to the relationship between John 13:1-12 and 13-20. Substantial opinion holds that vv. 13-20 are
a later addition to the tradition. As such they serve to add a paraenetic reflection
to a tradition which is essentially christological and soteriological in emphasis. Cf.
M.-E. Boismard, "Le lavement des pieds," *RB* 71 (1964) 5-24; G. Richter, "Die
Fusswaschung Joh. 13.1-12," pp. 301-320; "Die Deutung des Kreuzetodes Jesu in
der Leidensgeschichte des Johannesevangeliums (Jo. 13-19)," *BibLeb* 9 (1968) 21-
36; J.D.G. Dunn, "The Washing." On the other hand, Alfons Weiser has argued
vigorously against Richter's position. He holds that basically the verses have been
inserted into the narrative by the evangelist himself. Cf. A. Weiser, "Joh. 13,12-
20—Zufügung eines späteren Herausgabers?" *BZ* 12 (1968) 252-257.
107. A propos 13:15, Victor Furnish comments: "Jesus has provided not just
an ideal model or pattern to be imitated. His action becomes 'exemplary' insofar
as his disciples themselves have been served by his love." V. Furnish, *The Love
Command*, pp. 136-137.
108. Thus de Dinechin classifies the saying of 13:15 along with those found in
13:34 and 15:12 within the third of similitude found in John, i.e., "*agapē* as
similitude." Cf. O. de Dinechin, "ΚΑΘΩΣ", p. 208.
109. Even Bultmann and Käseman underscore service as the content of the
love commandment in John. Cf. R. Bultmann, *John*, p. 526; E. Käsemann,
Testament, pp. 61-62.
110. L. Cerfaux, "La charité fraternelle," p. 37. Cf. R. Schnackenburg, *Moral
Teaching*, p. 324; A. Feuillet, "La morale chrétienne," pp. 667, 670; J. Seynaeve,
"La charité chrétienne," p. 393.

When John returns to his exposition of the love commandment in 15:12-17, "love" (*agapē*) serves as the catch-word to link vv. 12 and 13 together. Thus, the love with which Jesus lays down his life for his friends (v. 13)[111] is implicitly proposed as a model for the disciples' love for one another.[112] Indeed the particularism with which the significance of the passion is formulated in v. 13 — lay down his life "for his friends" (*hina tis tēn psuchēn autou thē huper tōn philōn autou*) — is consistent with the particularism of the object of the love commandment and the particularism of that love for his own (13:1) which serves as the springboard for John's reflection on the significance of the passion. From the love of Jesus manifest in his passion, one can point to the intensity and extent of the love which ought to be characteristic of Jesus' disciples. In effect, Jesus' laying down his life for his friends is not only an example of great love; it ultimately constitutes the love of the brethren as Christian love.[113]

Thus it would seem not only legitimate but exegetically imperative to speak of an ethics of imitation[114] with respect to the Johannine formulation of the love commandment. The ethics of imitation is not foreign to Johannine thought. The soteriological-christological saying of John 12:24 is also followed (v. 25) by a call to imitation.[115] Thus, and with respect to the love commandment, Jesus' love for his disciples serves as the norm of fraternal love. More specifically Jesus' love for his own is normative with respect to its object, its intensity, and its quality as loving service.

111. The command may in fact be formulated according to some well-known proverb. Cf. Plato, *Symposium* 179B (Brown); Aristotle, *Nicomachaen Ethics* IX,8; 1119C, 18-20 (Feuillet); Tyrtaeus, 6: aff. (Bultmann).

112. Cf. R.E. Brown, *John. XIII-XXI*, p. 682.

113. Cf. D.J. Hawkins, "Orthodoxy and Heresy," p. 213; R. Schnackenburg, *Das Johannesevangelium*, 3, p. 124.

114. Cf. A. Feuillet, "La morale chrétienne,"; R. Thysman, "L'éthique," p. 172; J. Seynaeve, "La charité chrétienne," p. 399; A. Lacomara, "Deuteronomy," pp. 76-77; and A. Loisy, *Le quatrième évangile*, p. 736. Nevertheless Hendriksen remarks that "the love of Christ cannot *in every sense* be a pattern of our love toward one another." W. Hendriksen, *John*, p. 305.

115. Cf. A. Weiser, "Joh. 13,12-20," pp. 254-255.

The ethics of imitation proposed in 13:34 is grounded in the salvific act that Jesus is to accomplish as he departs from his disciples. The passion-glorification of Jesus inaugurates the time for the fulfillment of the love commandment and serves as the basis for the obligatory force of the commandment.[116] Because Jesus has loved his own and that unto his hour, the disciples must love one another. In this sense the memory of Jesus' love for his own should serve as a motivating force, urging the disciples to love one another. The disciples must love one another not only "as" Jesus loved them (the ethics of imitation) but "because" Jesus loved them (the motivation for brotherly love).

As with most covenant motifs, it is the memory of a divine favor in the past which creates future covenantal obligations. It is the memory of what Jesus is for the disciples which allows for the Johannine insertion of the love commandment in the farewell discourses. It is as the one who is about to accomplish that for which he has been sent, that Jesus can command the disciples to love one another. Indeed, as has already been suggested, the love commandment is no arbitrary decree of some despot but the legacy of the departing Lord. The very use of the word *entolē* suggests that the person of the Lawgiver is of importance for the obligatory force of the commandment. In no case is the commandment to be separated from the one who commands; but in the case of 13:34 the circumstances of the command give its fulfillment an urgency which it would not otherwise have. Thus fidelity to the memory of Jesus who loved them unto the end moves[117] the disciples to love one another.

To move the discussion one step further, we must agree with Bultmann that the *kathōs* of v. 34 expresses the integral connection between the "love one another" and Jesus' love which

116. Cf. R. Thysman, "L'éthique," pp. 172-173; A. Plummer, *The Gospel according to St. John* (Cambridge: University Press, 1882) *ad loc.* Jack Seynaeve comments that this Johannine love commandment derives its entire motivation from a christological fact — charity manifested by Christ himself. Cf. J. Seynaeve, "La 'charité' chrétienne," p. 396.

117. Cf. N. Lazure, *Les valeurs morales*, p. 220.

they have experienced.[118] One can then speak of Jesus' love as the foundation of the disciples' mutual love.[119] The disciples' love for one another is grounded in the love of Jesus in the sense that the disciples' love for one another is the fulfillment of the purpose of Jesus' love. The love which the disciples have for one another continues the love which Christ has for them. Jesus loves them in order that they might love one another.[120] His love culminates in their love,[121] one for the other. His love is the enabling force of their love. As Bultmann writes: "The imperative is itself a gift, and this it can be because it receives its significance and its possibility of realization from the past, experienced as the love of the Revealer: *kathōs ēgapēsa humas.*"[122] The commandment itself is the gift of Jesus and the possibility of its own realization.[123]

At the deepest level, the *kathōs* of 13:34 overcomes the extrinsicism of the commandment. What the departing Jesus leaves to his disciples is not so much an order, but his presence in another mode. The love of the disciples for one another has its

118. Cf. R. Bultmann, *John*, p. 525. In somewhat similar vein, Lacomara writes: "The love that is to be expressed in mutual charity is nothing less than the love that found supreme expression on the cross. It is because of this love, and according to the measure of this love, that the disciples are to love one another, the *kathōs* of 13:34 and 15:2 signifying both 'because' and 'as.' Because of the Passion, the formulation of this law is new and, strictly, unparalleled, the law of charity is not a repetition of a former stipulation, but the enunciation of a new code by which the new community is to be bound together and united to Jesus." Cf. A. Lacomara, "Deuteronomy," p. 77. Similarly, H. van den Bussche, *Le Discours d'Adieu de Jésus. Commentaire des chapîtres 13 à 17 de l'évangile selon saint Jean* (Tournai: Casterman, 1959) p. 58.

119. Bultmann often speaks of the "foundational" (*begründend*) sense of *kathōs*. Cf. R. Bultmann, *John*, pp. 527-528, and *passim*. Indeed, he states that, "The only thing that is specifically Christian is the grounding of the command and, in line with this, its realization." *John*, p. 542, n. 4. Cf. also H. Schlier, "Die Bruderliebe," p. 238, n. 1, p. 244; and R. Schnackenburg, *Das Johannesevangelium*, p. 60.

120. Cf. R. Bultmann, *John*, p. 525.

121. Cf. L. Cerfaux, "La charité fraternelle," p. 37; O. de Dinechin, "ΚΑΘΩΣ", p. 209.

122. R. Bultmann, *John*, p. 525. Cf. H. Schlier, "Die Bruderliebe," pp. 239-240.

123. Cf. R. Schnackenburg, *Das Johannesevangelium*, p. 60.

ontological root in the love of Christ which in turn is the love of God for them. It is, in fact, characteristic of Johannine theology to get back to the very foundation of the salvific realities.[124] Thus John, alone among the evangelists, offers a profound theological interpretation of love, an interpretation that is appropriately called "metaphysical."[125] Brotherly love means that the loving disciples participate in the very life of God.[126]

To grasp realities toward which the Gospel is pointing, we must begin with the love of the Father for Jesus.[127] Twice (John 3:35; 5:20) John notes that the Father's love for the Son is the source of all that the Son has. It is because of the Father's love that the Son has all things (3:35); because of that same love the Son is able to do the works of the Father (5:20). In effect, the mission of the Son results from the Father's love. In fulfilling his mission, the Son abides in the Father's love (15:10). The *menein en* formula of John 15:10 underscores the reciprocal immanence of the Son and the Father. The Son, by fulfilling his mission, has kept the Father's commandments. Thus the Son abides in the Father and the Father in Him.

Yet the very love of the Father for the Son is the exemplar of the love[128] which Jesus extends to his disciples (15:9). The

---

124. Cf. L. Cerfaux, "La charité fraternelle," p. 38.

125. Already Martin Dibelius had spoken of the double nature of *agapē* in John: its popular aspect and the "metaphysical" conception. Cf. M. Dibelius, "Joh. 15,13"; also A. Feuillet, "Le Temps de l'Église," pp. 69-70; *Le Mystère*, pp. 20, 84. Cipriani has, however, taken issue with Dibelius' metaphysical" interpretation. Cf. S. Cipriani, "Dio e amore," p. 218. A weakness of Dibelius' position was, in fact, his separation of the ethical from the ontic dimensions of the love commandment and finding only the latter to be characteristic of John. These two aspects compenetrate one another.

126. With somewhat more precision than a strict interpretation of the text warrants, Feuillet has even written that "the Christian life has become like a reflection of the Trinitarian relations." Cf. A. Feuillet, "La morale chrétienne d'après saint Jean," p. 666. Cf. also A. Feuillet, *Le mystère*, p. 58; "Un cas privilégié de pluralisme doctrinale: La conception différente de l'agapé chez saint Paul et saint Jean," *Esprit et Vie* 82 (1972) 497-509, p. 501.

127. Cf. H. Schlier, "Der Bruderliebe," pp. 235-239. Cf. also R. Schnackenburg, "Excurs 10. Die Liebe als Weseneigentümlichkeit Gottes," in *Die Johannesbriefe*, pp. 206-213.

128. John 15:9. Cf. A. Humbert, "L'observance," p. 204.

relationship is such that de Dinechin speaks of the *Analogatum Princeps* of similarity.[129] The Son's relationship with his disciples is like the relationship which the Father has with Him. The Father's love for the Son is thus the paradigm of the Son's love for his disciple: "As the Father has loved me, so have I loved you (*kagō humas ēgapēsa*)" (15:9). There is similarity, but there is no extrincism because the Son abides in the Father's love. Thus one can say that the Son loves his disciples with that love with which he is loved.[130]

When now Jesus commands his disciples to love one another, it appears that the love which he has for the disciples is the *tertium quid*, the mediating link, between the Father's love and the disciples' love for one another. Were one to combine, more immediately than the evangelist has done, vv. 9 and 12 of John 15, the text would read: "As the Father has loved me, so have I loved you; as I have loved you, so you love one another." In effect this means that the disciples are also the recipients of the Father's love, through the mediation of Jesus' love for them. This the evangelist states explicitly in the Priestly Prayer: "Thou has sent me and hast loved them even as thou hast loved me" (17:23). That love does not remain extrinsic to the disciples since the Father's love with which the disciples are loved is in them: "that the love with which thou hast loved me may be in them" (17:26).

Although the evangelist does not make use of the powerful *menein en* formula to speak of the disciples' being in the Father's love, he does so when he reflects on the love which the disciples have for one another: "abide in my love. If you keep my commandments, you will abide in my love, just as I have kept my Father's commandments and abide in his love" (15:9c-10). The commandment above all which the disciples are to keep is the love commandment which follows almost immediately (15:12). It

---

129. Cf. O. de Dinechin, "ΚΑΘΩΣ," pp. 198-199.

130. Cf. Jürgen Heise, who comments: "The love of the Son for his own is grounded in the love of the Father for the Son (cf. 3:35). In the love of the Son the Father's love has been revealed to the world." Cf. J. Heise, *Bleiben. Menein in den Johanneischen Schriften*. HUT, 8 (Tübingen: Mohr, 1967) p. 89.

is clear that to "abide in my love" is the same as to "abide in me and I in you."[131] Thus the reciprocal immanence of Christ and the disciples is the existential situation of those disciples who truly love one another as Jesus has loved them. Such reciprocity is not a reward for keeping the love commandment.[132] Rather the love commandment is gift. Here, as so often in the Fourth Gospel, the Giver abides in the gift which He gives.[133]

Thus within the broad context of Jesus' mission, understood both in terms of commandment and of Jesus' participation in the life of the Father, falls the love commandment in its specifically Johannine formulation. The disciples' love for one another is caught up in a series of participatory relationships[134] in which we can discern two main motifs. On the one hand there is the Father's command to the Son bearing upon the totality of the Son's mission, and the command of the Son to his disciples at the hour of fulfillment of that mission. In a real sense, the mission of the Son is fulfilled in the love commandment. On the other hand, there is the Father's love for Jesus, Jesus' mediating love for the disciples, and the disciples' love for one another. The love of the disciples for one another has its true source in the love of God as Father.[135] In a very real sense, then, there is reciprocal intimacy between the Father and Jesus, between Jesus and his disciples, and between the Father and the disciples because of the reality of love.[136]

131. John 15:4. Cf. J. Heise, *Bleiben*, p. 90.
132. Cf. J. Heise, *Ibid.*, p. 90.
133. With Brown and Feuillet one can cite the influence of Wisdom motifs. Divine *Sophia* abides in men and makes them God's friends. Cf. R.E. Brown, *John. XIII-XXI*, pp. 682-683; A. Feuillet, *Le mystère*, pp. 42-43.
134. Cf. A. Humbert, "L'observance," pp. 188, 215; O. Prunet, *La morale chrétienne*, p. 99.
135. Cf. J.L. Boyle, "The Last Discourse," p. 218. Prunet distinguishes this "theological" sense from the eschatological and the ecclesiastical sense of the love commandment. Cf. O. Prunet, *La morale chrétienne*, "ΚΑΘΩΣ," p. 98.
136. Cf. O. de Dinechin, ΚΑΘΩΣ, pp. 214-215; H. Schlier, "Der Bruderliebe," p. 241. The point is well emphasized by David L. Mealand, who writes: "It is because God has known his own from the beginning, and has revealed himself to them in his Son, that they in turn know and trust him. But above all it is in the dynamic of *agapē* that the mutuality consists. Dodd expresses this very well when

"Love One Another"

Now the significance of "love one another" (*hina agapate allēlous*) as the content[137] of Jesus' new commandment comes to the fore. The evangelist has sought to interpret the meaning of Jesus' glorification-return to the Father. To do so, he has employed the genre of the farewell discourse. The genre which he has chosen requires that the Departing One have something to say about the relationship which ought to obtain among those whom he is about to leave. Departure is not the moment for universal legislation; rather, it is the moment for memory and family spirit. Thus John's Jesus speaks of mutual love rather than of love of enemy[138] or love of neighbor[139] precisely because he is presented as giving instructions to his own as he is about to leave them: they are to be one among themselves even as he is one with them.

Yet it is not only the choice of literary genre which has dictated the particularism of the Johannine formulation of the love commandment. The Johannine dualism,[140] so apparent in the exposition of the love commandment in 1 John 2 but also present in the farewell discourse, especially in its second part, has also contributed to a shaping of the apparently restrictive object of the love commandment in its Johannine formulation.[141] In Jesus the

he speaks of indwelling as due to the love which is 'the very life and activity of God.'" Cf. D.L. Mealand, "Language," p. 31 with reference to C.H. Dodd, *The Interpretation of the Fourth Gospel*, p. 196.

137. The *hina* clause is to be taken epexetically so that "love one another" constitutes the commandment. Cf. R.E. Brown, *John XIII-XXI*, p. 607; R. Schnackenburg, *Das Johannesevangelium* 3, p. 60. Bultmann comments: "And in so far as the content of the *entolē* is *hina agapate allēlous*, the care for oneself is changed into a care for one's neighbor." Cf. R. Bultmann, *John*, p. 525. Cf. 2 John 5 where the *hina* clause, pace Brooke (*Johannine Epistles*, p. 173), relates to *erōtō*. Cf. R. Schnackenburg, *Die Johannesbriefe*, pp. 311-312.

138. Cf. Matt 5:43 (44-48). Cf. Luke 6:27-28, 32-36.

139. Mark 12:31 and par.

140. Cf. N. Lazure, *Les valeurs morales*, p. 232.

141. In this respect it is to be noted that Jesus' love is also directed to "his own." Cf. John 15:9. The Father's love is, however, directed to the world. Cf. John 3:16.

final times have arrived for those who are his disciples; they indeed belong to the light, and not to the darkness. The eschatological salvation of the future[142] is made present in the love of the community.[143] In effect, the love commandment in John is particularistic in its formulation because it is a reflection on the Church in the situation of Jesus' absence-presence. In somewhat similar fashion, but without the depth of theological reflection present in John's formulation of the love commandment, even the love commandment of the Old Testament was rather particularistic in its formulation. "Love thy neighbor as thyself" (Lev 19:18) speaks more of love among the Israelites than it speaks of a universal love. Yet this prescription is not so restrictive as it is a covenant stipulation bearing upon the relationships which ought to obtain among those who are convenanted with God and with one another. The love commandment of John is also a covenant reality—the way of those who belong to the new covenant, abiding in the Father through the mediation of Jesus' love.

If the literary genre adopted in John 13-16, Johannine dualism, and the covenant connotation of the love commandment in John prompt a formulation of the commandment in terms of "brotherly love," one can speak of the sectarian character of John's formulation of the love commandment. It is sectarian in the sense that it is a reflection on the Johannine church against a dualistic background, but it is not sectarian if that means that hatred for those outside of the brotherhood is the necessary concomitant of those who belong to the brotherhood. Oftentimes the dualism of the Fourth Gospel has prompted a comparison between it and the Qumran writings.[144] Both speak of love within the community.[145] Indeed it would appear that brotherly love is the

142. Cf. John 14:2.
143. Cf. J. Becker, "Die Abschiedsreden," pp. 230, 232; O. Prunet, *La morale chrétienne*, p. 106.
144. Cf. James Charlesworth, "A Critical Comparison of the Dualism in 1 QS 3:13-4:26 and the "Dualism' Contained in the Gospel of John," *NTS* 15 (1968-1969) 389-418.
145. Cf. 1 QS 1:9-11 and 2:24-25; 5:4, 24-26; 6:25-27, 7:4-9; 8:2; 10:17-18; 11:1-12; CD 6:20; 7:2-3; 13:18.

binding force of the members of the sect according to the views of
the Qumran sectarians. Thus some commentators suggest that
John's exposition of the love commandment is similar to that of
Qumran's.[146] But the parting of the ways comes with the realization
that John's love commandment never explicitly challenges the
disciples to hate those who do not belong to the brotherhood.[147]
His reflection simply bears upon the relationship which ought to
obtain among the disciples themselves.[148]

Indeed in 13:35 John appears to have defined discipleship in
terms of "love for one another."[149] The gift-commandment of
brotherly love forms Jesus' followers into a community and
provides that community with its identity before the world.[150]
Since the community is constituted by Jesus' love, the mutual
love which it evidences before the world is its mark of recognition
and its sign of credibility.[151] The community is composed of

146. For example, Lucetta Mowry who has written: "To be sure, the evangelist
hesitates to press his exclusion to an attitude of hatred for outsiders, but by
implication he approaches the Qumran point of view." L. Mowry, *The Dead Sea
Scrolls and the Early Church* (Chicago: University of Chicago, 1962) p. 30. Cf.
E. Käsemann, *Testament*, p. 59. Still more nuanced is the view of Leon Morris: But
we should not without further ado assume that the attitudes of Qumran and of
John are the same, or even basically similar... Nevertheless if is of interest that the
Qumran exhortations to brotherly love should be more nearly paralleled in John
than in other parts of the New Testament. L. Morris, *Studies in the Fourth Gospel*
(Grand Rapids, MI: Eerdmans, 1969) pp. 338-339. In a similar vein, cf. R.E.
Brown, "The Qumran Scrolls and the Johannine Gospel and Epistles," *CBQ* 17
(1955) 403-419, 559-574, pp. 561-564.

147. Cf. P.C. Fensham, "Love in the Writings of Qumrân and John," *Neo-
testamentica* 6 (1972) 67-77, esp. pp. 69, 75.

148. It is surprising, therefore, that Schnackenburg speaks, in context, of the
university of Christian love in contrast to the particularism of Judaism. Cf.
R. Schnackenburg, *Die Johannesbriefe*, p. 111.

149. In v. 35 John uses one of his descriptive definitions. Cf. 16:30; 1 John 2:3,
5; 3:16, 19, 24; 4:9, 13; 5:2, in each of which is found a following *hoti* clause. Cf.
R. Bultmann, *John*, pp. 525, n. 1; 539.

150. Cf. V. Furnish, *The Love Command*, p. 139; R.E. Brown, *John. XIII-XXI*,
p. 613; P. van Boxel, "Glaube und Liebe," p. 23; C. Spicq, *Théologie morale*,
pp. 493, 506. The latter speaks of the "institutional law of the Church" and the
"constitution of the Church."

151. Cf. N. Lazure, *Les valeurs morales*, p. 229; S. Cipriani, "Dio e amore,"
p. 229; A. Feuillet, "Le temps de l'Église," p. 69.

those to whom the gift of the love commandment is given. As love is a concrete expression of the life of God in the world, those who receive the gift of the love commandment are those who are begotten of God.[152] John joins love and faith together.[153] As those who believe are begotten of God, so those who love are begotten of God. It is to the children of God that the love commandment is given. Thus it is most appropriate that the proclamation of the love commandment in its Johannine formulation formed a traditional part of the baptismal catechesis within Johannine circles.

The love which is given and which constitutes believers as members of the faith community is, however, not a static reality. Love must produce its fruits. In fact, John 15:9-17, with its theme of love, is really an interpretation of the idea of bearing fruit which is found in the parable of the vine and the branches.[154] A life of love must be the normal occupation of the disciple. To love is the way which the disciple has to do righteousness.[155] His loving is the visible manifestation of the fact that he is the child of God. Thus love is more than a commandment for the disciple. it is his way of life, his mandate.[156]

Thus it is the ecclesial situation of the Johannine community which has prompted the seemingly restrictive formulation[157] of the new commandment of love, but it is the christological gift inherent in that commandment which yields its richness. To

152. Cf. 1 John 2:29-3:10. Cf. N. Vallanickal, *Divine Sonship*, pp. 295, 313-314.

153. Cf. R. Schnackenburg, *Moral Teaching*, p. 325; H. Schlier, "Die Bruder-liebe," pp. 240-241; R. Bultmann, *John*, p. 529. Bultmann considers John 15:1-17 to be a commentary on 13:34-35. He notes that, "The exposition of the command of love as the essential element in the constancy of faith makes it clear that faith and love form a unity; i.e., that the faith of which it can be said *kathōs ēgapēsa humas* is authentic only when it leads to *agapan allēlous*.

154. Cf. R.E. Brown, *John. XIII-XXI*, p. 680; R. Schnackenburg, *Das Johannes-evangelium* 3, p. 127.

155. Cf. N. Vallanickal, *Divine Sonship*, p. 295; A. Humbert, "L'observance," p. 209; H. Schlier, "Die Bruderliebe," p. 244.

156. Cf. N. Lazure, *Les valeurs morales*, pp. 144-145; "Louange," p. 79.

157. Cf. N. Vallanickal, *Divine Sonship*, p. 299.

separate the Johannine formulation of the love commandment, "that you love one another," from its Johannine context, "a new commandment I give to you ... even as I have loved you, that you also love one another," is to misrepresent Johannine thought. Yet it is only by means of such an exegetically unwarranted separation that one can arrive at the conclusion that John intended to restrict the scope of application of the traditional (i.e., Synoptic) logion on love.[158]

The Johannine love commandment is not so much a precept as it is a gift. It does not so much imply a dictate from above as a presence from within. Looked at as one of the salvific gifts which Jesus gives to his own, the love commandment is indeed for those whom he has chosen and to whom he gives the gifts of salvation. The salvific gifts are given to those who are his disciples, for it is among and with them that Jesus abides. Thus Jesus' love for his disciples, as the revelation of the Father's love, is made present in the love which they have for one another. It is this pregnant theological reflection which constitutes the new commandment as an expression of that Revelation which the Revealer has come to make known. It is the reality of this participatory love, which is Jesus' abiding in them, that is significant for all men, past and present:[159] "By this all men will know that you are my disciples, if you have love for one another" (John 13:35).

---

158. A more accurate reflection on the limited scope of the Johannine formulation of the love commandment is offered by Feuillet who writes of "a privileged case of doctrinal pluralism." Cf. A. Feuillet, "Un cas priviligié."

159. Abbott already called attention to the frequent use of the present subjunctive in the farewell discourse(s): the precept extends to all future generations. Cf. C.A. Abbott, *Johannine Vocabulary*. Diatesserica, 4 (London: A. & C. Black, 1905) p. 2529. From another point of view, a similar point is made by N. Lazure (*Les valeurs morales*, pp. 216-217).

INDEX OF PERSONS

Abbott, C. A., 256.
Achtemeier, P J., 187
Aland, K., 40, 70, 76, 102, 113, 169.
Ambrose, 30.
Arenillas, P., 42.
Aristophanes, 140.
Aristotle, 246.
Arndt, W., 198.
Artemidorus, 136.
Augustine, 209.

Balducci, E., 30, 31.
Barosse, T., 10, 11.
Barrett, C. K., 135, 139, 140, 141, 177, 198, 214, 223.
Barsotelli, L., 31.
Barth, G., 160.
Barth, M., 173.
Barthélemy, D., 201.
Bartina, S., 29, 125.
Bassler, J. M., 142.
Beasley-Murray, G. R., 2.
Becker, J., 223, 231, 253.
Becker, H., 5, 224.
Benoit, P., 121.
Berg, L., 220.
Bernard, J. H., 5, 111, 177, 220, 236, 243.
Bertram, G., 104.
Best, E., 71, 73.
Billerbeck, P., 114, 137, 139, 145, 148, 176.
Bligh, J., 21.
Blinzer, J., 143.
Bode, E. L., 3, 34, 41.
Boismard, M.-E., 9, 19, 20, 80, 97, 107, 110, 177, 186, 192, 223, 245.
Bonneau, N. R., 16.
Bonsirven, J., 240.
Bornkamm, G., 160.
Bowen, C. R., 96.
Boyle, J. L., 225, 243, 251.

Braun, F.-M., 108, 175.
Brooke, A. E., 230, 243, 252.
Brown, C., 191, 197.
Brown, R. E., 4, 5, 6, 9, 29, 36, 37, 79, 81, 83, 84, 102, 103, 108, 110, 111, 113, 123, 128, 129, 140, 143, 149, 162, 169, 176, 177, 185, 218, 220, 221, 223, 225, 242, 243, 244, 246, 251, 252, 254, 255.
Brown, R. P., 226, 242, 244.
Bruce, F. F., 137-138, 140, 143.
Brunner, A., 168.
Bruns, J. E., 15.
Bultmann, R., 2, 3, 4, 5, 9, 14, 15, 18, 21, 25, 30, 36, 38, 39, 41, 63, 96, 100, 102, 116, 117, 129, 135, 136, 137, 139, 141, 148, 160, 163, 164, 175, 177, 185, 224, 225, 229, 230, 231, 232, 233, 239, 241, 244, 245, 246, 247, 248, 252, 254, 255.
Burney, C. F., 97.

Cerfaux, L., 226, 241, 242, 245, 248, 249.
Charlesworth, J. H., 109, 253.
Chisda, 145.
Christ, F., 162.
Chrysostom, 139, 177, 219.
Cipriani, S., 242, 249, 254.
Clamer, A., 107.
Collins, R. F., 31, 101, 111, 120, 121, 161, 163, 166, 169, 179, 184.
Conzelmann, H., 95, 229.
Cross, F., 207.
Crossan, J. D., 31.
Cullmann, O., 4, 55, 97, 162.
Culpepper, R. A., 129, 228.
Cyril of Alexandria, 177.

Dauer, A., 30, 42, 178.
de Dinechin, O., 222, 225, 244, 245, 248, 250, 251.

de Goedt, M., 12, 100, 179.
de Halleux, A., 232.
Deissmann, A., 227.
de Jonge, M., 15, 58, 135, 230, 232.
de la Potterie, I., 15, 16, 31, 32, 108.
de Lubac, H., 120.
de Pinto, B., 108.
Descamps, A., 95, 232.
de Solages, B., 42.
Dibelius, M., 227, 249.
Dodd, C.H., 108, 140, 143, 144, 163, 167, 168, 203, 220, 223, 240, 251, 252.
Dunn, J.D.G., 226, 242, 245.

Eltester, W., 121.
Enang, K., 195.
Ephraem, 169.
Epictetus, 136.
Eusebius, 134.
Eyquem, M.B., 162.

Farmer, W.R., 143.
Feiereos, K., 30.
Fensham, P.C., 254.
Ferrar, W.H., 191.
Feuillet, A., 2, 31, 32, 103, 106, 107, 108, 120, 162, 219, 222, 232, 242, 243, 246, 249, 251, 254, 256.
Forestell, J.T., 120.
Fortna, R.T., 5, 18, 142, 161, 164, 166, 185.
Freedman, D.N., 114, 207.
Furnish, V.P., 229, 241, 242, 243, 245, 254.

Gächter, P., 143, 223.
Gartner, B., 28.
Geoltrain, P., 178.
Giblet, J., 71.
Gingrich, F., 198.
Glombitza, O., 41.
Goguel, M., 210.
Grant, R.M., 114.
Greeven, H., 104.
Gregory of Nyssa, 169.
Griesbach, J.J., 68.
Guntner, J.J., 80.

Haenchen, E., 9, 130, 132, 135, 136.
Harris, J.R., 203.
Harrisville, R.A., 241.
Hartdegen, S., 168.
Hartmann, G., 40.
Harvey, A.E., 99.
Hawkins, D.J., 242, 246.
Heil, J.P., 90.
Heise, J., 18, 100, 101, 250, 251.
Heitmüller, W., 223.
Held, H.J., 160.
Hemelsoet, B., 57.
Hendriksen, W., 233, 246.
Henze, C.M., 162.
Hillel, 238.
Hirsch, E., 5, 223.
Hobbs, E.C., 142.
Hoffmann, F., 30.
Horace, 146.
Horsley, R., 71, 72.
Hoskyns, E.C., 101, 198, 240, 243.
Humbert, A., 229, 236, 239, 249, 251, 255.
Hunter. A.M., 139.

Janssens de Varebeke, A., 123.
Jeremias, J., 166.
John Hyrcanus, 213.
Johnson, S.E., 142.
Johnston, G., 223.
Josephus, 136.

Kähler, M., 87.
Käsemann, E., 217, 220, 241, 245, 254.
Kee, H.C., 187.
Kilmartin, E.J., 166, 168.
Kloppenborg, J.S., 77.
Klos, H., 4.
Knox, J., 143.
Kragerud, A., 3.
Kuss, O., 143.
Kysar, R., 108.

Léon-Dufour, X., 135.
Lacomara, A., 235, 236, 246, 248.
Laconi, M., 5, 6.
Lagrange, M.-J., 2, 96, 225.
Lake, K., 75.

Lamouille, A., 80, 186.
Laurentin, R., 123.
Lazure, N., 221, 224, 233, 234, 236, 237, 239, 242, 247, 252, 254, 255, 256.
Leal, J., 6.
Lightfoot, R.H., 148.
Lindars, B., 5, 6, 10, 12, 57, 97, 110, 111, 113, 114, 118, 119, 134, 135, 136, 138, 139, 142, 143, 144, 147, 163, 164, 173, 225.
Loisy, A., 2, 30, 68, 103, 242, 243, 244, 246.

MacDonald, J., 18, 213.
MacGregor, G H. C., 5, 242, 244.
Maimonides, 176.
Manns, F., 165.
Marconcini, B., 11.
Marsh, J., 214.
Martin, J.P., 26.
Martyn, J.L., 21, 22, 57, 99, 109, 129, 130, 133, 135, 165.
Mastin, B.A., 141.
Matthiae, K., 72.
Matus, T., 36.
Maynard, A.M., 83.
Mbiti, J.S., 195, 196.
Mealand, D.L., 228, 231, 251, 252.
Meeks, W.A., 17.
Merx, A., 223.
Metzger, B.M., 70.
Milik, J.T., 201.
Moeller, H.R., 108.
Moloney, F.J., 58, 225.
Montefiore, H., 220.
Moody, D., 208.
Moran, W.L., 235.
Moreno Jiminez, F., 42, 44.
Morris, L., 244, 254.
Morton, A.Q., 5.
Moule, C.F.D., 1, 4, 143.
Mowry, L., 254.
Murtonen, A., 163.
Mussner, F., 143.
Naumann, P.S., 237.
Neirynck, F., 96.
Nestle, E., 40, 70.

Nicholson, G.C., 82, 83, 141.
Niebuhr, R.R., 143.
Niewalda, P., 4.
Noack, B., 5.

O'Connell, M.J., 234, 235.
O'Rourke, J.J., 134.
Olivieri, R., 5.
Origen, 1, 142, 177.
Osty, E., 107.
Ottoson, K., 219.

Painter, J., 108.
Papias, 43, 203.
Parnham, F.S., 174.
Perkins, P., 130.
Pesch, R., 76.
Philo, 104.
Pirot, L., 107.
Plato, 246.
Plautus, 136.
Plummer, A., 247.
Polycrates, 43.
Prete, B., 17, 20.
Prunet, O., 239, 251.

Randall, J.F., 221.
Reese, J.M., 222, 223, 224.
Reim, G., 224.
Ricca, P., 31.
Richter, G., 223, 226, 242, 245.
Rigaux, B., 72, 232.
Rissi, M., 162.
Ristow, H., 72.
Robinson, J.A.T., 177, 183.
Roloff, J., 42.
Ruchstuhl, E., 166.
Ruddick, C.T., 24.
Ruppert of Dietz, 2.

Sabbe, M., 96.
Sabugal, S., 16, 17.
Sanders, E.P., 191.
Sanders, J.A., 196.
Sanders, J.N., 141.
Sandvic, B., 232.
Schürmann, H., 30, 72.
Scheffczyk, L., 30.

Schlatter, A., 96, 115.
Schlier, H., 232, 234, 248, 249, 251, 255.
Schmid, J., 143.
Schnackenburg, R., 5, 6, 19, 39, 72, 83, 103, 109, 129, 131, 132, 135, 143, 144, 147, 162, 169, 175, 185, 217, 223, 229, 230, 231, 232, 240, 241, 243, 245, 246, 248, 249, 252, 254, 255.
Schneider, J., 229, 230, 231.
Schneiders, S.M., 135.
Schulz, S., 12, 15, 16, 17, 24, 29, 30, 38, 102, 103, 116.
Schumann, F.K., 244.
Schwank, B., 42.
Schwartz, E., 5.
Schweizer, E., 114.
Seynaeve, J., 226, 242, 245, 246, 247.
Shepherd, M.H., 142.
Siegman, E.F., 19.
Simeon b. Eleazar, 145.
Simon, M., 210.
Simonis, A.J., 177, 214.
Slenger, W., 26.
Smith, D.M., 5, 185.
Sobosan, J.G., 113.
Spicq, C., 162, 168, 222, 233, 235, 237, 239, 254.
Stanley, D.L., 236.
Stauffer, E., 220.
Strack, H.L., 114, 137, 139, 145, 148, 176.

Tarphon, 145.
Tatian, 169.
Teeple, H., M., 129.
Theodore of Mopsuestia, 169.

Thysman, R., 226, 246, 247.
Titus, E.L., 167.
Torrey, C.C., 97.
Toussaint, D., 176.
Trilling, W., 72.
Tyrtaeus, 246.

Uzin, D., 31.

Vaccari, A., 168.
Vallanickal, M., 229, 231, 232, 255.
Van Belle, G., 84, 129, 161, 183, 185.
van Boxel, P., 226, 227, 234, 243, 254.
van der Bussche, H., 248.
van der Ploeg, J., 234.
Vanhoye, A., 99, 115, 133, 167, 169, 237.
van Unnik, W.W., 7.
Vawter, B., 4.
Vespasian, 192.
Villescas, J., 160.
Viteau, J., 9.

Wead, D.W., 97.
Weber, J., 107.
Weiser, A., 245, 246.
Wellhausen, J., 5, 164, 223.
Wikenhauser, A., 5, 116, 223.
Wind, A., 7.
Windisch, H., 137.
Wrede, W., 220.
Wright, G.E., 207, 235.
Wulf, F., 102.

Zahn, T., 115.
Zimmermann, H., 100, 119, 222, 223, 224.

INDEX OF SCRIPTURAL REFERENCES

Genesis 1:1-2:4   144, 203.
1:1   203.
12:8   209.
13:3-4   209.
18:10-22   209.
22:1-14   24.
24   16.
24:29   16.
28:12   52.
49:11-12   174.

Exodus 2   16
7:3   192.
12:46   90.
20:1   234.
24:9-10   24.
25-27   207.
25-26   205.
25:8   199.
25:22   204.
29:4   214.
29:42-43   204.
30:36   204.
33:9   214.
34:10-16   172.
36-40   205.
37-38   207.
40-48   207.
40:21   199.
40:34   199.

Leviticus 10:16   109.
19:18   219, 235, 238, 253.
26:12   207.
13:31-16:33   221.

Numbers 2   208.
21:8-9   93.
21:9   65.

Deuteronomy 236, 237, 242.
1:1   236.
5:2-10   172.

5:5   234.
5:22   234.
10:12   235.
11:1   235.
11:22   235.
15:15   194.
15:18   194.
19:9   235.
22:2   109.
24:16   118.
32:45   236.
33:1   236.

Joshua 22:24-25   167.

Judges 11:12   167.
20:18   209.
20:26   209.
21:2-5   209.

1 Samuel 10:3   209.
28:78   109.

2 Samuel 7:6-7   200.
7:13   200.
11:3   109.
16:10   167.
19:23   167.

1 Kings 6:13   200.
8:8-9   207.
8:10-11   200.
17:17-24   96.
17:18   167.
2 Kings 3:13   167.
4:32-37   96.

Isaiah 6:9-10   195.
8:14   211.
9:1-2   25.
25:6   174.
29:17   174.
42:6   146.

51:1   106.
54:4-5   173.
54:5   172.
56:6-8   208.
58:11   175.
60:4-7   208.
62:5   173.
64:1   106.
64:7   105.
65:6-7   105.
66:1   105.
66:18-21   208.

Jeremiah 1:8   64.
2:2   172.
3:29   173.
7:11-15   211.
7:14   215.
10:21   106.
11:15   172.
17:12-13   211.
29:10   105.
29:13-14   105, 106.
31:5   174.

Ezekiel 3:19   118.
8:4   200.
9:3   200.
10:3-4   200.
10:18-19   200.
10:18   211.
11:15-16   211.
16:8-13   172.
18:24   118.
18:26   118.
43:4-5   200.

Hosea 1:2-9   172.
2:4-25   172, 173.
2:9   106.
2:24   174.
5:6   106.
5:15   106.
7:10   106.

Joel 3:17   201.
4:18   174.

Amos 5:1-6   106.
5:4-6   105.
8:11-12   106.
9:13   174.

Nahum 2:7   109

Zephaniah 1:6   106.
2:3   106.

Haggai 1:8-9   201.
1:14   201.

Zechariah 2:14   201.
8:3   201.
8:22   106.
14:16-19   208.

Malachi 3:1   106.

Psalms 9:11   106.
22   88.
24:6   106.
34:21   90.
40:17   106.
69:33   106.
70:5   106.
83:17   106.
104:15   174.
105:3-4   106.
118:20   214.

Job 31:8   140.

Proverbs 1:24-28   106.
3:13   106.
3:16   106.
8:35   106.
30:4   139.

Canticle 3:1-4   120.

Qoheleth 15.
11:5   139.

Lamentations 3:25   106.

Daniel 3:41   106.

Nehemiah 4:7   215.

2 Maccabees 5:19   215.

Sirach 16:21   139.
24:8   203.

Wisdom 1:1-2   106.
6:12-16   107.
6:12-13   107.
6:13   107.
6:14   107.
6:16   107.
8:2   106.
8:18   106.

Matthew   233.
1:22   95.
2:15   95.
2:17   95.
2:23   95.
3:2   94.
3:15   94, 95.
3:17   95.
4:1   84.
4:5   84.
4:8   84.
4:10   84.
4:12   94.
4:13-16   94.
4:14   95.
4:15-16   25.
4:17   94.
4:18-20   39, 47.
5:6   95.
5:10   95.
5:17   94, 95.
5:19-30   143.
5:19-20   143-145.
5:20   95.
5:43-48   219, 252.
5:43   252.
6:1   95.
6:33   95.
7:7   114.
7:22   192.
8:5-13   19, 190.
8:5   20.

8:13   20.
8:17   95.
8:23-27   159, 160, 186.
8:26   186.
9:9-13   76.
9:9   76.
9:17   175, 240.
9:18-19   190.
9:23-26   190.
10:1-4   75.
10:1-2   74.
10:1   75, 77.
10:2-4   74, 76.
10:2   74.
10:3   23, 76.
10:5-14   78.
10:7   77.
11:1   75.
11:2   193.
11:7   139.
11:20   192.
11:21   192.
11:23   192.
12:17   95.
12:27   189, 191.
12:46-50   179.
13:13-15   195.
13:35   95, 144.
13:44   95.
13:52   140.
13:54   142, 192.
13:57   142.
13:58   192.
14:2   192.
14:3   23.
14:13-21   159, 160, 190.
14:22-23   159, 190.
15:32-39   159, 160.
16:8-12   72.
16:9   72.
16:13-23   83.
16:13-20   38, 40.
16:13   23.
16:15-16   82.
16:17-18   39.
16:17   133.
16:23   84.
17:24-27   159.

18:3   62.
19:28   71.
20:12-13   159.
20:17   75.
21:4   95.
21:18-20   159.
21:32   95.
22:1-14   165, 173.
23:32   95.
24:15   215.
24:24   192.
25:1-13   165, 173.
25:24   141.
15:34-35   241.
26:6-13   28.
26:8   28.
26:20   75.
26:23   28.
26:28   240.
26:29   240.
26:33   37.
26:47   74.
26:54   95.
26:56   95.
27:3-10   79.
27:9   95.
27:47-56   28.
28:1-10   151.
28:1-8   33.
28:16-20   78.
28:16   74.
28:17   35, 85.

Mark 1:9-11   9.
1:11   95.
1:13   84.
1:14   94.
1:15   56, 94.
1:16-20   46.
1:16-18   39, 47.
1:19-20   47.
1:24   83.
2:13-17   76.
2:13-14   46, 47.
2:14   76.
2:21   240.
2:22   175, 240.
3:13-19   179, 180.

3:14-19   28, 70.
3:14-16   73.
3:14-15   46, 70.
3:14   70, 71, 73.
3:16-19   76.
3:16   39, 70, 71.
3:18   23.
3:21   189.
3:31-35   179.
3:35   179.
4:10   73.
4:12   195.
4:35-41   159, 160.
5:22-24   190.
5:34-43   190.
6:3   144.
6:4   142.
6:7-11   225.
6:7   73.
6:17   23.
6:32-44   159, 160, 190.
6:37   72.
6:41   72.
6:43   72.
6:45-52   159, 190.
7:31-37   188.
8:1-10   159, 160.
8:19   72.
8:27-33   83.
8:27-30   40.
8:27   23.
8:29   82.
8:31   92.
8:33   84.
9:31   92.
9:35-40   225.
9:35   73.
10:13-16   62.
10:15   62.
10:17-22   61.
10:17   61.
10:32   73.
10:33   92.
11:11   73.
11:12-14   159.
11:20-21   159.
12:17-22   61.
12:28-34   219.

12:31   238, 252.
13:9-13   225.
13:22   192.
13:26-26   225.
14:3-9   28.
14:4   28, 240.
14:10   73.
14:17   75.
14:18-21   225.
14:20   28, 73.
14:24   240.
14:25   240.
14:26-30   225.
14:29   37.
14:32-52   123.
14:32-50   88.
14:32-40   124.
14:43-52   28.
14:43   73.
14:50   124.
15:21-41   88.
15:26   13.
15:34   88.
15:37   88.
16:1-8   33.
16:9-20   74.
16:11   35, 85.
16:14   35, 74, 85, 152.

Luke 1:35   83.
2:11   95.
2:41-52   180.
2:48-50   123.
2:49   95, 180.
3:1   23.
3:20   95.
3:21   95.
3:22   95.
4:1   84.
4:16   80.
4:21   95.
4:23   142.
4:24   142.
4:25-27   96.
4:34   83.
5   38.
5:1-11   39, 47, 159, 190.
5:26   95.

5:27-32   76.
5:27   76.
5:36   240.
5:37-38   175.
5:37   240.
5:38   240.
5:39   175.
6:13   70, 74, 77.
6:14-16   77.
6:14-15   77.
6:14   23, 39.
6:15-16   77.
6:15   77.
6:27-28   219, 252.
6:32-36   219, 252.
7:1-10   19, 190.
7:4-5   20.
7:6-7   20.
7:9   20.
7:11-17   96, 190.
7:24   139.
7:36-50   28.
8:10   195.
8:16   143.
8:19-21   179, 180.
8:21   180.
8:22-25   159.
8:40-42   190.
8:49-56   190.
9:1-6   78.
9:1   78.
9:10-17   159, 160, 190.
9:18-22   83.
9:18-21   40.
9:20   82.
10   30.
10:12   75.
10:13   75.
11:9   114.
11:19   189, 191.
11:27-28   180.
12:28   95.
13:6-9   159.
13:32   95.
13:33   95.
15:24   173.
16:17-19   47.
16:19-31   25.

17:22　114.
18:17　62-63.
18:18　61.
19:5　95.
19:9　95.
19:21　141.
22:3　28.
22:14　75.
22:20　240.
22:21　28.
22:30　71.
22:33　37.
22:34　95.
22:47-53　28.
22:47　74.
22:61　95.
23:43　95.
24:1-12　33.
24:9　74.
24:12　40.
24:33　74.
24:34　41.
24:36-43　35, 85.

John 228.
1-20　130.
1:1-18　7, 9, 131, 151-157.
1:1 24, 109, 132, 153, 206, 210.
1:6-8　9, 48.
1:6　10.
1:7　10,11.
1:8　11.
1:11　142.
1:12　237.
1:14　109, 132, 195, 198-216.
1:15　9, 11, 48, 156.
1:16-17　177.
1:16　155, 156.
1:18　65, 154.
1:19-12:50　213.
1:19-2:12　36.
1:19-2:11　97.
1:19-51　50.
1:19-34　9, 48.
1:19-28　10, 165.
1:19　10, 11, 48, 59.
1:21　169.
1:22-24　9.

1:25　10.
1:29-51　3.
1:29-34　13, 48, 165.
1:29　11, 48, 110.
1:32　11, 53.
1:33　53.
1:34-39　107.
1:34　11, 48.
1:35-51　23, 48, 51, 133.
1:35-42　107, 165.
1:35-41　12, 47, 81.
1:35-39　13, 46-55, 96, 98, 100, 102,
　　103, 108, 110, 115, 116.
1:35-36　50.
1:35　12, 48, 120.
1:36　48, 110.
1:37　51, 98.
1:38　12, 29, 34, 51, 54, 59, 96, 100,
　　102, 103, 104, 107, 109, 111, 172.
1:39　97, 100, 102, 103.
1:40-42　39, 41, 46, 54, 100.
1:40　48, 80, 101, 134.
1:41-42　81.
1:41　12, 39, 51, 82, 100, 104, 107.
1:42　47, 80, 100, 101, 133.
1:43-51　12, 23, 166.
1:43-50　35, 46, 47.
1:43-46　81.
1:43　23, 80, 107.
1:44　51, 80.
1:45　12, 80, 104.
1:46　80, 100.
1:47-51　13.
1:47　100.
1:48　17, 80.
1:49-51　83.
1:49　12.
1:50　103.
1:51　13, 14, 17, 22, 35, 46, 209.
2:1-12　98, 133, 158-182, 189.
2:1-11　2, 138, 162, 165, 176.
2:1-8　163, 164-165.
2:1-2　172.
2:1　161, 165.
2:2　164.
2:3-5　166.
2:3-4　53, 165, 166-172, 178, 179, 180.
2:3　164, 177.

2:4   31, 32, 99, 133, 161, 162.
2:5-6   165.
2:5   166, 168.
2:6   160, 161.
2:7-8   165.
2:7   164.
2:8   164, 174.
2:9-10   163, 164, 165.
2:9   161, 174.
2:10   137-139, 149, 171, 174, 177-178, 192, 195.
2:11-12   163-164.
2:11   161, 162, 164, 181, 183, 184, 185, 191, 195, 210.
2:12   130, 164.
2:13-25   209, 210, 212.
2:13-22   91, 98, 152, 176.
2:13   91.
2:18-19   53.
2:18   183, 184, 193, 194.
2:19-21   212.
2:19   210, 211, 212.
2:20   210.
2:21   98, 210, 211, 212.
2:23-25   66.
2:23   183, 185, 191.
2:24   66.
2:25   100.
2:33   91.
3   58.
3:1-15   14, 15, 56-57, 176, 194.
3:1-11   133.
3:1-10   16, 58.
3:1   14, 57, 58, 61, 134, 184.
3:2   15, 34, 59, 61, 64, 103, 183, 184, 189, 181, 192, 193.
3:3   59, 60, 61, 62, 110.
3:4-5   53.
3:4   65, 169, 195.
3:5   59, 60, 61, 62, 63, 110.
3:6-8   63.
3:8-48   158.
3:8   59, 139-140, 148.
3:9   64.
3:10   14, 15, 57.
3:11-21   58.
3:11   59, 60, 64.
3:12   64.

3:13-14   82.
3:13   59, 65.
3:14-15   14, 65, 92, 93.
3:14   59.
3:15   60, 61, 64.
3:16-21   64.
3:16   175, 208, 252.
3:17   112.
3:18   175.
3:22-30   9.
3:22-26   9.
3:22   130.
3:23   10.
3:25-30   9.
3:26   9, 11, 103.
3:27-30   9.
3:29   11.
3:29   173, 178.
3:31-36   58, 64.
3:32   11.
3:33   11.
3:34   112, 154, 237.
3:35   249, 250.
3:36   175.
4   16.
4:1-42   17.
4:1-15   174.
4:1-3   9.
4:1   9, 16.
4:2-4   16.
4:2   9.
4:7-26   58.
4:7   111, 174.
4:9   17.
4:10-15   16.
4:10   175, 237.
4:11-12   169.
4:11   174.
4:12   99.
4:14   175, 237.
4:15   174, 237.
4:16-19   16.
4:16   17.
4:17-18   100.
4:19-24   212.
4:19   22.
4:21-24   209.

4:23   112, 176.
4:24   212.
4:25   16, 101, 104.
4:26   17, 22, 111.
4:27   103, 111, 169.
4:28   25.
4:29   16.
4:31-38   17, 24, 141.
4:31   103.
4:34   111, 112.
4:35   140-141.
4:37-38   17.
4:37   140-141.
4:39-42   18.
4:39   18.
4:40   18.
4:42   18.
4:43   156.
4:44   141-143.
4:45   142.
4:46-54   19, 142, 158, 165.
4:47   142.
4:48-49   19.
4:48   183, 184, 192.
4:50   20.
4:51-53   19, 20.
4:51   20.
4:53   20.
4:54   59, 183, 185, 191.
5   21, 58, 190.
5:1-18   21.
5:1-9   21, 144.
5:1   130.
5:2-9   158, 189.
5:4   191.
5:5   21.
5:7   193.
5:8   21.
5:9-47   144.
5:9   21, 177.
5:10-47   158.
5:10   21.
5:14   22, 130.
5:15   23.
5:16   21, 23.
5:17   177, 191.
5:18   21, 123.
5:19-20   59.

5:20   249.
5:23   112.
5:24   112, 175.
5:25-29   60.
5:30-47   1.
5:30   112.
5:33-36   9, 11.
5:33   11.
5:34   11.
5:36   11, 112.
5:37   22, 112.
5:38   112.
5:39-40   13.
5:41   210.
6   58, 242.
6:1-15   23, 158, 160, 189.
6:1   130.
6:2   183, 185, 191.
6:4   91.
6:5-7   24.
6:5   80.
6:6   24.
6:7   80.
6:8   39, 80, 134.
6:11   237.
6:14   183, 185, 191.
6:15-21   190.
6:15   91.
6:16-21   158, 189.
6:20   29.
6:22-65   158.
6:22-26   110.
6:22-25   110.
6:22-24   110.
6:24   110.
6:25   103.
6:26   110, 183, 193.
6:27   237.
6:29   112.
6:30   169, 183, 184, 191, 193, 194.
6:31-33   52.
6:31   237.
6:32   237.
6:33   237.
6:34   237.
6:35   29, 110, 175.
6:37   237.
6:38   112.

6:39   112, 237.
6:40   175.
6:41   184.
6:42   169.
6:44   112.
6:46   65.
6:51   29, 237.
6:52   237.
6:57   112.
6:64   134.
6:65   112, 237.
6:66-71   78-84.
6:66-67   86.
6:66   83.
6:67-71   28, 40, 80, 81.
6:67   80.
6:68-69   82, 83.
6:68   39, 80, 82.
6:69   82.
6:70-71   84.
6:70   81, 100.
6:71   28, 79, 80, 84, 134.
7   113, 190.
7:1   123, 130.
7:3   164.
7:4   149.
7:8   128.
7:10   128.
7:14   205.
7:16   112.
7:18   112.
7:19   123.
7:20   123.
7:25   123.
7:28   112.
7:29   112.
7:30   123, 170, 171.
7:31   183, 191, 193, 194.
7:33-36   119.
7:32-36   113, 115, 116.
7:33   112, 116.
7:34-36   118.
7:34   59, 113, 115, 116, 118.
7:35   99, 169.
7:36   59, 113, 115, 116, 118.
7:37-39   175.
7:37-38   175, 209.
7:37   175.

7:38-39   152.
7:41-42   169.
7:47   169.
7:50-52   57.
7:50-51   14.
7:70   14, 57, 134.
8   152.
8:2   205.
8:12   29, 51, 117, 118, 147.
8:16   112.
8:18   112.
8:20   170, 171, 205.
8:21-29   117, 119.
8:21-22   59.
8:21   112, 116, 118.
8:22   99, 116, 117.
8:23   117.
8:24   29, 117.
8:25   13, 117.
8:26   112, 117.
8:28   29, 92, 93, 117.
8:29   112, 117.
8:30   117.
8:31   44, 170.
8:34-59   180.
8:37   123.
8:40   123.
8:42   112, 152.
8:43   13.
8:44   13.
8:46   169.
8:53   99.
8:56   216.
8:57   99.
8:58   29.
9   21, 133, 192.
9:1-34   21.
9:1-7   21, 158, 189.
9:1   21.
9:2   99, 103.
9:3-5   146.
9:3   22.
9:4-5   147.
9:4   112, 145-146, 148.
9:5   29, 177.
9:7   21.
9:14   21, 177.
9:16   21, 183, 184, 191, 193, 194.

9:19   169.
9:22   152.
9:24-34   66.
9:26   169.
9:27   169.
9:35-39   21.
9:35   22.
9:38   27.
9:39   14.
10:1-21   242.
10:3   34, 214.
10:4   34, 51.
10:7-9   209.
10:7   29, 213, 214.
10:9   29, 213, 214.
10:11   29, 215.
10:14   29.
10:15   51, 215.
10:16   34.
10:17   215.
10:18   215, 233, 235.
10:23   205.
10:27   51.
10:28   237.
10:31   123.
10:36   82, 112.
10:39   123.
10:40-42   9.
10:40   10.
10:41   183, 191.
11:1-12:8   148, 190.
11:1-45   26.
11:1-44   25, 26, 91, 158.
11:2   134.
11:3   26.
11:4   37, 149.
11:5   26.
11:6   26.
11:8   103, 123.
1:9-10   146-149.
11:11   26.
11:16   36, 37.
11:17   26.
11:21   27.
11:24   27.
11:25   27, 29.
11:27   27, 82.
11:32   27.

11:36   26.
11:39   26.
11:40   27.
11:42   112.
11:43-44   134.
11:44   26.
11:47   183, 184, 191, 194.
11:48-50   209.
11:48   215.
11:52   91.
11:55   91, 92.
11:56   169.
11:57   233.
12:1-11   25, 30.
12:1-8   28.
12:1   134.
12:3   134.
12:4   28, 134.
12:6   28, 30.
12:9   134.
12:11   26.
12:16   51.
12:18   183, 185, 191, 193.
12:20-36   23, 24.
12:20   115.
12:21-22   24.
12:21   80.
12:22   25, 80.
12:23   170.
12:24   149, 215, 246.
12:25   246.
12:27   169, 170, 185.
12:32-34   92.
12:32   92, 116, 208, 215.
12:33   134.
12:34   53, 92, 169.
12:35   112, 117.
12:36-43   92.
12:38-40   195.
12:37   183, 185, 186, 189, 191, 192.
12:41   209, 215.
12:44-50   92.
12:44   112.
12:45   112.
12:49-50   235.
12:49   112, 233, 235.
12:50   233, 235.
13-21   123.

13-19 245.
13-17 37, 90, 119, 222, 223, 225, 227, 243, 248.
13-16 223, 253.
13-14 222, 223, 224.
13 58, 226, 242.
13:1-20 218, 226, 242, 245.
13:1-12 242, 245.
13:1 90, 115, 227, 245, 246.
13:2 28, 30.
13:3 112.
13:6 39, 80.
13:8 80
13:9 29, 39, 80.
13:12-20 245, 246.
13:13-20 245.
13:15 222, 226, 245.
13:16 112, 225.
13:18 81.
13:20 112, 225.
13:21-30 134.
13:21-26 42.
13:21 39, 225.
13:22-26 134.
13:22-24 82.
13:23-26 44.
13:23 44, 134.
13:24 39, 80.
13:25 44.
13:26 28.
13:27-30 28, 30.
13:27 29, 30.
13:30-32 181.
13:30 30, 102.
13:31-16:33 221, 222, 225, 235.
13:31-14:31 218, 222, 223, 224.
13:31-38 223, 224, 225.
13:31-33 221.
13:31 124, 225.
13:32 117.
13:33-38 226.
13:33 112, 119, 123, 221, 223, 225.
13:34-35 218, 221, 223, 224, 226, 238, 239, 255.
13:34 152, 208, 217-256.
13:35 134, 152, 254, 256.
13:36 39, 80, 86, 112, 128, 223.
13:37 37, 80.

13:38 225, 226.
14 223.
14:1-14 23.
14:2-3 101.
14:2 253.
14:4-5 112.
14:5 37.
14:6 29, 108.
14:8-9 24.
14:8 80.
14:9 80, 210.
14:10 53.
14:11 53.
14:12 112, 141, 144, 225.
14:15 233, 236, 238.
14:16 122, 237, 238.
14:19 112, 117, 154.
14:21 233, 236, 237, 238.
14:22 80.
14:23 237.
14:24 112.
14:25 101.
14:26 112.
14:27 86, 237, 238.
14:28 112.
14:31 128, 218, 222, 223, 233.
14:33 116.
15-17 223.
15-16 218, 222, 223, 224.
15 54, 226, 242.
15:1-16:4 223, 224.
15:1-17 225, 242, 255.
15:1-11 54, 218.
15:1-8 242.
15:1 29.
15:4 101, 251.
15:5 29.
15:7-8 227.
15:7 101.
15:9-17 226, 255.
15:9-10 250.
15:9 249, 250, 252.
15:10 101, 233, 236, 238, 249.
15:12-17 246.
15:12 152, 208, 218, 220, 222, 223, 226, 233, 236, 238, 244, 246, 248, 250.
15:13-16 41.

15:13-15 227.
15:13 226, 227, 246, 249.
15:14 233, 236.
15:15 44.
15:16-17 227.
15:16 54, 81, 100.
15:17 218, 226, 227, 233.
15:18-16:4 224.
15:19 81.
16:21 2.
16:4-33 223, 224.
16:5-6 222.
16:5 112, 128.
16:7 130.
16:11 130.
16:16-33 222.
16:16-19 112, 117.
16:19 123.
16:20 225.
16:21 149.
16:28 112, 115.
16:23 225.
16:30 254.
16:32 124.
17 89, 90, 217, 225, 238.
17:1 90, 170.
17:2 237.
17:3 112, 156.
17:8 83, 112, 237.
17:14 222, 237.
17:16 222, 227.
17:18 112.
17:20-21 141.
17:21 112.
17:22 227.
17:23 112, 250.
17:24 101, 237.
17:25 112.
17:26 250.
18:1-19:30 30.
18:1-11 88, 122-125.
18:1 36.
18:2-12 28.
18:2-5 28.
18:2 134.
18:3 30.
18:4-8 29, 125.

18:4 29, 102, 103, 120, 122, 123, 124, 125.
18:5 29, 79, 124.
18:6 29.
18:7 29, 104, 120, 122, 123, 125.
18:8 29, 88, 123.
18:10 39, 80.
18:11 80.
18:15-18 39, 203.
18:15-16 42.
18:15 39, 42, 80.
18:16 80.
18:17 80, 131.
18:18 80.
18:20 205.
18:25 39, 80, 131.
18:26 80.
18:27 80, 131.
18:28 90.
18:33-38 91.
18:39-47 66.
18:39-40 90.
19:20 88.
19:12 123.
19:13 101.
19:17-30 88.
19:17 88.
19:19-22 88.
19:24-27 13, 15.
19:25-27 2, 30, 32, 42, 166, 171-172, 178, 181.
19:25 178.
19:26-27 31, 32, 44, 178.
19:26 44, 88.
19:27 32, 170.
19:28 88, 130.
19:30 66, 88, 89, 90.
19:31-37 90.
19:34 209, 216.
19:35 45.
19:38 130.
19:39 14, 57, 134.
19:41-42 36.
19:41 238.
20-21 121.
20 36, 40.
20:1-8 121.

20:1-2   33, 120, 151.
20:1   131.
20:2-10   134.
20:2   33, 34, 39, 42, 44, 80.
20:3-10   39, 40, 42, 43.
20:3   40, 42, 80.
20:4-7   27.
20:4   39, 42, 80.
20:6-9   43.
20:6   39, 80.
20:7   42.
20:8   43.
20:9   43.
20:11-18   33, 34, 59, 120, 121, 131, 151.
20:11   33.
20:13   96, 120.
20:14-15   33.
20:14   120.
20:15   33, 96, 103, 120, 123, 169.
20:16   33, 34, 101, 103, 120.
20:17   33, 34, 120, 121.
20:19-23   35.
20:19   43, 86.
20:21   112.
20:24-29   35, 36, 37.
20:24-25   86.
20:24-29   152.
20:24   36, 40, 78, 79, 84-85, 133.
20:25   85.
20:26   85.
20:28   37, 85.
20:29   20, 37, 43, 141.
20:30-31   6, 18, 60, 128, 130, 131, 153, 185, 186, 187.
20:30   183, 185, 191, 192.
20:31   128, 156, 193.
21   7, 9, 36, 38, 41, 43, 128, 130, 131, 132, 133, 136, 137, 153.
21:1-14   130.
21:1-11   158, 190.
21:1-2   36.
21:1   41, 130.
21:2-7   42.
21:2   12, 39, 41, 78, 79, 80, 132, 133.
21:3   39, 41, 80.
21:7   39, 41, 43, 44, 80, 136.
21:10-11   82.

21:10   44.
21:11   39, 41, 80.
21:14   41, 130, 131.
21:15-25   42.
21:15-17   41, 131.
21:15   39, 41, 80, 133.
21:16   133.
21:17   80, 133.
21:18-33   135.
21:18-19   134.
21:18   134-137.
21:19-24   42.
21:19   51, 135, 136, 137.
21:20-23   39, 41.
21:20   44, 51, 80, 133, 135.
21:21-23   26.
21:21   80.
21:22   51.
21:24-25   45.

Acts 1:8   78.
1:13   77, 80.
1:18-19   79.
1:26   74.
2:14   74.
2:22   192.
2:43   192.
4:30   192.
5:12   192.
6:8   192.
6:13   215.
6:14   215.
6:21   74.
7:8   215.
7:36   192.
8:4-28   17.
14:3   192.
15:12   192.
17:30   36.
21:28   215.
28:26   195.

Romans 15:19   192.

1 Corinthians 1:22   104.
12:1-11   192.
12:2   192.
12:28   192.

15:5   41.

2 Corinthians 6:2   146.
12:12   192.

Ephesians 5:25-27   173.

Colossians 1:15-20   153.

1 Thessalonians 4:13-18   26.

2 Thessalonians 2:9   192.

Hebrews 2:4   192.

1 John   222, 228, 239.
2   252.
2:3   233, 236, 254.
2:4-5   234, 237.
2:4   233, 236.
2:5   254.
2:7-11   240.
2:7-8   218, 219, 228-232, 238, 239.
2:7   229, 233.
2:8   230, 231, 233.
2:18   229.
2:24   219.
2:29-3:10   255.
3:10-24   232.
3:11   229, 237.
3:14   231.
3:16   254.
3:19   254.
3:22   233, 236.

3:23   233.
3:24   233, 236, 254.
4:3   229.
4:7-21   232.
4:7-10   232.
4:9   254.
4:10   219.
4:13   254.
4:16   83.
4:20   219.
4:21   233.
5:2   219, 233, 236, 254.
5:3   233, 236.

2 John   228.
4   233.
5   218, 228, 230, 232, 238, 239, 252.
6   232, 233.

3 John   228.

Revelation   228.
6:10   26.
7:15-17   212.
7:15   202.
11:19   212.
12:17   233.
14:12   233.
14:13   26.
16:17   212.
21:3   202.
21:10-14   72.
21:22   212.

INDEX OF SUBJECTS

Abiding, 53, 101, 226, 250.
Absence of Jesus, 119, 146, 225, 227, 238, 243, 253.
Allegory, 1.
"Amen, Amen," 62-63, 135, 144.
Andrew, 39, 46-47, 100, 134.
Apologetic interest, 34, 36, 38, 121.
Apostles, 74-75, 86.
Aretalogy, 187, 196.
Arrest of Jesus, 29, 88, 122-125.
Ascension, 35, 59, 120-121, 151.

Baptism, 9, 21, 59, 63-64, 95.
Beloved Disciple, 3, 8, 30, 31, 38, 39, 42-45, 48, 133-137, 149.
Bethel, 209-210.
Brothers of Jesus, 164, 179-181.

Cana, 30, 32, 133, 158-182, 194-195.
Catechesis, 229.
Church, 3, 30-31, 38-39, 63, 78, 99, 122, 152, 179, 255.
Circular style, 59.
Commandment, 208, 219, 232-238.
Covenant, 200, 206-207, 234, 242-243, 253.
Cross, 30-31, 66, 117, 126, 134, 178-179, 181.
Crypto-christian, 57.

Departure, 90, 224-225, 238, 252.
Dialogue, 50, 58, 80, 132, 161.
Disciple, 39, 40, 41, 44-45, 46-55, 72, 86, 100, 100-103, 238, 241, 244-245, 255.
Displacement theory, 5.
Divine name, 118-119, 125, 202.
Double meaning, 59, 97, 135.
Doubt, 36-37, 85.
Drama, 33, 46, 47-48, 50, 85, 98, 100, 101-102, 115, 117-118, 133, 165, 184.
Dualism, 117, 240, 252, 254.

Ecclesiastical redactor, 2-3, 38, 63.
Eleven, the, 74.
Epilogue, 9, 41, 78, 128, 131-132, 153.
Eschatology, 1, 60, 71, 72, 94-95, 159, 200-202, 208, 213, 231, 240-241.
Evangelist, 6.
Excommunication, 22, 152.
Exorcisms, 73, 189, 191.

Faith, 6-7, 8, 15, 18-19, 20, 22, 27, 31, 33, 37, 43, 45, 58, 63-64, 66-67, 82-83, 121, 181, 186, 191-195, 196, 229, 255.
Farewell discourse(s), 58, 89-90, 119, 218, 221-227, 228, 247.
Father, 13, 35, 53-54, 109, 112, 115-116, 119, 124, 143-145, 146, 149, 154, 209, 224, 226, 233, 236, 243, 249-251.
Feasts, 152, 177, 208-209.
Final redactor, 6.
Following, 51, 98, 101, 135.

Gentiles, 20.
Gifts, 17, 66, 174, 175, 178, 237, 241, 248, 251.
Glorification, 33, 37, 44, 89, 91, 93, 117, 119, 120, 121, 170, 179, 181, 243.
Gnostic, 64, 114, 154, 220, 230, 232.
Gospel of Thomas, 113-114, 142, 148.
Greeks, 25, 115.

Homiletic tradition, 5-6, 7-8, 45, 56, 77, 151, 152.
Hour, 29, 31, 32, 90, 102, 115, 120, 161, 168-171, 178, 181, 195, 225, 247.

"I Am" (*Egô Eimi*), 4, 17, 27, 29, 92, 108, 110, 115, 117, 125, 126.
Inclusio, 36, 80, 227.

Individuals, 1-2, 4, 6, 8.
Interrogation, 50, 58, 80, 99-100, 115, 117, 125, 161, 167, 169, 223.
Irony, 113, 215.

Jesus, bridegroom, 173, 178.
Jesus, rabbi, 59, 149.
Jewish institutions, 138-139, 152, 155, 176-177, 210.
Jewish tradition, 12, 16, 26, 65.
Jews, the, 13, 14, 15, 21, 22, 24, 57, 91, 112, 115, 117, 123, 143, 152, 215.
Johannine school, 129, 228, 238.
Johannine note, 24, 84, 98, 134, 161, 211.
Johannine "we," 82.
John (the Baptist), 8-11, 45, 48, 50, 94-95, 100.
Judas, 8, 28-30, 74, 77, 78, 79, 81, 84, 134.

Kingdom of God, 56, 59-62.

Lame man, 8, 21-23, 189, 191, 192-193.
Lazarus, 8, 25-27, 43, 91, 134, 146-147, 158, 189-190.
Life, 3, 8, 20, 27, 41, 66-67, 105, 118, 148-149, 157, 222.
Light, 3, 10, 147-148, 222.
Loaves, 24, 58, 72, 110, 159, 160, 184, 189.
Love command, 119, 152, 208, 217-256.

Man born blind, 8, 21-23, 27, 45, 133, 189, 191-192.
Martha, 25-26.
Mary of Bethany, 25-26, 33, 124.
Mary Magdalene, 8, 33-35, 43, 103, 120-122, 131, 151.
Mary, mother of Jesus, 2, 8, 30-33, 44, 161, 165, 166-169, 170, 178-181.
Matthew, the tax collector, 76.
Messiah, 11-12, 13, 17, 32, 40, 103-104, 188, 195, 211.
Midrash, 65, 66.
Miracles, 19, 21, 26, 31, 58, 59, 158-160, 163, 168, 171, 186-191, 196.

Misunderstanding, 15, 16, 17, 24, 59, 117, 120.
Moral demand, 238.
Moses, 65, 155, 177, 194, 199, 204, 236.
Mount Gerizim, 177, 213.

Narrative, 49-50, 58, 163-165.
Nathanael, 3, 8, 11-14, 23, 27, 35, 45, 47, 78, 209.
New commandment, 218-219, 228-232, 238-242.
Nicodemus, 8, 14-16, 24, 30, 34, 56-67, 134, 140, 184, 193.
Night, 3, 15, 56, 102, 134, 145, 146-149.

Parables, 59, 163-164, 195, 214, 218, 226, 255.
Parousia, 26, 27, 36, 122.
Passion, 28, 29, 30, 32, 83, 87-93, 124, 225-226, 246.
Passover, 75, 90-92.
Persecution, 224.
Peter, 3, 8, 38-42, 43, 45, 51, 71, 80, 81-83, 85, 131, 133-137.
Pharisees, 14, 17, 30, 57, 122, 184, 193, 194, 215.
Philip, 8, 23-25.
Philosophical quest, 104.
Preaching, 6, 7-8, 56, 77, 152.
Priestly prayer, 89-90, 250.
Prologue, 9, 109, 131, 132, 151-157, 177.
Prophetic 'oth, 3.
Prophets, 105-106.
Proverbal sayings, 128-150, 246.
Purification, rites of, 176.

Q-source, 19, 71, 77, 114-115, 173 189.
Qumran, 43, 62, 152, 219, 253-254.

Rabbinic dialogue, 15, 58.
Redactions, 5, 129, 185-186, 222-223.
Representative figures, 1-45.
Resurrection, 26-27, 34-35, 36-38, 41, 98, 121, 211, 215.
Revealer, 18, 22, 40, 64-66, 82, 154, 156.

Revelation, 29, 30, 36, 234, 235.
Rhetoric, 147.
Royal Official, 8, 19-20, 142, 165, 184.

Sabbath, 21, 177.
Sacramentalism, 4, 63, 162.
Samaritan Woman, 3, 8, 16-19, 27, 58, 111, 140, 173, 176, 212.
Samaritans, 16-17, 18, 25, 140-141, 142, 213.
Scripture, 12, 13, 14, 52, 65, 88, 90, 91, 93, 95, 103, 109, 152.
Sectarianism, 152, 217, 253.
Seeing, 51, 53-54.
Seeking, 52, 94-127.
Self-revelation, 14, 17-18, 27, 29, 46, 67, 83, 89, 110, 116, 117, 125, 126, 181, 204.
Seven (the number), 3, 12, 36, 59, 78, 132, 176.
Shekinah, 202.
Sign-source, 19, 163-164, 165, 185.
Signs, 3, 15, 19-20, 31, 59, 64, 66, 91, 158, 181-182, 183-185, 190-195.
Son of Man, 13-14, 59, 65-66, 67, 92-93, 117, 118, 225.
Son of Zebedee, 42, 47, 69, 76, 78, 80.
Sources, 5, 129.
Spirit, 11, 16, 53, 59, 63, 78, 89, 121, 139-140, 152, 213.

Stage duality, 15, 164-165.
Symbolism, 2-4, 33, 39, 49-54, 68-69, 116, 135, 160, 226, 242.
Synopsis, 68-69.
Synoptics, 9-10, 19, 23, 28, 36, 39, 47, 48, 51, 61, 62, 68-78, 92, 96, 189, 192, 195, 197, 219-220, 225, 240, 256.

Tabernacle, 152, 199-216.
Temple, 91, 152, 177, 199-216.
Text criticism, 40, 52, 70-71, 102-103, 107, 113, 120, 147, 208.
Theophany, 24, 125, 209.
Thomas, 3, 8, 35-38, 45, 78, 84-85.
"Today," 95-96.
Tomb, 34, 43.
Transcendence, 206.
Twelve, the, 23, 28, 36, 40, 44, 46, 68-86.

Wedding feast, 138, 166, 172-173, 183.
Wine, 3, 166, 171-176, 192.
Wisdom, 106-112, 126.
Wisdom tradition, 15, 203.
Witness, 10-11, 18, 23, 44, 48-49, 59, 100-101.
Word, the, 109-110, 154, 198-216.